What were *your* forefathers and mothers like? Did they glitter on stage or swashbuckle at sea? Were they notorious or celebrated? Shepherds or shieks?

Track down your pedigree with these low-cost, easy methods of genealogical tracing.

You may be surprised—and enchanted—at the interesting people you will meet at the roots of your own family.

Finding
Your Roots

How *Every* American Can Trace His Ancestors—At Home and Abroad

Jeane Eddy Westin

Foreword by
John J. Stewart
Founder and Past President
The Genealogy Club of America

BALLANTINE BOOKS • NEW YORK

Library of Congress Catalog Card Number: 76-62675

ISBN 0-345-32554-0

This edition published by arrangement with J. P. Tarcher, Inc.
Illustrated by The Committee

Manufactured in the United States of America

First Ballantine Books Edition: June 1978
Eleventh Printing: September 1989

Dedicated to my ancestors, the saints and the scamps; and to my husband, Gene, a bit of both

ACKNOWLEDGMENTS

Many people deserve thanks for helping make this book possible—so many that I cannot mention them all, which in no way lessens my gratitude to them.

A special word of thanks must go to those who made significant contributions: Cheri R. Smith, Managing Editor of the *Genealogy Digest*, whose expertise is matched by her unending enthusiasm for family history; Shirley Linder Rad, who gave special insights for the chapter on family associations; Effingham P. Humphrey, Jr., former editor of *The Pennsylvania Genealogical Magazine*, and Jimmy B. Parker of Utah, who helped with sources on American Indians; Dr. Mary Matossian of the University of Maryland for her kind permission to quote from her research into psychohistory; and William D. Rowe at the Library of Congress Local History and Genealogy Reading Room and James D. Walker of the National Archives in Washington, D.C., who helped me see into the hearts of those two exciting institutions; and Norman Dawson, who taught me the importance of names.

I would also like to thank dozens of reference librarians, who never once refused my seemingly endless requests for information; the staff at the LDS (Mormon) Genealogical Library in Salt Lake City and at the branch library in Sacramento, California; and the many ancestor hunters who allowed me to study their personal family history books and handle their precious photographs.

The illustration in Chapter 10 of the heraldic components, plus the pedigree chart, family group record, family inquiry sheets, and the United States Census Summary Chart, are reproduced by permission of The Genealogy Club of America and *Genealogy Digest*.

The illustration in Chapter 11, which originally appeared in *Science Digest*, May 1976, is reproduced with the permission of Dr. Mary K. Matossian.

CONTENTS

JOURNEY TO YOUR PAST
BY JOHN J. STEWART

Among my fondest childhood memories is a marvelous train trip I took with my mother to visit my grandparents in a far-distant city. I remember especially my excitement at arriving at our destination, and the warmth and affection that grew stronger in all of us as we became familiar with each other once again. *Finding Your Roots* is much like that childhood experience. By starting out with your mother and father, you embark on a journey to meet your ancestors. As you travel back into your family history, you are bound to experience the pleasure and excitement of discovering warm and fascinating characters whose blood flows in your veins.

Genealogy is one of the oldest pursuits of mankind —and possibly one of the most interesting. (The Bible itself is a monumental genealogical record.) You are fortunate to have in your hands an excellent guidebook for this pursuit. Jeane Westin's *Finding Your Roots* will help you take an enjoyable and challenging journey into the past. The author is a skillful writer, well acquainted with her subject. She has prepared a practical and easy-to-follow, step-by-step itinerary of where to go, how to do it, and what to do when you get there.

As one of the founders of the Genealogy Club of America, I have seen that many people in all walks of life are eager to pursue their family biography but have no idea how or where to begin. Jeane Westin's book will provide anyone interested in undertaking this search with concise and invaluable information.

There are many rewards to be derived from your ancestral quest. One is the sheer pleasure and excitement of engaging in this fascinating hobby. As moving as it is to read about the journey of immigrants from all over the world to this country, consider how much more poignant it would be to find the story of a great-grandparent's hazardous, months-long voyage across continents and oceans to reach America. And especially when you yourself have discovered that story on the pages of a yellowed diary while digging through an old family trunk.

Another reward for investigating your family's past is this: The better you get to know your forebears, the better you will come to know yourself. Through a genealogical search you can come to a much more complete understanding of who and what you are. What worthier effort, then, can we make than to seek out the story of our ancestral past and record and preserve it for future generations in a Family History Book? The benefits are first your own, but the legacy to your children and grandchildren will be priceless.

One final thought: When you and I and a sufficient number of other people start finding our roots, the whole world may recognize at last that we are all one family, and that it is time we learned to live in love and peace and goodwill toward all mankind.

John J. Stewart
Logan, Utah
April 1977

1

GENEALOGY—YOUR
GREATEST ADVENTURE

Today thousands of Americans of all kinds are searching for their forebears—from American Indians to
those whose English ancestors stepped off the *Mayflower* to those whose African, Asian, Latin-American,
and European ancestors arrived much later. These
searchers have been gripped by one of the oldest and
now fastest-growing avocations: genealogy, tracing your
roots and making a family history.

The word "genealogy" is fast losing its stuffy association with elderly aunts, upper-class statesmen, and
cobwebbed scholars. In fact, ancestor hunting has become one of the most democratic and popular pursuits
around, one of the greatest forms of collecting—except
that, instead of acquiring Indian-head pennies or first-
day covers, you are collecting the historical pieces of
yourself.

Genealogy is truly for every American—as much for
those of eastern and southern European, American
Indian, Oriental, African, or Spanish-speaking descent
as it is for those of Anglo-Saxon or northern European
heritage, with which it has been traditionally associated.
There are family records of nearly all cultures, and
much of the past is recoverable.

Moreover, to be a successful family historian you
don't have to identify all of your forebears back to the
beginning of time. Just doing the three or four generations that almost any of us can trace back to provides

a world of enjoyment. You may trace them only as far as you want to. You can choose to seek out living relatives rather than long-gone ones. The idea is to learn more about your family and to have some fun doing it.

The promise of ancestor hunting is not just in the finding but also in the looking. As one fan of detective stories told me, "Trying to solve mysteries in your own family is more fun than seeing them solved in Agatha Christie or John D. MacDonald." In addition, it need not be expensive; most of it can be done from your living room with letters. Yet if you want, it can carry you to new towns and new countries in an ever-widening search.

Is ancestor hunting important, considering all the other things we could do with our time? I think so—and so do thousands of other Americans joining in the search. Americans are *hungry* to uncover the buried secrets of their heritage. Most of us live far from the homes that our ancestors—even our parents—established. Many of us don't know much about our grandparents, let alone our great-grandparents. The freedom of mobility in our society takes its toll in that many of us feel rootless and yearn for a sense of family. As you begin to understand who your forebears are, you begin to understand who *you* are.

But perhaps best of all is the fun of it and where it can lead you. My story is typical of what you will hear from thousands of others who have joined in the ancestor hunt.

I began to explore my ancestral past by talking with older relatives. (Indeed, this can be one of the most pleasant things about searching for family roots.) One of my earliest talks was with Great-uncle Joseph, who sometimes forgot my name but remembered every detail of events that occurred seventy-five years ago. He was able to give me dates, names, and anecdotes about long-dead ancestors, important to every family historian, but best of all, he mentioned that his father, Thomas Moffitt, had come from northern Ireland in the 1850s.

After interviewing all my living relatives, in person and by mail, I sought access to family Bibles and other records that many families had stored away in attics and basements. After that, I turned to library, government, and other public records to search for my ancestors, Thomas Moffitt in particular.

Acting on advice from a librarian, I went to the local branch of the Mormon library in Sacramento, California, where I live. The staff there ordered for me the 1880 federal census for Harrison County, West Virginia. It showed Thomas Moffitt had married and had eight children. The Harrison County library in turn answered my request for information about my ancestor with a photocopied sheet from a printed 1890 county history, which listed his birthplace as County Fermanagh, Ireland. It did not, however, list where in County Fermanagh.

Great-uncle Joseph had told me that Thomas had arrived in New York City on a ship from Belfast in the summer of 1852, but he did not know the name of the ship or exactly when it reached port. While on a business trip to Washington, D.C., my brother Dick took up the search and spent three hours in the National Archives scanning passenger list microfilms. Finally, there he was, on the manifest of *Sea Nymph,* captained by L. B. Hale: *T. Moffitt, arrived in America, July 11, 1852.* Most exciting of all, this record listed his point of origin: *Enniskillen, County Fermanagh.*

My search for Great-grandfather Thomas led me to a summer reunion with Moffitt cousins in Ohio, and eventually to northern Ireland. During a long-saved-for European vacation, my husband and I drove from Belfast about 80 miles across a moss-green Irish landscape to Lough Erne and the island town of Enniskillen.

It had been over a century since my ancestor lived there, and no one alive remembered him or knew about his family.

"Never mind," Patrick and Joanna Moffitt, owners of the Guards Inn, told me over a glass of Guinness stout. "While you're here, we'll be your family."

Who knows? Maybe they were. They *felt* like family.

Alex Haley, in *Roots,* has told perhaps the most sensational genealogical story of our time, but he is far from being the only black to have traced his ancestors. A Vaughn family in Chicago has charted its past back six generations to a slave ancestor named Scipio. Using census and country historical records, a slave inventory, family Bibles and interviews, Mrs. Aida Stradford, born a Vaughn, was able to piece together an epic tale. Born in 1784, Scipio was a member of the Ega family of the Yoruba tribe in Nigeria. He was captured and sold to a South Carolina planter named Wilie Vaughn. After becoming a valued iron worker, Scipio eventually helped two of his thirteen children buy their freedom in 1853 and return to Nigeria. With this background, the Vaughn family has been able to trace and contact Scipio's descendants—their relatives—on two continents.

Another story. Orphaned in this country in 1930, Helga Pehrson had not even known her own middle name and very little of her Danish immigrant family's history. She wrote to many parish *Folkregisters* in Denmark, until she made a contact. The clerk at Norup recognized the family name, and took the letter to her father's sister. Five days later Helga got an air-mail letter from an aunt she had never heard of, inviting her to come to Denmark and meet her family. The result of her trip was that she met an unknown half brother and two half sisters—and was reunited with her past.

Charles Wing of Honolulu had a similar kind of experience. After tracing an immigrant forebear through early Episcopal missionary registers and Oahu island tax records to the province of Canton, he wrote to a public official in his ancestral village. To his astonishment several weeks later he received a large package wrapped in rice paper from mainland China. In it was the Wing clan genealogy, meticulously hand-copied from ancient temple tablets.

The element of surprise in genealogy is never far away. While most immigrants to America were not from the noble classes, genealogical tracing sometimes comes up with the exceptions. While researching his great-great-great grandfather's ties, Kerry Ross Boren found he had Irish royalty hanging all over his family tree back to A.D. 347. When the Chief Herald of Ireland confirmed the discovery, Boren caused to be posted on the walls of Dublin Castle this rather grand public notice:

THAT I, Kerry Ross Boren, by right of title and blood, do hereby proclaim my rightful ascent to the throne of Eir, through the gracious blood of my ancestor, Brian Boru, 175th Monarch of Erin, and by right of whole blood I descend into the 29th generation, and whose proof of lineage is hereby attached, do hereby declare that I am herewith and for all time PRINCE KERRY OF IRELAND.

Quite often genealogy is the joy of finding the unexpected. Almost all ancestor hunters can tell you about an experience in which a seemingly blocked channel in their search was suddenly opened up by a chance conversation with someone, by a comment from a relative passing through town who knew of the connecting link, or by the unexpected gift of a family diary or Bible. These are occasions of *serendipity*—fortunate discoveries made quite by accident. It happened to the John Lindholm family of Denver when the succeeding owners of a former Lindholm family home told them they had found an old ironing board, on the back of which on March 18, 1899, Mrs. Augusta Lindholm, for some unknown reason, had written her thirteen-member family's names and birthdates.

Perhaps, you will also thrill to see the names and birthdates of a long-dead forebear and all his family flash across the screen of a microfilm reader. Maybe you will conjure up a mental image from 1908 immigration records of a frightened Polish girl in a white babushka. Perhaps you will feel rage at finding your forebear in a North Carolina slave sale record. This pulling together of your family's history is something like presiding at your own reincarnation—finding little pieces of yourself in the past that make up the total of who you are today.

In this book, I deal with all the major ethnic groups which provided America with immigrants. You will learn about fascinating sources for all your forebears, sources that are more than just written records of the past. They will lead you to all the romance, adventure, humor, and pride which is your family treasure. It will also draw the bonds of your own family unit closer together. Enlist your children in the search, for they *are* interested. My daughter recently asked me why her hair had a reddish cast. I told her that her great-great-grandmother was an Irish redhead. My response brought a flurry of interest in things Irish. The enthusiasm of others can enrich the family history search, especially a vacation visit to the ancestral hometown or homeland.

The Irish and the Welsh had oral accounts of their ancestors covering 1,500 years, the Elizabethans painted their heritage on their ceilings, and the emperor of Japan is able to trace a 2,600-year family history. Historians will write the biographies of famous families, but possibly no one but you will trace your family history. The story of your family—a family whose experiences helped build the world we live in today—must be written by you. And with each passing year, as older family members die, you risk losing some part of your heritage forever.

You can't start a moment too soon.

2

WHAT'S IN A NAME?
A FIRST CLUE
TO YOUR ROOTS

When you begin your search for where you came from you start with the obvious: your name.

Your name is one of your most personal possessions. It defines to the world who you are. As psychologists point out, a name can predispose others to like or dislike us. Indeed, even today, some primitive tribes keep their names secret to prevent enemies from acquiring power over them. In terms of history, your name is a fingerprint, perhaps the first clue as to who you are. Some knowledge of naming practices in your ancestral country could help you trace your early ancestors to a town, an occupation, or give you a clue to their physical characteristics.

NAMING NAMES—FIRST AND MIDDLE

First names, of course, are called "given" or "Christian" names, after early Christians who converted their pagan first names to Christian ones after baptism. Most of the first names in use in the United States today come from five languages: Hebrew, Teutonic (which includes Germanic), Greek, Latin, and Celtic (which includes Irish, Welsh, Scotch). No matter what their ethnic background, these are the names most immigrants have given their children. The reason? To "Americanize" them. A second-generation Japanese, for example, might be named not, say, Masa, but Philip, which is Greek.

Hebrew contributed biblical names, and accounts for about half of all first names (see box). The Teutonic tongues gave us names associated with warlike characteristics. The Greek, Latin, and Celtic languages often gave us names for personal characteristics and abstract qualities.

The origin of most first names is in the Bible. In A.D. 325 the Church outlawed the use of pagan names (like Marcus or Diana, which referred to pagan gods), and much later, in 1545, made the use of a saint's name mandatory for Catholic baptism. As a result, in all Western countries during the Middle Ages, there were only about twenty common names for infant boys and girls. And then as now, John and Mary led the name parade.

In the 1600s, Protestants, rejecting anything Catholic, turned from the saint names of the New Testament to Old Testament names, such as Elijah, Joshua, Patience, Priscilla, Rejoice, Truth—even He-Soundeth-the-Trumpets-for-Jehovah (imagine a child going through school with *that*).

As any parent can attest who has struggled with what to name the baby, there is far more choice in girls' names than in boys'. As name authority Elsdon C. Smith points out, this is because a boy's name can be made feminine by putting a feminine ending on it: Christina for Christian, Charlotte for Charles, Juanita for Juan. Because of the ancient cultural bias against applying feminine names to the male, however, it didn't work the other way around.

Middle names, usually a second "first" name, were first used as a status symbol by German nobility in the fifteenth century. They did not come into widespread use until several hundred years later, and were not common in the United States until after the Revolutionary

COMMON AMERICAN FIRST NAMES
AND THEIR ORIGINS AND MEANINGS

Names of Hebrew origin: *Meaning:*

Adam	Earth
Ann	Grace
Dan	He judged
David	Beloved
Elizabeth	Oath of God
Eve	Life
James	May God protect
John	Gracious gift of Yahweh
Joseph	He shall add
Judith	Praised
Mary	Bitter
Samuel	Name of God
Thomas	Twin

*Names of Teutonic
(including Germanic)
origin:*   *Meaning:*

Amelia	Industrious
Arnold	Strong as an eagle
Arthur	Fearless
Charles	To become adult
Edward	Guardian of property
Ethel	Noble
Francis	Free
William	Resolute protector

Names of Greek origin: *Meaning:*

Andrew	Manly
Barbara	Stranger
Basil	Most noble
Cynthia	Of the moon
Dorothy	Gift of God
Eugene	Well-born
Eunice	Fair victory

COMMON AMERICAN FIRST NAMES
AND THEIR ORIGINS AND MEANINGS
(continued)

Names of Greek origin:	*Meaning:*
George	Tiller of the soil
Peter	Rock
Philip	Lover of horses
Sophia	Wisdom

Names of Latin origin:	*Meaning:*
Camilla	Free-born
Clarence	Famous
Claude	Limping
Emily	Industrious
Florence	Flower
Laura	The air
Genevieve	White enchantress
Martin	Warlike
Patricia	Noble
Paul	Small
Rufus	Red
Sylvia	Of the woods
Victor	Victory in battle
Virginia	Pertaining to spring

Names of Celtic origin (including Irish, Scotch, and Welsh):	*Meaning:*
Alistair	Defender of men
Brian	Strong
Donald	A lord
Dougal	Dark-complexioned
Duncan	Brown warrior
Eileen	Light
Kevin	Gentle and beloved
Leslie	From the gray stronghold
Morgan	Sea Dweller
Morna	Soft
Owen	Well-born

War, when the fashion was to use the mother's maiden name as a middle name.

Highly unusual first names may be of some use in tracing family history, but valuable, tantalizing clues are often found in last names. This is one of the aspects of family tracing that makes it a great adventure.

LAST NAMES: 200 YEARS OF SMITH

There are over 1,500,000 family names (surnames) in the United States today. Although enormous numbers of German, Italian, Polish, Russian, and other immigrants brought their own surnames to this country during the last century, the family name picture in America is very close to what it was in revolutionary times. The first federal census, taken in 1790, lists the most common surnames as follows: Smith, Brown, Johnson, Jones, Davis. Today the five most common are (see chart next page): Smith, Johnson, Williams, Brown, Jones. Americans no longer need try to keep up with the Joneses, only with the Smiths (all 2.2 million of them).

Why have the predominant family names changed so little in almost 200 years? The answer is that many of the people whose names mean "blacksmith"—Schmidt from Germany, Kuznetzov from Russia, Ferraro from Italy, and so on—simply "Americanized" their names and disappeared into those 2.2 million Smiths we now have. And many other names were similarly translated, such as Woods from the German Holtz, the Dutch Bos, the French DuBois, the Polish Borowski, and the Spanish Silva. Or Hills from the German Buehler, the French Dumont, the Italian Costa, the Hungarian Hegy, the Irish Bryant, the Czechoslovakian Kopecky, the Polish Zagorski, and the Scandinavian Berg.

Some of the ethnic groups in our country have not, in general, Americanized their last names. For example, the Chinese. Surnames first appeared in China in 2852

THE FIFTY MOST COMMON SURNAMES IN AMERICA*

1. Smith	18. Clark	35. Mitchell
2. Johnson	19. Lewis	36. Campbell
3. Williams	20. Walker	37. Phillips
4. Brown	21. Hall	38. Carter
5. Jones	22. Robinson	39. Evans
6. Miller	23. Allen	40. Turner
7. Davis	24. Young	41. Collins
8. Wilson	25. King	42. Parker
9. Anderson	26. Nelson	43. Murphy
10. Taylor	27. Wright	44. Rodriguez
11. Moore	28. Baker	45. Edwards
12. Thomas	29. Hill	46. Morris
13. Martin	30. Scott	47. Peterson
14. Thompson	31. Adams	48. Cook
15. White	32. Green	49. Rogers
16. Harris	33. Lee	50. Stewart
17. Jackson	34. Roberts	

* From the records of the Social Security Administration.

B.C. when the Emperor decreed that all families were to choose a name from a sacred poem (Po-Chia-Hsing). Since the poem contained only 438 characters, the result is that today there are only about 1,000 Chinese surnames and only 60 are common. Chew ("mountain"), Chan ("old"), Fu ("teacher"), and Wing ("warm") are four of the most common Chinese surnames in America. Because the Chinese have extremely strong family and ancestral ties and because the names are short and easy to pronounce, very few Chinese family names have changed.

The practice of using surnames was not adopted in Western countries until about A.D. 1000, when the growth in population and commerce caused Europeans to take them up (merchants needed to know which John owed them money). Surnames were first used by noblemen in Venice, and from there the practice spread to France, England, Germany, and then the rest of Europe.

Experts generally agree that family names originated in all *Western* countries in much these same ways: according to place, occupation, patronymics (son of), or nicknames. In the United States, surveys show the percentage of descent to be:

place names	43.13%
occupational	15.16%
patronymics	32.23%
nicknames	9.48%

In England, to which William the Conqueror brought the custom of family names from Normandy, nobles usually took their surnames from the names of their estates (Somerset, for example), then passed both estate and name on to their sons. But by the end of the thirteenth century, the peasants, who made up about 70 percent of the population, had begun to imitate their manor lords and adopted the use of family names.

Quite often the common people took the name of their village or a distinguishing geographical feature. When the local priest wanted to differentiate between the many Johns on his parish rolls, he would write "John atte [at the] water" or "John river" or "John near the mill" or "John by the [village] green"—which of course eventually became Atwater, Rivers, Mill, and Green.

Occupational names are, of course, based on trade or occupation, such as Miller or Farmer (see the box).

One of the most common ways of forming surnames in many Western languages is patronymics. Williamson in English means "son of William," Petersen in Danish means "son of Peter," O'Brien is Irish for "descendant of Brien," MacGregor is Scottish for "son of Gregory,"

Janowicz is Polish for "son of Janos," Pieterzoon is Dutch for "son of Peter," Mendelssohn is German for "son of Mendel," Antonescu is Romanian for "son of Anton," Sanchez is Spanish for "son of Sancho," Bertucci is Italian for "son of little Berto," Mohammed ibn Ali is Arabic for Mohammed "son of Ali," and Isaac ben Jacob is Hebrew for "Isaac, son of Jacob."

It took a few centuries for the patronymic as we know it to stabilize. At first, in England, Robert the son of Peter became Robert Peterson. His son John would not be John Peterson but John Robertson, and so on, changing the surname every generation. Then, in 1413, Henry V decreed that the surname of an individual be listed on every official paper, and this tended to start the legal process of standardizing family names, which was completed when parish registers were established in 1538.

Nicknames form the last class of words from which surnames are derived. If your family name is Stout, it is possible that centuries ago you can claim an ancestor who was more than a little overweight; if Little, a forebear who was small of stature; if Reid, a red-haired ancestor; if Longfellow, a person who was tall or long-legged; if Goodman, a man kind to his neighbors.

THE ORIGIN OF OTHER LAST NAMES

Although most Western countries formed surnames in the four ways I mentioned—place names, patronymics, occupation, nicknames—some countries had slightly different methods. If your heritage can be found among any of the following, this section will be of interest to you: African, American Indian, Chinese, German, Japanese, Jewish, Russian, Scottish, Spanish and other Spanish-speaking nationalities, Norwegian, Swedish, Greek, Arabic, Indian.

OCCUPATIONAL NAMES AND THEIR TRANSLATIONS

English:	German:	French:	Italian:	Polish:
Archer	Reisman	Flèche	Battaglia	Luczak
Baker	Becker	Boulanger	Fornari	Piekarz
Carpenter	Schreiner	Charpentier	Martello	Cieslak
Coward (cowherd)	Schweiger	Bouvier	Vaccaro	Krowa
Farmer	Bauer	Gagnon		Kmiec
Fisher	Fischer		Pisciolo	Ryback
Miller	Müller	Meunier	Farina	
Miner		Ménier	Carbone	Weglarz
Priest	Pabst		Prete	Kaplan
Shepherd	Schaefer	Berger	Pecora	
Taylor	Schneider	Tailleur	Sartori	Krawczyk

African

African-naming customs vary from tribe to tribe, but most are descriptive. For example, the children of some western African tribes receive what amounts to a name based on the order of their birth ("first born," "second born," and so on). The Ashanti tribes of Ghana name their children for the day of the week on which they are born, and give them a second name which further pinpoints their birth order. For example, "Kofi" means Friday, but if you are the second child born on Friday your name would be "Kofi Buo," meaning "Friday who has come again."

During the two centuries blacks were brought to this hemisphere as slaves, except in the West Indies, they rarely kept their African tribal names. Usually the slave's owner arbitrarily picked a first name (such as Toby, which was forced on Kunte Kinte, *Roots* author Alex Haley's Mandinka ancestor), often a fancy classical name such as Cicero, Scipio, or Caesar. Then the slave owner often ignored even this name in his property records, listing instead "a male Negro, strongly made." No surname was allowed until the slave was freed. And, contrary to popular belief, it is not true that most freed slaves took the names of their former masters. Although some did, many wanted no reminder of their days in slavery.

Freed slaves generally chose familiar or prestigious family names from the South, and since these names were primarily English, Scottish, Welsh, and Irish in origin, that is why the most common are patronymical, such as Johnson, Jackson, and Robinson. But black family names were often changed until the northern migration, World War I draft, and Social Security made change more difficult.

American Indian

Among native Americans, names generally described traits of character. The Shawnee, for instance, had a "name-giver" (a man often as important as the tribal chief) who gave each child a name never used before. Other tribes simply called all first sons a name that translated as "First Son" and first daughters "First Daughter," and the same with second sons and daughters. Later, this name was replaced when the child had a unique experience or acquired a distinctive personality trait. Most tribes had a manhood initiation ceremony for boys at puberty, requiring them to choose their own adult names based on a spirit vision during a fast in the wilderness. (The Dakota chief Crow-Flies-High, for example, received his name from a spirit disguised as a crow.) The initiation rites for women often accompanied the first menses, after which the girl could choose an adult name.

Most tribes allowed for name changes throughout life, and so surnames were not needed until Indians ran up against the white man's passion for record keeping. Then Indian names that were lyrically beautiful in their native tongues defied English phonetic spelling, Or their translation proved to be too unwieldy (such as "Buffalo-Bulls-Back-Fat" or "She-Who-Bathes-Her-Knees"). And so, on most reservations the surname that was assigned was often ignored by Indian families. This produced such great confusion in record keeping that in 1903 President Theodore Roosevelt urged Dr. Charles Eastman, a Sioux, to rename every person on a large Sioux reservation. The result was a codifying of family names, and today American Indians researching their ancestry have some records to start searching.

Chinese

Traditional Chinese placed their surname first (Chiang Kai-shek, for example, is really Kai-shek, a member of the Chiang family).

Usually of one syllable, a few are place names such as Chew, after the province, and Pei, meaning "north." The most common, however, are descriptive, such as Chan ("old"), Chang ("draw-bow"), Fu ("teacher"), Gee ("well-mannered"), Li ("plum tree"), Moy ("plum flower"), Wang ("yellow"), Wong ("field or wide water").

Chinese Americans no longer place their surname first, but follow the Western custom.

German

Unlike English surnames, which are predominantly derived from place names, German family names most usually come from occupations, such as Schmidt ("smith"), Kaufman ("merchant"), or Richter ("judge").

Among other German names, colors predominate, such as Schwarz ("black"), Weiss ("white"), Roth ("red"), Braun ("brown"), Grün ("green"), Silber ("silver"), Gold ("gold"), and Rosen ("rose").

Other name forms are descriptive, such as Gross ("big"), Klein ("little"), Baum ("tree"), and Blume ("flower").

Location names account for the last definable group of German surnames, such as Wald ("forest"), Brück ("bridge"), Sachs ("Saxony"), Hess ("Hesse"), Schlesinger ("Silesian").

Japanese

The nobility had surnames as early as the fifteenth century, but most common Japanese surnames (taken primarily from locations) were assumed late in the last century when Emperor Mutuhito declared that everyone must take a family name. Whole villages took the same name, so that there are only about 10,000 surnames in Japan today. Examples of such names taken from locations are Takahashi ("high bridge"), Nakagawa ("middle river"), Nakamura ("middle village"), and Yamashita ("mountain below").

Other Japanese family names are descriptive, such as Suzuki, which means "bell tree," and Matsumoto, "pine origin."

Another group of surnames are composed of two words, usually taken from nature but seemingly not related to each other—for example, Ito ("only, wisteria"), Kato ("add, wisteria"), Sato ("help, wisteria"), and Saito ("festival, wisteria").

Jewish

For most of their history Jews favored patronymics, but during the early 1800s persecution forced them to abandon their own system and adopt permanent family names.

The Jews in Germany were made to take surnames by law. Those who were willing to pay the officials were allowed to choose names for their natural beauty, such as Blumberg ("flower mountain") or Rosenthal ("rose valley"). Those who refused to pay off were purposely assigned contemptuous or silly names such as Ziegellaub ("brick branch"), Bettelarm ("destitute"), Durst ("thirst"), Eselskopf ("ass's head"), Saumagen ("hog's paunch"), and even plain Stinker.

In Bohemia (now part of Czechoslovakia) Jews were restricted by law to Hebrew names, which accounts for the prevalence of Levy ("priestly tribe"), Cohen ("priest"), Isaacs ("he who laughs"), Rubin ("behold a son"), Abrams ("high father"), and Katz ("priest of righteousness").

Other distinctive Jewish names are occupational, although they are few because Jews were limited by most European countries to a few professions. Some examples are Perlman ("dealer in pearls"), Dayan ("rabbinic judge")͵, Chalfen ("money changer"), and Lehrer ("teacher").

Place names were also favored, such as Rothschild ("at the sign of the shield"), Moscovitz ("son of Moscow"), Dávila ("one from the Spanish city of Avila"), and Sacks ("one from Saxony").

Russian

When researching a family tree that includes Russian ancestors, one should be aware of the masculine and feminine name endings of the second name. Each child receives three names at birth: first name, followed by a second derived from the father's name (for example, the son of Ivan would be Ivanovich, the daughter, Ivanovna), and the surname. After the revolution of 1917, many former peasants changed their last names, since they were often offensive or derisive names given their grandfathers as serfs. Many a Durakov ("fool") changed his name to Umnov ("wise"). At the same time, religious names were changed to ones more appropriate for Communist revolutionaries.

As in other countries, many Russian families have surnames derived from places where their ancestors were born: Minsky ("from Minsk"), Tchaikovsky ("from Czajkowo"), Umansky ("from Uman").

Scottish

During the late Middle Ages in Scotland because of infant mortality it was not uncommon to give two or even three brothers the *same* first name. It's possible to trace a family line back to a James Campbell and then find there were three in the family. One might also find the Campbells were really MacDonalds or Frasers, for it was a common practice back then to change surnames with every change of residence in order "to please the laird." Finally, until the last century many good Scottish wives did not take their husband's surname on marriage but retained their own—remnant of an even older custom in which men took their wives' surnames after marriage.

Spanish (Including Mexico, Latin America, the Caribbean, and the Philippines)

Legend says that family names in Spain actually began as cries of Christian families to each other, warning of approaching Moors. If this is so, the cries have long since disappeared into the common patronymic so popular in Spanish-speaking countries, such as Rodríguez, Fernández, González, Martínez, Pérez, López. The unusual Spanish system calls for the giving of two surnames, the first from the father's family, the second from the mother's, sometimes (but not always) connected with a y, meaning "and." For example, a former president of Mexico was named Adolfo Ruiz Cortines —Ruiz from his father and Cortines from his mother. A woman named Maria Teresa de la Fuente y Fernández inherited de la Fuente from her father and Fernández from her mother.

Other common Spanish surnames are place names such as Acota ("long coast"), Alvara ("from Alvado"), Aguilar ("from Aguilas"), Cardoza ("from Cardoso"), Contreras ("from Cuevas Contrerias"), Cortez ("court" or "town"), Espinosa ("thorny thicket"), Estrada ("paved road"), Vargas ("steep hill"), and Silva ("thicket of briars").

Other Nationalities

Norwegians quite often have farm names. Family farms have been important enough to carry names since A.D. 1100, so the tradition is very old. Some examples are Eggerud ("ridge farm"), Bjornstad ("Bjorn's farm"), and Askeland ("ash tree farm").

Swedish surnames are of recent origin and are usual-

ly patronymic. Because of the confusion when everyone
in a country is named "son," for the last seventy-five
years the Swedish government has encouraged Swedes
to manufacture new family names. The *Släktnamns-
kommitté* or national Family Name Committee has ap-
proved 56,000 new names, usually combining two nature words, such as Bergstrom ("mountain, stream"),
Blomberg ("flower, mountain"), Holmgren ("river island, branch"), Wahlgren ("field, island"), Strandberg
("shore, mountain"), and Skoglund ("forest, grove").

The most popular Greek surname is Pappas, which
indicates descent from a priest. (The Greek Orthodox
Church allows its priests to marry.) Other Greek names
are descriptive, such as Makris ("long") and Mavros
("dark skinned"). Patronymics such as Demetriou
("son of Demetrius") and place names such as Vlahos
("from Wallachia") are also common.

The patronymic predominates for Arab names, such
as Ahmed ibn Hassan which is "Ahmed son of Hassan."
There is no such name as Abdul; it is a Western con-
traction of Abd al, meaning "slave of Allah"—for example, Abd al-Nasir ("slave of Allah of Nasir"), whom
we knew as Nasser. Many Arabs, especially in small
villages, do not have surnames at all but carry nicknames (often unflattering) which do not stick from
generation to generation.

In Indonesia, there is the curious custom of having
only a surname, no first name at all—for example, ex-
President Sukarno. Since in a country undergoing mod-
ernization—which implies keeping records—this creates
confusion in families with more than one child, the
custom will probably give way to the use of two names.

In modern India (as in Russia during its industrializ-
ing era), many lower-caste people are choosing such
names as Vikas ("development"), Yojana ("plan"),
and Pragati ("progress").

HOW YOUR FAMILY NAME VARIES

It would make family tree tracing a lot easier if our last names were distinctive, and spelled the same way our ancestors spelled them hundreds of years ago, but that probably isn't so.

In England, for instance, most records were kept by churchmen—and they were sometimes kept in Latin, sometimes in Norman French, and finally, toward the end of the Middle Ages, in English. The result was a wide variation in spellings of family names, sometimes even on the same piece of paper. In one 1623 document described by English genealogist L. G. Pine, the name Pierce was spelled Peirs, Pearce, and Peers—all on the same page.

Of course, it wasn't always officialdom that mutilated your ancestors' names. Sometimes your forebears did it to themselves. A famous Kentucky trapper of the late 1700s, for instance, sometimes signed his name Bone or Boon as well as Daniel Boone. The famous maker of Levi pants often spelled his name Levy.

And for some of us, our most recent family baptism may have been at the hands of United States immigration officials who couldn't understand our foreign names and so changed the spelling completely or gave up and changed the name into the nearest English sound. Thus, some Polish forebears arrived at New York's Ellis Island—the processing center for millions of immigrants—bearing the name Wallachinsky, and left it with the name Wallace. Among them was the father of novelist Irving Wallace. The father of Senator Edmund Muskie was originally Marciszewski, and my own husband's ancestors became Westins because a clerk didn't want to bother with Westinetsky.

Because of this lack of standardization, there are now thirteen versions of Smith, thirty-one different Snyder spellings, thirty-seven ways to write Burke, and forty-six ways of spelling Baer. And there are 400 possible spellings of Shakespeare. Canooles, Knowles, and Knolles are all names on one family tree, which demonstrates there has been not only a change in spelling over the centuries but also a change in pronunciation.

Knowing different possible spellings of your name is important, because otherwise you could miss another branch of your family tree. The information will be helpful later when you begin your search through public records. The real challenge, of course, is figuring out what these different spellings are. Here are some tips:

1. Sit down and list every possible spelling you can think of. (My list includes Eddy, Eddie, Ede, Eddye, Edde, Edy, Eddi, Edie, Edye.)
2. Say your name out loud, and see if this brings to mind other possibilities.
3. List the way other people frequently mispronounce your name; you can be sure that somewhere on your family tree it is spelled that way.
4. Next try pronouncing your name several different ways—for example, "Ride" for Reid. Next change the soft consonants to hard ones and vice versa. For instance, if your name is Keegan, pronounce it "Seegan" or "Keejan."

One woman whose maternal name was Crockett made a list of her ancestors as follows: Crocket, Crockette, Crockit, Crockitt, Cruckett, Crucket, Crukett, Cruket. She found most of these spellings before her search ended with an English gentleman born in 1271, Thomas de Cruket.

While at first it might seem that making a list of all the possible spelling variations would make your ancestor hunt more difficult rather than less, actually it will not. After all, you will not be searching for a name alone but a name coupled with a birthdate or a birthplace or both.

When you have listed the possible spellings for your family name, you may also want to check them in a surname encyclopedia (see bibliography) to discover their origin and probable meaning. They will help convey the fascination and adventure that you will encounter as you search for your family's roots.

Now let's look at where your ancestors came from and how they got here—which determines in good part where and who *you* are.

3

THE AMERICAN FAMILY HISTORY: HOW OUR ANCESTORS GOT HERE

Throughout history, in good times and bad, most of the world's population has stayed right where it was. Your forebears did not. Historian Arthur Schlesinger uses the phrase "the choosing people" to describe Americans, and except for those who came as slaves, the expression is apt.

For 350 years people have chosen America—39 million of them. Although they often had the compelling reasons of religious and political oppression and economic hard times, still they chose the difficult course of leaving their homes. As you retrace your immigrant ancestors and chart their progress from their homeland and through America, perhaps some of their spirit will be rekindled in you.

WHERE THEY CAME FROM

It is impossible to do justice here to 39 million people, but let me briefly in the next few pages try to describe the major immigration tides, for some of your ancestors may very well have been part of those waves.

The first immigrants—the ones who stepped off the *Mayflower* in 1620 and thereafter—were overwhelmingly English. Then in 1700 Germans and Scotch-Irish also began to emigrate. After the Revolutionary War, when the first census was taken in 1790, there were a little under 5 million people in the United States and, except for 750,000 black African slaves, most were descended from these three original groups. During the next fifty years, a million more immigrants arrived, again most of them from England and Germany. Although thousands more black Africans were brought in as slaves, they were not even considered immigrants. (Only 104,000 Africans—both black and white—have emigrated, in the choosing sense of the word, since 1820.)

In the middle of the nineteenth century the tide of immigration became a flood. Between 1841 and 1860 nearly 3.5 million came from Ireland and Germany. Another million came from England, Scandinavia, France, and Switzerland. And, beginning in 1850, thousands of Chinese began arriving in California, and later Japanese also. From 1880 until World War I, the growth of American industry attracted more than 15 million southern and eastern Europeans—Italians, Russians, Poles, and Hungarians.

Most European immigrants, no matter what their country of origin, left from one of two German ports, Bremen or Hamburg. And while waiting to board ship they usually stayed in an inn especially designed to house them and their families. If they wandered around the evil port cities they were most likely to be bilked of whatever money they had—which is one reason why the average immigrant arrived in America with less than $20. Because steamship companies had to bring rejected immigrants back to Europe at company expense, everyone had to undergo a medical inspection. And if lice were found, he and his bundles were fumigated.

The ocean voyage, of course, was not quite up to the advertisements. An immigrant might be in a 6-by-6-foot cabin with triple-decker bunks and five other passengers who were sick all the way. Often mothers were too ill even to care for their children.

Immigrants who made the Atlantic crossing after 1855 were processed through Castle Garden, a converted amusement park on the tip of Manhattan. This was replaced in 1892 by Ellis Island, which remains forever associated with boatloads of immigrants sailing in past the Statue of Liberty and yearning to breathe free. Originally, Asian immigrants were processed at the Pacific Mail Steamship Company warehouse in San Francisco, but after 1910 they were quarantined on Angel Island in San Francisco Bay—sometimes for weeks or months—because of official fear of cholera and other epidemic diseases. Since 1920, despite a quota system, Canada, England, Germany, and especially Mexico and the Caribbean have helped keep the immigrant tradition alive. From 1971 to 1975, an average of 387,000 people have emigrated to America each year.

That, in brief, is the story of how and when most of our immigrant ancestors came to be Americans. If you want to learn more about your own ancestors' journey, I've listed some books in the bibliography. You can also learn more by checking with ethnic organizations, which you can find through a directory of organizations at the library. In the following pages, however, I've listed in alphabetical order how the immigration tides ran for the principal ethnic groups in this country.

Africans

In the beginning, American colonists who depended on cheap labor relied mainly on European indentured servants, people who sold their labor for seven years in return for passage to America. Soon, however, the needs of Southern planters outstripped the supply of bond servants, and black slaves were imported to take their place. The increase in the slave trade was so great, in fact, that by 1776 *20 percent* of the colonial population had African ancestors. Twenty-five percent of the blacks captured in Africa and sold to slavers came from Angola, another 25 percent from Biafra, and the rest from the Gold Coast, Senegambia, Sierra Leone, and other parts of West Africa.

An African's trip to America, described in Alex Haley's *Roots,* was almost unimaginable. Shackled hand and foot to a plank, with only 18 inches of head room, he or she was forced to lie in body wastes for days, even weeks. If one could free himself, he often committed suicide. Often half of those taken aboard did not survive the trip.

When the Civil War brought an end to the slave trade there were approximately 4.5 million persons of African descent in America, 90 percent of them living in the South.

Canadians

Like the United States, Canada has been a mecca for European immigration, and in turn has contributed an enormous number of emigrants across the border to the U.S.

Among the first were the Acadians, 8,000 French Catholics who had settled in Nova Scotia and who were ordered out of the country by the British in 1755. They settled in Louisiana, where many of their descendants call themselves "cajuns."

Since 1862 four million Canadians have emigrated to the United States, many such as Scotch highlanders who came to Ontario province in droves before 1850 and later crossed over into the United States.

By 1890, large numbers of French-Canadians had moved into New England to work in the textile mills, and until the 1930s they proved to be one of the least assimilable groups of immigrants, fiercely maintaining their own French-speaking schools and churches, much like their counterparts in Canada today.

Chinese

The Chinese began arriving on the West Coast during the 1850s and at first worked at resifting the dirt at

worked-over gold-mining camps. Later many moved
on to jobs building the Central Pacific railroad, helping
to hack through mountains by hand. They were such
valued and inexpensive workers (their wages were often
two cents a day) that agents were sent to Canton to re-
cruit thousands more.

After the railroads were built in the 1870s, trade
unions and other white labor groups protested the im-
portation of such cheap labor, resulting in the Chinese
Exclusion Act of 1882, which stopped large-scale immigration, although thousands of Chinese able to pay
their passage to Hawaii or California continued to
come.

English

Most Americans—82 percent, in fact—can trace at
least one line to English ancestors. The first of five million English immigrants to America arrived in James-
town in 1607, adventurers and artisans sent by the
London Company for the purpose of colonizing. They
managed to gain a foothold on the swampy Virginia
land. Surviving starvation, Indian troubles, and personal squabbles, they unknowingly set the stage for
future disaster by buying the first black slaves, twenty
persons from a Dutch trader in 1619.

In 1620 an even more famous band landed to the
north at Plymouth Rock, the Pilgrims, who were sep-
aratists from the Church of England. Barely half the
company of 100 survived the rigorous first winter, but
during the next thirty years about 20,000 English immigrants arrived in the Massachusetts Bay Colony,
which gradually overflowed into what was to become
Rhode Island, New Hampshire, and Connecticut.

If your forebears came from England in those early
days, they underwent a terrible journey. The horribly
overcrowded ships took six to twelve weeks to make the
trip and often ran out of food, even though passengers
were promised by the investors who financed such ex-
peditions, "salt beefe, Porke, Salt Fish, Butter, Cheese,

Pease Pottage, Water-grewell, and such kinds of vict-
uals, with good Biskets and sixe-shilling Beere." One
early immigrant ship lost 108 of its 156 passengers to
starvation. Then voyages were, despite their discom-
fort and deaths, very expensive. The average Puritan
family of eight with a ton of freight spent 30 pounds
on the trip (over $1,000 in our money today).

One group of English immigrants came involuntarily
—in chains. From 1717 to 1775, 50,000 English convicts quite naturally chose deportation to the colonies
for seven years rather than hang. But one should not
think harshly of these convicts, for in those days the
penalties for crimes were unduly stiff—indeed, 150
crimes were capital offenses, including stealing a sheep,
cutting down trees in avenues, sending threatening letters, or merely standing mute in front of one's "bet-
ters." The convicts were not unwelcome in America.
Southern planters were eager to pay 10 pounds to acquire their services, and many eventually achieved posi-
tions of responsibility. George Washington, for instance,
was taught by a convict servant his father bought for
a schoolmaster. For many, what was intended as pun-
ishment turned out to be their good fortune, and many
a person transported as a felon became rich.

Another group of English people who arrived in this
country before the Revolutionary War were indentured
"bond" servants. Many respectable but destitute people
actually sold themselves into temporary slavery to reach
this country. In fact, half of all the English who emigrated came under a labor contract called an "in-
denture." This was an agreement, in exchange for passage to America, to work as a servant for a number of
years (usually four, but in the case of children the term
ran until they were twenty-one years old). Upon arrival
in America they were auctioned off by the ship's captain
to the highest bidder.

Many captains engaging in this trade made enormous
profits so there were bound to be abuses. Starving
families often sold one or two of their young children
for a few coins. If a ship heading for the Colonies did

not have its full complement of indentured men and women, a press gang would go out and shanghai the rest.

But the traffic was not entirely one way. In the 1780s, one group of English emigrated *from* the newly created United States. Americans loyal to the English King fled in numbers estimated to be as high as 100,000. Since families were split, with son against father and brother against brother, many descendants of Loyalists, as they were called, still live in America. If it is possible your ancestors were Loyalists, look for them in the records of England, Canada, and Nova Scotia (see Chapter 9).

French

There have been French immigrants in America since the 1600s. They were planters, fur traders in the Mississippi Valley, and merchants in Louisiana.

About 15,000 Huguenots—Protestants driven out of Catholic France in the 1700s—settled around Charleston, South Carolina. A few others went to New York and Rhode Island.

In the century between 1820 and 1920, about one million French-speaking immigrants came from France, Belgium, and Switzerland.

Germans

Before the Revolutionary War more than 200,000 Germans had congregated in New York and the Pennsylvania back country, where they became known as "Pennsylvania Dutch." Many of them emigrated from the German Rhineland, called the Palatinate, in order to practice a number of dissenting religions. They were called Mennonites, Dunkards, Moravians, Schwenkfelders, or sometimes were all lumped under the common title of the "Plain People." Later, Lutheran Germans came. Although they were industrious and sober settlers and usually welcomed, Thomas Jefferson, for one, was afraid of the influx of Germans, and warned against

foreigners deluded by "maxims of absolute monarchies."
He needn't have worried about any such democratic
backwardness. During the Revolutionary War, the Germans already in America so successfully propagandized
the 30,000 Hessian mercenaries hired by the British
that nearly half of them deserted and settled in New
England and Pennsylvania.

After 1848, a time of destructive revolution, bad
crops, and avaricious landlords in the German states,
a new wave of 1.5 million German immigrants arrived
to help develop the Middle West. They settled in Ohio,
Wisconsin, Indiana, Michigan, Iowa, traveling even as
far as Texas, where one of their number is said to
have originated a very un-German dish called chili con
carne.

Hungarians—Including Czechs, Slovaks, Slovenes, Croats, Serbs

From 1880 to 1920, almost four million immigrants
arrived from the old Austria-Hungary empire. There
were not many Austrians. Instead there was a mix of
ethnically distinctive groups such as Hungarians,
Czechs, Slovaks, Slovenes, Croats, and Serbs. In this
country they became collectively known as Slavs.

Few of these southern and eastern Europeans were
drawn to the land (most of the good homestead land
was gone by then anyway), but preferred the gregari-
ous social life of their own ethnic neighborhoods.

Concentrating in Pennsylvania, and in the cities of
Chicago, Akron, Toledo, Milwaukee, and Detroit,
Slavic laborers provided much of the muscle needed
for America's iron, steel, and coal industries.

Irish

St. Patrick's Day was celebrated with a grand feast
by Boston Irish as early as 1737, but if you have Irish
ancestry, the chances are they were immigrants after

1845. In that year a potato blight in Ireland caused that food staple to rot in the ground, and thousands chose America over starvation. Many of those who left were so weak they did not survive the trip; in 1847 alone, 15,000 Irish died aboard ship. Nevertheless, over two million Irish, mostly Catholics from central and southern Ireland, came in thirty years. In all, nearly 4.4 million Irish have come (and are still coming) to this country as immigrants.

They clustered together in eastern cities and along the industrially developing shores of the Great Lakes. Although most had been farmers at one time, because the land had betrayed them they turned their backs on it, preferring to trust their stomachs to wages instead of crops. Many took tough construction jobs for 30 cents a day, and few early canals or railroads were built without their labor.

Italians

More than 5.3 million Italians have come to America since the first one, Nicholas Biferi, arrived in Georgia in 1774 and billed himself as the "Musician of Naples."

Many of those who arrived in the late nineteenth century headed for California, where they worked in agriculture and developed the wine industry. Most came from northern Italy, but after 1900 it was the Italians from Mezzogiorno (the southern half of the peninsula and Sicily), fleeing poverty, overpopulation, and economic oppression. These former *contadini* (rural laborers) shunned the agricultural life, settling in cities north of the Ohio and east of the Mississippi.

Everywhere they replaced earlier immigrants (the Irish, in particular) in low-paid, pick-and-shovel jobs, building subways and railroads, and working in textile mills and the needle trades. Some became small merchants or opened restaurants. In many eastern cities at one time, barbering was virtually an Italian monopoly.

About 40 percent of Italian male immigrants returned to Italy to see their families, to obtain brides, or to live out their lives on the luxuries made possible by American wages. The majority re-emigrated, but the back-and-forth travel continued until World War I.

Japanese

Until 1890, the Emperor of Japan refused to allow emigration, and those who did emigrate to America were not allowed to return to their homeland. After the edict was rescinded, over 100,000 Japanese quickly boarded ships to escape poverty, ruling class oppressions, and military conscription. Most settled in Hawaii and on the West Coast and became small farmers, cannery workers, and the like. Although 400,000 Japanese immigrants have come to the United States since 1861, there are today only 600,000 Americans of Japanese ancestry.

Jewish

Between 1880 and the first World War, two million Jews emigrated to America, one-fourth of the world's Jewish population. They settled in ethnic neighborhoods in large cities—1.4 million in New York City alone, with additional large enclaves in San Francisco and Los Angeles.

Most of the immigrants were *Ashkenazim,* a Hebrew word meaning "German," but used to describe eastern European Jews as well. For the most part they were escapees from savage pogroms, forced conversion, army conscription, and laws denying them a livelihood.

They were not the first Jews to come to America fleeing persecution. In 1654, twenty-three Jewish *Sephardim* (Spanish or Portuguese in origin), escaping the Inquisition, landed in what was then New Amsterdam. Four years later, a small group arrived at Newport, Rhode Island. By the time of the Revolutionary War there were 300 Jews in New York, with smaller groups in Philadelphia and Charleston, South Carolina. Later, between 1820 and 1870, 400,000 German Jews became established along the eastern seaboard.

Today one-third (5.5 million) of the world's Jews are Americans, twice as many as live in Israel.

Polish

The total numbers of Polish immigrants are buried in the statistics for Russia and Austria-Hungary, which both dominated Poland at different times, but more than two million Poles flocked into America's expanding industrial cities after 1880.

The largest Polish communities grew up near the stockyards of Chicago, the steel mills of Pittsburgh, the auto plants of Detroit, and the metal industries of Buffalo. Many Poles also vied with incoming Italians, Irish, and French-Canadians for jobs in the textile mills of New England.

Russians

The bulk of Russian immigrants were Jews from western Russia, but more than 1.2 million others were Russians, Lithuanians, and Ukrainians.

The largest immigration came between 1880 and 1920, much of it the result of an economic depression brought on by the disastrous Russo-Japanese war, forced military service, and the political unrest that resulted in the revolution of 1917.

Scandinavians

The Scandinavians—Norwegians, Swedes, Finns, and Danes—who came after 1840 went west and north to Minnesota, Wisconsin, and the Dakota territory, where the country more nearly duplicated the climate of their homeland. Their glowing letters home emptied whole Scandinavian villages. "Anyone who wants to make good here has to work," one Swede wrote, "but here everything is better rewarded." Norwegian immigration was stirred by public readings in Norway of a book entitled *True Account of America for the Information and Help of the Peasant and Commoner.*

Immigrants were lured not only by compatible climate but also by the promise of free land, the result of the 1862 Homestead Law, which promised every adult immigrant 160 acres of land if he lived on it and farmed any portion of it for five years. In all 2.5 million Scandinavian immigrants helped fill up the Midwest, and they prospered perhaps more than any other ethnic group.

Scotch-Irish

Millions of Americans are descended from the 250,000 Scotch-Irish immigrants who came to America between 1717 and 1775. These people were actually transplanted lowland Scots who, in one of many English schemes to subdue the Irish, had been urged to emigrate to Ulster in Northern Ireland a century earlier by James I. It was thought that hard-nosed Presbyterian Scotsmen could better control the Irish than England's standing army, but by 1717 the Scotch-Irish were in trouble themselves. A depression in the flax industry, higher rents, severe frosts, a sheep disease, and a smallpox epidemic scourged Ulster.

They emigrated in waves to the Shenandoah Valley of Virginia, the Piedmont country of North Carolina, to New Jersey, Delaware, Maryland, New Hampshire, Maine, and Pennsylvania. By the time the Declaration of Independence was written, one out of every ten Americans was Scotch-Irish.

The Scotch-Irish brought an ethnic personality well fitted to westward-moving pioneers: they were religious, stubborn, and moral. After discovering that the prime land along the eastern seaboard had been taken by earlier arrivals, they quickly fanned out toward the Appalachians. Their sons and daughters were in the forefront of the western migrations each succeeding generation.

Spanish-Speaking

The Spanish and Mexicans had done some colonizing of southern Texas and New Mexico as early as the seventeenth century, and in the next century moved into California. But the biggest influx of Spanish-speaking people has been since 1920 with the immigration of roughly two million people from Mexico, one million from the West Indies, another million from South and Central America, 650,000 from Cuba, and 200,000 from the Philippines.

A total of 4.8 million Spanish-speaking Americans have been recent immigrants, and this figure excludes large numbers of Puerto Ricans—a group not counted as immigrants because they are American citizens. Adding these groups together, the total of Spanish-speaking mainland Americans probably is nearer six million, the largest ethnic group in the country.

Other Immigrants

America, called "half-brother to the world," has been more receptive to immigration than any other country. Almost every nation is represented in our ethnic makeup: Portugal has sent 850,000 immigrants, Greece 500,000, the Netherlands 350,000, Switzerland 350,000, Spain 250,000. From Turkey have come 380,000 people, primarily Armenians, Syrians, and Lebanese. From Australia have come 100,000, descendants of immigrants themselves. Finally, from Vietnam have come 125,000 Vietnamese, most arriving in 1975 after the war.

If I have not mentioned your ancestral group—or even if I have—you will find a decade-by-decade description of the flow of your people to this country in a wonderful table in the 1975 *Annual Report* published by the Immigration and Naturalization Service of the U.S. Department of Justice. Ask a librarian to help you find it.

THE INNER MIGRATIONS: THE COMING OF THE ROADS

A great many, perhaps most, Americans no longer live near where their ancestors settled when they arrived in this country. If your forebears came after 1869, they may well have traveled by train from their arrival point, since by then the nation's rail system had begun to be well along. Or if they arrived more recently, of course, they may have migrated across the country by car or plane. But in the early days of America, the inner migrations followed the coming of the roads.

"Westering," the lure of the western unsettled lands, took hold of early immigrants almost as soon as they arrived. They began by pushing out from Massachusetts to Connecticut. Axmen widened Indian trails to accommodate horses, then made them wider still for wagons loaded with household goods. Within fifty years after the *Mayflower* arrived, the King's Highway (later the Boston Post Road) carried mail—and migants—from Boston to New York.

A stagecoach ride down the King's Highway was a rough experience. "You are fully exposed to inclement weather," one migrant wrote, "and soaked as if you were out of doors. You are crushed, shaken, thrown about, bumped . . . Every mile there is a new accident and you must get out into the mud while the damage is repaired. It is not unusual to see coaches shattered, the passengers crippled, and the horses downed."

After 1685, the King's Highway was extended from New York to Philadelphia, then on south to Norfolk, Virginia, and finally all the way to Charleston, South Carolina. And after 1744, the Great Road funneled Scotch-Irish and German migrants from Philadelphia

west and then southwest along the eastern edge of the
Appalachians. Eventually the Great Road linked up
with Daniel Boone's Wilderness Road, which passed
through the Cumberland Gap and on to Louisville,
Kentucky. By 1780, 12,000 settlers had crossed into
Kentucky; by 1783, 22,000.

The Pittsburgh Pike, another early road from the
original Thirteen Colonies, wound through the Pennsylvania forests from Harrisburg, taking migrating English, Scotch-Irish, and German settlers to the Ohio
River, which by the early 1800s had become the quick-
est way to get to the newly opened western territories.
A flatboat ride down the Ohio from Pittsburgh to
Louisville, past sandbars, rocks, and inhospitable Indians cost $40, and migrants had to share accommoda-
tions with pigs and livestock. Later the Ohio became
the tributary feeding boats into the Mississippi, the
major river road to the South and to Texas.

Early roads began as blazed trails and became wagon
tracks, but the federal government began to get into the
roadbuilding business in the 1800s with the National
Road, a vast project that extended from Cumberland,
Maryland, to the Indiana territory, which was built
principally for military reasons because of American
concern about the French presence in Louisiana. Once
again this extended the westward migration. A traveler
on the National Road in 1817 wrote, "Old America
seems to be breaking up and moving westward. We
are seldom out of sight of family groups before and
behind us."

To the south, the government built the Federal Road,
which wound from Athens, Georgia, to just north of
Mobile, Alabama. This became the jumping-off point
for emigrants to New Orleans or Nashville. Far to the
north, in upper New York state, the Erie Canal was
opened in 1825, and was a big factor in the early settlement of the Northwest Territory. The canal was safer,
cheaper, and shorter than the roads and rivers, and was
a favorite mode of migration until the development of
the railroads.

One group of inner migrants, the American Indians, had little choice. By 1830 Congress had passed the Indian Removal Act, enabling the government to transfer the remaining eastern Indians west of the Mississippi River. In one of these removals, the trek of the Cherokees to Oklahoma, many died of hardship and disease on their trail of tears.

By 1850, the population of Ohio, Indiana, Illinois, and Michigan alone was 6,100,000, and the days of the canals and the old roads were over. Then railroads were carrying migrants (in specially marked "immigrant cars") to where the "new West" began at the Mississippi River. With immigrants crowding eastern cities and farms, the West offered "elbow room" for which every pioneer yearned.

The first wagon train for Oregon started West in 1842; the first for California in 1844. Riding in a covered wagon meant a bone-rattling trip, jammed into a 10-by-4 foot space with all the utensils, belongings, and other family members, across a 2,000 mile stretch of plains, alkali flats, deserts, and mountains. Most of the trains were made up in Independence, Missouri, headed along the south side of the Platte River to western Wyoming, then turned northwest on the Oregon Trail or went southwest through the High Sierras to the gold rush in California. The Santa Fe trail took migrants south to New Mexico and then over the Old Spanish Trail through the desert to California.

Although we tend to think of the wagon train (and steamboat and railroad train) as the principal way our ancestors traveled West, many of them, believe it or not, actually walked—"shanks mare," it was called. If a migrant was a little better off than average, he could afford a horse to carry his wife and a handcart in which to push some family belongings.

A lot of inner migrants never made it. There was no protection against sickness, and many of us have ancestors or their relatives who perished from cholera, childbed fever, or weariness. They left their names on markers such as this alongside the trail:

Jno. Hoover, died, June 18.49
Aged 12 yrs. Rest in peace,
sweet boy, for thy travels are over.

By 1870, rails were carrying migrants West, and by 1890, the last wild frontier was conquered. Yet still the inner migrations continued—and are continuing—as wars, depressions, hard times, personal misfortunes, and also simply the promise of something better, have impelled people to pull loose from their roots and re-settle elsewhere.

Now let us begin that search back to your roots.

4

FIRST STEP BACKWARD: HOW TO TAKE A FAMILY HISTORY AND GATHER AVAILABLE RECORDS

Now that you have some background—a sense of how names vary, and perhaps a sense of the immigration and migration patterns that might have affected your forebears—let us get down to the main task of actually finding your roots. While very few people can trace *every* branch on their family tree, there is hardly any family historian who cannot use the techniques I'm about to describe to trace back to an early ancestor in *some* line of the family.

In this chapter, I'm going to show you how to start by interviewing your living elderly relatives in order to gather a history of the family. This might well be a kind of oral history—that is, spoken memories (which you might want to tape-record). Although oral history is a tradition older than books, it has only recently become widely popular among students and scholars. For instance, the oral-history interviews of southern Appalachian mountaineers by high school students resulted in the best-selling *Foxfire* books. Many colleges in the country are rapidly building oral-history libraries, recording the recollections of older local people. You can do the same with your own family. Or if you can't do it in person you can probably get a family history by interviewing by mail.

Before we get to this, however, let me describe the equipment you need and the procedures to follow.

SETTING UP YOUR FAMILY HISTORY PROGRAM

Unlike photography, golf, and almost every other leisure-time pursuit, ancestor hunting requires very little equipment, and most of it is paper and pencil (or pen). Here's what you need:

Two Loose-Leaf Binders. Old ones recycled from school days are fine. One is for your notes and unfinished research. One is for your permanent Family History Book.

Pedigree Charts. See the examples in Figures 1 and 2. The Family History Book is really the culmination of your search. In it, in alphabetical order by surname, should go everything you acquire during your ancestor hunt—photographs, maps, letters, clippings, vital statistics, deeds, wills, and so on, including the Pedigree Charts and Family Group Sheets, described below.

You should give some thought to the paper you use inside. Ordinary bond paper will turn yellow and brittle in forty years or less even with maximum protection —which means storage in a cool, dark, temperature- and moisture-consistent place. Both words and pictures should be recorded on permanent paper. Fifty percent cotton content or rag bond, Permalife document bond, or ledger-mounting stock will last 500 years or more. All city, county, and national records are recorded on permanent paper stock. So why not spend a few cents more at a stationery store and make your Family History Book also a lasting record? You can draw a copy similar to the one shown here onto 8½-by-11-inch white bond paper, and photocopy (Xerox), say, twenty-five copies for starters. Or you can order a supply printed on special durable or acid-free paper from the nearest genealogy club you'll find listed in Appendix I in the back of this book.

I found the word "pedigree" awfully stuffy at first, since it reminded me of poodles and race horses, but that's the term genealogists use. It doesn't mean these charts are only for people whose blood runs bluer than that of the French kings. They are for everybody.

Family Group Sheets. See the example in Figure 3. Like the Pedigree Chart, you can draw a copy similar to the one in this book and duplicate it, or you can order some sheets from the Genealogy Club of America.

Both the Pedigree Charts and the Family Group Sheets are your personal road maps to your family history, worksheets to show you how much information you have on your ancestors and how much more there is to discover. The reason for having both in standardized form is so that later you can exchange them with other members of your expanded family— and they'll be able to understand what you've done.

Family History Questionnaires. See the example in Figure 4. You'll need this when you go out to start gathering oral history from the relatives, so you won't forget the important questions to ask.

Tape Recorder and Cassettes. These are not mandatory, but they are helpful when you're talking with the relatives—especially if you tend to be a slow writer, as I am. More on this later.

How to Fill Out the Pedigree Charts

Pedigree Charts are really quite simple to fill out. Most family historians follow a few standard rules, which make charts consistent and thus easy to read

FIGURE 1. Example of Pedigree Chart
and how to fill one out.

PEDIGREE CHART

CHART NO. *1*

NAME OF PERSON MAKING OUT THIS SHEET

STREET ADDRESS _____
CITY _____
STATE _____ ZIP _____
DATE _____

No. 1 on this chart is
the same person as no. _____
on sheet no. _____

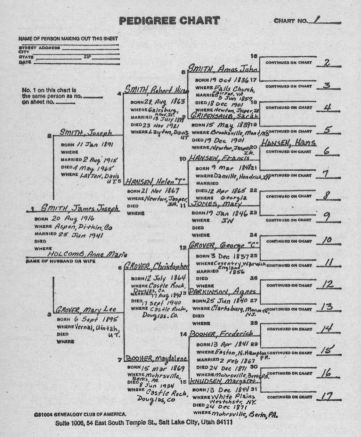

16		
8 SMITH, Amos John		CONTINUED ON CHART *2*
BORN 19 Oct 1836 17		
WHERE Falls Church, Fairfax, VA		CONTINUED ON CHART *3*
MARRIED 3 Jun 1859		
DIED 18 Dec 1901		CONTINUED ON CHART *4*
WHERE Newton, Jasper, IA		
9 GRIPENSAUB, Sarah		
BORN 15 May 1839 19		CONTINUED ON CHART *5*
WHERE Brooksville, Mont, MS		
DIED 19 Dec 1901		HANSEN, Hans
WHERE Newton, Jasper 20 IA.		CONTINUED ON CHART *6*

4 SMITH, Robert Hiram
BORN 28 Aug 1863
WHERE Galesburg, Knox, Ill.
MARRIED 19 July 1888
DIED 23 Nov 1921
WHERE Layton, Davis UT

2 SMITH, Joseph
BORN 11 Jan 1891
WHERE
MARRIED 2 Aug 1915
DIED 4 May 1965
WHERE Layton, Davis UT

10 HANSEN, Francis
BORN 9 Mar 1841 21
WHERE Danville, Hendrick, IN
MARRIED
WHERE Georgia 22
JONES, Mary
BORN 19 Jan 1846 23
WHERE IN
DIED
WHERE

5 HANSEN, Helen "T"
BORN 21 Nov 1867
WHERE Newton, Jasper, IA.
DIED
WHERE

CONTINUED ON CHART *7*
CONTINUED ON CHART *8*
CONTINUED ON CHART *9*

1 SMITH, James Joseph
BORN 20 Aug 1916
WHERE Aspen, Pitkin, Co
MARRIED 25 Jun 1941
DIED
WHERE
HOLCOMB, Anne Marie
NAME OF HUSBAND OR WIFE

24
12 GROVER, George "C"
BORN 3 Dec 1837 25
WHERE Coventry, Warwick England
MARRIED 1856
DIED
WHERE
26
PARKINSON, Agnes
BORN 25 Jun 1840 27
WHERE Clarksburg, Monm, NJ.
DIED
WHERE
28

6 GROVER, Christopher
BORN 12 July 1864
WHERE Castle Rock, Douglas, Co.
MARRIED 11 Aug 1893
DIED 17 Sept 1940
WHERE Castle Rock, Douglas, Co.

CONTINUED ON CHART *10*
CONTINUED ON CHART *11*
CONTINUED ON CHART *12*
CONTINUED ON CHART *13*

3 GROVER, Mary Lee
BORN 6 Sept 1895
WHERE Vernal, Uintah, UT.
DIED
WHERE

14 BOOHER, Frederick
BORN 13 Apr 1841 29
WHERE Easton, N. Hampton PA.
MARRIED 2 Feb 1867
DIED 24 Dec 1871 30
WHERE Mohrsville, Berks, PA.
KNUDSEN, Margaret
BORN 13 Dec 1844 31
WHERE White Plains Westchstr, NY.
DIED 24 Dec 1871
WHERE Mohrsville, Berks, PA.

7 BOOHER, Magdalene
BORN 15 Mar 1869
WHERE Mohrsville, Berks, PA.
DIED 8 Jun 1934
WHERE Castle Rock, Douglas, Co

CONTINUED ON CHART *14*
CONTINUED ON CHART *15*
CONTINUED ON CHART *16*
CONTINUED ON CHART *17*

FIGURE 2. Example of how to continue a line of the family onto another sheet of the Pedigree Chart.

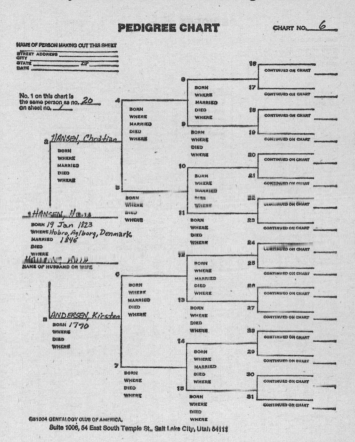

PEDIGREE CHART   CHART NO. 6

NAME OF PERSON MAKING OUT THIS SHEET
STREET ADDRESS
CITY
STATE _____ ZIP
DATE

No. 1 on this chart is
the same person as no. 20
on sheet no. 1

2 HANSEN, Christian

1 HANSEN, Hans
BORN 19 Jan 1823
WHERE Hobro, Aglborg, Denmark
MARRIED 1846
DIED
WHERE
NAME OF HUSBAND OR WIFE

3 ANDERSEN, Kirsten
BORN 1770
WHERE
DIED
WHERE

GS1004 GENEALOGY CLUB OF AMERICA,
Suite 1006, 54 East South Temple St., Salt Lake City, Utah 84111

FIGURE 3. Example of Family Group Sheet
and how to fill one out.

HUSBAND BIGLER, Jacob
Born 1752-53   Place Bucks Co. PA.
Chr.   Place
Marr. 29 Mar 1779   Place
Died Will proved Sep 1829   Place Clarksburg - Harrison WV
Bur.   Place Enterprise Cemetery Harrison Co WV
Husband's Father BIGLER, Mark (Immigrant)
Husband's Mother Catherine
Husband's other wives

WIFE BOOHER, Hannah
Born 1760   Place Philadelphia, PA.
Chr.   Place
Died 17 July 1853   Place Shinnston, Harrison, PA.
Bur.   Place Saltwell Righter Cemetery Harrison WV
Wife's Father BOOHER, Henry
Wife's Mother KOON, Catherine
Wife's other husbands

SEX M/F	CHILDREN SURNAME (CAPITALIZED) GIVEN NAMES	WHEN BORN DAY	MONTH	YEAR	WHERE BORN TOWN	COUNTY	STATE OR COUNTRY	DATE OF FIRST MARRIAGE / TO WHOM	WHEN DIED DAY MONTH	YEAR
1 F X	BIGLER, Sarah	30	Jan	1780		Bucks	PA	26 Apr 1795. RIGHTER, John	7 July	1880
2 F	BIGLER, Hannah	30	Jan	1783	Shinnston	Harrison	WV	18 Apr 1799. McCAULLY, James	23 Sept	1851
3 M	BIGLER, Mark	19	May	1785	Shinnston	Harrison	WV	7 Nov 1805. OGDEN, Susannah	25 Sept	1839
4 F	BIGLER, Ruth	28	Apr	1788	Shinnston	Harrison	WV	4 Sept 1806. WHITEMAN, Able		1830
5 F	BIGLER, Nancy	29	Apr	1790	Shinnston	Harrison	WV	1 Sept 1812. WHITEMAN, Henry		1842
6 M	BIGLER, Jacob	9	Jun	1793	Shinnston	Harrison	WV	24 Mar 1814. HARVEY, Elizabeth	3 Sept	1853
7 M	BIGLER, Henry	24	Apr	1796	Shinnston	Harrison	WV	30 Oct 1822. DICKERSON, Hannah	2 Sept	1857
8 F	BIGLER, Bathsheba	29	Jun	1798	Shinnston	Harrison	WV	30 Sept 1821. SMITH, William	17 Nov	1826
9 F	BIGLER, Maria	29	Jan	1801	Shinnston	Harrison	WV	FLOWERS, William		
10 F	BIGLER, Rebecca	About 1805			Shinnston	Harrison	WV		About	1805

and understand no matter who makes them. Starting off with a consistent form will save a lot of recopying later. Here's how you do it.:

1. Study the five-generation Pedigree Chart in Figure 1. It will give you at a glance the names, births, marriages, and deaths of four generations of direct ancestors. The fifth generation is shown by name only, but each fifth-generation name is repeated as the first generation on the next consecutively numbered Pedigree Chart of that line (see Figure 2). In that way, you can extend any family surname back as far as you are able to and the numbering system will be simple to follow.

2. Record each person's full name, capitalizing the entire surname. For example, BARNES, John Joseph.

3. Record the day, then month, then year, like this: 16 Apr., 1853.

4. Always record the smallest geographical area first: Johnston City, Williamson County, Illinois, becomes Johnston City, Williamson, IL. Use standard Postal Service abbreviations for states, but do not abbreviate cities or counties.

5. Any information such as a birthdate which is in doubt should be followed by a question mark in parentheses.

How to Fill Out the Family Group Sheets

A Family Group Sheet should be started for the marriage or marriages of every person shown on your Pedigree Chart. If your great-grandfather went to the altar five times, then he should have five separate sheets. (As you go back farther into your past, you'll find a number of men and women who were married more than once. In those days wives frequently faded after eleven children and husbands collapsed under back-breaking work.)

FIGURE 4. Example of Family History Questionnaire.

VITAL STATISTICS

Your full name _____ (maiden name, if any) _____ Date and place of birth _____ Residence _____ Religious affiliation _____

Father's name _____ Date and place of birth _____ Mother's name _____ (maiden name) _____

Education _____ Date and place of marriage _____ Spouse's name _____

YOUR CHILDREN

Sex	Name	When born where	When married where	Married to	If dead, when and where
1					
2					
3					
4					
5					
6					
7					
8					

FAMILY HISTORY INFORMATION

What do you know about the family surname? _____

Are there traditional first, middle, or nicknames? _____

Do you know the name of your immigrant ancestor? _____

What country did he come from? _____

When and how did he arrive in this country? _____

What was his occupation? _____

Which ancestors served in the military? _____

Is there a family cemetery? _____

Are there any notorious characters, famous people, knights, or royalty in the family? _____

Do you know anyone in the family working on genealogy? _____

Does anyone still own old photos, letters, family Bible, etc.? _____

Here are a few guidelines the experts suggest to help you complete neat, consistent Family Group Sheets:

1. Record names, dates, and places in the same way you did on your Pedigree Chart.
2. Initials (if you do not know the full name) should be placed in quotation marks. For example, SMITH, John "P."
3. All uncommon first names—such as Evelyn for a boy or Georgie for a girl—should be *underlined* to show you know they are unusual and that they are not mistakes on your part.
4. If there were other marriages for either husband or wife, reference them by name so that they will be easy to find in your Family History Book.
5. In the upper right-hand corner mark the name and address of the Family Group Sheet preparer, also indicate what relationship you are to this family, such as great-granddaughter.
6. Place an X next to the number of the child who is your direct ancestor.
7. If any children are twins, adopted, stepchildren, or stillborn, place the information in parentheses after the child's name.

That's all there is to it. After you get the Pedigree Charts and Family History Sheets drawn up, you can start getting the information you'll need to begin filling them in.

START WITH YOURSELF

You will probably be able to complete parts of these charts right now—perhaps back through your grandparents' generation. As soon as you collect more family history from interviews and the Family History Questionnaire I'll show you about in a bit, you should be able to fill in missing details and add another generation or two. Here's how to proceed.

Since chronologically you are the first person in your family history, you should start with yourself. Sit down with scratch pad, Pedigree Chart, and Family Group Sheet and spend a couple of hours searching your mind for family information. Who are your parents? Your aunts and uncles? Your grandparents? When and where were they born, married, and so on? Who are their children? You can use the Family History Questionnaire as your own guide. You'll be surprised how many family facts you have tucked back in the corners of your memory. Enter names, places, and dates right on your charts. If you're not sure of some, put a question mark in parentheses after the entry. Then you'll know to check it later with some other family member.

After you've put down as much information as you can gather from out of your head or from your own records (birth certificates, letters, old photographs, diaries, family Bibles, and so on), make out a list of older (and other) relatives you need to interview. You'll then be ready for the next step.

INTERVIEWING YOUR FAMILY ELDERS AND OTHER RELATIVES

The most critical thing you have to do as a family historian is to hurry to your oldest relatives before it is too late and get every scrap of information you can. This is the advice professional genealogists give all amateurs. Few older relatives will refuse to cooperate. In fact, most will be flattered that they have information the younger generation wants.

There are three ways to extract these family facts. Using the Family History Questionnaire (Figure 4) as a guide, you can:

1. talk to your elders face-to-face
2. interview them by mail, if they live some distance away
3. ask another relative or family friend to talk to them for you

The way to approach relatives is to inform the family in general that you're working on the family history—and to invite their comments and solicit their help. One professional genealogist tells me you can expect one of three answers when you tell members of your family you're doing their genealogy: (1) "Wonderful, I was hoping someone would!" (2) "I knew there was a nut loose in this clan." (3) "Mind your own damn business and leave it alone." It may well be that the one who gives the third answer is the one you want to talk to first; you can bet that person hasn't forgotten any juicy particulars he or she ever heard. If any relatives balk, the genealogist advises, you can win them over easily with one statement: "Whatever I find out, I'm going to share with all of you."

A word of caution: Don't think just because you were particularly close to a certain older relative that you know all he or she has to tell. In researching my own Eddy line, I talked with many relatives, thinking I had heard all the family stories my grandmother knew. As I came to know more about my family, I realized I had made a mistake, but by then grandmother was in a convalescent home, senilely rocking away with the personalities, loves, tragedies, dates, names, and places of four generations locked in her mind.

Now let me describe the three methods of interviewing relatives.

1. Face-to-Face Interviewing

The word "interview" sometimes sounds a bit too professional to new family historians, but all it is, really, is just another term for a thorough conversation.

You may be talking to family elders across a gap of several years, but you have a lot in common, for you're exploring important memories. Even a cranky aunt will be happier when she's recalling a time when she *was* happier.

Face-to-face interviewing is preferable to the other

HOW TO RECORD YOUR INTERVIEWS WITH RELATIVES

There are two ways to record an interview—(1) using a tape recorder, or (2) taking notes in your workbook.

The tape recorder (which you can rent from a camera store) is by far the better technique. It frees you to listen more fully; you can be sure you are getting every word said; it allows you to be alert to every change of expression; and you won't have to decode your own handwriting days later. With tape you can record a real oral history of your family.

Recorders with built-in microphones are best, I've found. The interviewee usually forgets the recorder is there if he doesn't have a mike in his face.

The tapes needs not be high fidelity. They can be cassette tapes of the least expensive variety—unless you want high-quality tapes to save some of the most important or colorful conversations or the ones of special grandparents. Obviously, the sound of their voices and the accent or colloquial expressions they use will be extremely precious years later.

Be sure to mark the outside of the tape or cassette with date, time, place, and person interviewed.

If you rely on or prefer note taking, begin by identifying each interview as to date, time, place, and person in your workbook. Then, as the interviewee talks, write like crazy. And try to remember that *you* will be the one to unscramble all those sentences that curve around the edge of the page. Obviously, it's a good idea to transcribe or type your notes as soon as possible after the interview.

types of interviewing. As I mentioned, it is better to use a tape recorder (see box, p. 52), but it is not necessary. You can pick up nuances of feeling—sadness, joy, fear, evasiveness—that can quickly tip you off about whether you should pursue or drop a particular line of questioning. People also tend to go on longer when they're talking than when they're writing. When, during a face-to-face interview, you let an elder talk he will probably reveal many more insights and tidbits of family lore than you would have thought to ask. Indeed, he might give you some information that leads you in an entirely new direction.

When I first started tracing my family history I interviewed a great-great-uncle who was 104 years old. At the time I found it a terribly frustrating experience. He talked on for hours as if he were still living on the Cherokee Strip in the Oklahoma Territory, and reminisced about the prairie town that swelled to 5,000 people overnight, where drinking water cost fifty cents a dipper and raucous saloon girls mixed with desperate outlaws and even more lawless lawmen. While I tried to pin him down to dates and names, he meandered down verbal paths of his own choosing. Since then, however, I have learned to be less impatient with elders. Although statistics are significant to every family historian, it is obvious to me now that living details about the past flesh out these numbers and are every bit as important. In general, you can look forward to meeting your relatives on a genealogical level. Most interviews, in fact, serve to pull the family ties even tighter.

Interviewing an older relative requires thoughtfulness as well as tact. Here are a few courtesies you should observe:

1. Make the appointment no longer than an hour and a half. The idea is to make it pleasant, not exhausting. Make a second and a third appointment, if necessary.
2. Don't assume they can't hear well and shout at

them. Just talk slowly, pronouncing words distinctly.

3. The five Ws of reporting—who, what, where, when, why (and sometimes how)—are good guidelines for phrasing questions.

4. Interview the relative alone, if you can, to preclude any possible influence from others present. (Sometimes after individual interviews, a joint interview, with each person jogging the other's memory, will get new information or correct and clarify the old.)

5. Ask important questions first. If you do, you'll have all the vital information in case your visit must be cut short for any reason.

6. Don't try to make them stick to your question if they don't want to. Let the conversation flow. Try to listen more than talk. Later you can come back and say, "Now, what was great-grandma's maiden name again?"

7. Send them a copy of the transcribed interview for their corrections. The value of this is great, for often they will add as much as they correct.

8. Don't overlook family friends and long-time neighbors when you interview. Even if they have no new facts, they may give a fresh perspective to the information you already have.

2. Interviewing by Mail

If you aren't in a position to take a vacation or business trip near the home of some relative you'd like to interview, then you'll need to do it by mail. This is not unusual. Indeed, my own family history research has been accomplished at least 75 percent by mail. The way to do it is to mail out Family History Questionnaires. Here's how:

1. Write a cover letter explaining that you are compiling a family history and need their help (see sample in Figure 5).

2. Be sure to thank them in advance. They don't *have* to help, you know.

3. Assure each relative that you plan to share your mutual family's history with them.

4. Make one original and a copy to keep, so you will not duplicate requests, and will have a complete record of your family search right from the start.

5. Always include a self-addressed, stamped envelope with every request.

You should include a copy of your own Pedigree Chart to show them what you already know and a blank Pedigree Chart for their use. To make things even easier for them, send along a blank Family Group Sheet (see Figure 3) for them to complete about their own marriage—but be sure to explain how to fill it out, so it won't confuse them.

3. Interviewing a Family Friend or Another Relative

If you equip them with the Family History Questionnaire as a basic guide, you may be able to interest a relative or trusted family friend in interviewing a distant relative for you. Usually several people in your family will be interested in the family's history. But they may not want to take on the entire job. Still, they usually don't mind helping out—especially when you promise to share your family-tree research results with them.

Be sure to tip your friends to a common family problem: You know that Uncle Jack has been a fount of information for years, but he's also been the family gossip. Unfortunately, Uncle Jack and your mother had a falling-out ages ago and he vowed never to speak to her again. Assuming the family feud extends to your generation, it is smarter (if a bit sneaky) to send Uncle Jack's favorite nephew Norman to do the interviewing.

FIGURE 5. Cover letter for interviewing relatives by mail about your ancestor.

Dear (name of relative):

I am trying to gather information on our family in hopes of putting together a history of it and making it available to other relatives.

I would be grateful if you could find the time to fill in the blank Pedigree Chart attached to this letter. Please fill it in as completely as you can and return it to me in the stamped self-addressed envelope enclosed. I am also enclosing a copy of my own Pedigree Chart to show you how far I've been able to go with my side of the family.

It would also be very helpful if you could refer me to others in our family who might have information about our forebears. And, of course, I'd appreciate any information you could give me on family and related public documents (Bible records, certificates, photos, diaries) that I might copy and return. I sincerely want to record and preserve our family's heritage as accurately and completely as possible.

Thank you for your time and help.

Cordially,

Don't make the mistake of approaching the gentleman and being refused. This might just make him suspicious of anyone who comes around asking for family information, even Norman. It is also a good idea to remain in the background. Don't brag about fooling him—because Uncle Jack may also have other treasures, such as the family Bible or photos, and you'll want them later on.

Incidentally, be careful about probing emotional relationships too deeply. Some relatives may be ashamed of skeletons in their family's history. Of course, today's ancestor hunters live in a more relaxed moral climate, and most wouldn't be at all aghast at finding an illegitimacy, a prison sentence, insanity, a horse thief, or a pirate. Sometimes they actually add glamour to a modern family's history and make the people human. But respect the sensibilities of the people you are interviewing.

ATTIC ARCHAEOLOGY: FINDING FAMILY RECORDS

A family history can contain more than vital statistics. Letters, diaries, old photographs, memoirs, albums, clothing, and other family artifacts add flesh and blood to the ancestral bones and show your forebears' personalities. They also add a thrill of discovery, an awareness of the continuous line that stretches back to the past, of which you are a part.

Even with the mobility of the modern American family, a great mass of information about family heritage exists if you know where to look for it. When interviewing a relative, in person or by mail, always inquire if he or she has old Bibles, photos, scrapbooks, legal papers, or letters of your family ancestors that you can photocopy and return. It's amazing what you can find when you rummage through attics, basements, trunks, closets, and old shoeboxes.

Here is a checklist of items to look for that will add luster to the Family History Book:

1. *Personal records*—journals, diaries, letters, newspaper clippings, photos, baby books, wedding albums, funeral albums, employment and retirement papers.
2. *Legal papers*—contracts, tax bills, wills, deeds, mortgages.
3. *School records*—diplomas, yearbooks, awards, alumni papers.
4. *Religious records*—marriage, baptismal, christening, church membership, family Bible.
5. *Government records*—military discharge papers and awards, citizenship or naturalization papers, passports, business licenses, Social Security cards, income tax forms.
6. *Health records*—vaccination, hospital, insurance, doctor bills.

Unless you are interviewing or writing your own parents, it is a good rule never to ask to borrow or keep personal treasures. Extract all the information you can from what you find, and suggest you might like to see the items again sometime. Often enough, on the second or third visit, I have received a spontaneous gift. A great-aunt gave me my great-great-grandfather's farm journal with a hand-drawn map of his orchard and several 125-year-old grocery shopping lists. Another relative (this one a cousin I met only by questionnaire) sent me a perfectly preserved picture of my great-grandfather in his Union Army uniform and his yellowing discharge certificate, dated June 14, 1865.

Remember the serendipity factor and watch for every possible clue. One family archaeologist came to the razing of a family home expecting to make some kind of find and, sure enough, located a box of century-old love letters hidden between the walls in a bedroom.

Here are some things to watch for as you check family records.

1. *Family Bible.* You'll find that you can't always trust Bible data. One story I heard concerned a family Bible which had two complete lists of the same children, both written in the same handwriting but each list obviously written years apart. Since the first child entered had been born in 1899, the family detective checked the Bible's publication date, which was 1914. From that, she understood that the first list of entries was probably made from memory after 1914. The second complete list of children with their death dates was made years later, as indicated by the shaky handwriting and unfaded ink. Although the two lists contained good genealogical material, they also presented a problem. On the first list, a child was named Arthur Albert, on the second, Albert Arthur. Which was right? The searcher would have to go to vital records for a birth certificate. Obviously, a family Bible cannot always be considered—you'll pardon the expression—the gospel truth.

2. *Letters.* In addition to what is revealed by their contents, make a note of their postmarks (postmarks started back in the sixteenth century), dates, and return addresses.

3. *Household effects.* Needlework keepsakes such as samplers and friendship quilts (still popular through the 1930s) often give names, dates, and place clues. Spoons and teapots may also bear family names.

4. *Books.* Scrapbooks, photo albums, and other compilations of memorabilia are good sources for the ancestor hunter. And our ancestor's library shouldn't be overlooked. Not only will the choice of books give a valuable clue to his interests and character, but there may be solid gold hiding in the pages. In our grandparent's day, books were storage chests as well as reading matter. Flowers were pressed between their pages, calling cards and greetings were dropped in for safekeeping,

and sometimes newspaper clippings, too. While leafing idly through a volume of my Grandfather Righter's set of *Lee's Lieutenants,* a fifty-year-old newspaper article fell out in my lap. It was a full-page interview (dull to anyone but me) on the occasion of his father's investiture as commander of the local post of the Grand Army of the Republic. It gave great-grandfather's version of the family history back to the Revolutionary War.

The important thing to remember is: don't try to remember. Whenever you are checking through family records, have your loose-leaf workbook handy for notes. Don't trust to memory. In genealogy, memory is never as good as documentation. If wills, deeds, or letters are too long, then have them photocopied or take extracts of the most important parts. Or, of course, you can use a tape recorder to tape your notes.

There you have it. Once you have drawn up or ordered the forms, you're ready to go.

NOW LET'S GET GOING

There is precious little time to waste in beginning to trace your family. A friend of mine tells a story about how a month after his mother died he went through her personal things, with other members of the family, and found a photo album with some very old tintype pictures in it—some more than a hundred years old. No one could identify the pictures. It's sad to have photos of great-grandparents and others and not know who they are. That's something we should be trying to discover now, not after our grandparents and relatives are gone.

That's not the note I want to end the chapter on, however. I once asked a long-time professional genealogist what she advised beginners to do, expecting a very learned reply. Her answer: "Have fun!" So, start having fun with your own search for roots. You can, if you wish, carry your family search just to the extent I've described in this chapter—that is, interviewing relatives. That may well give you over a century of family history, compiled in charts and memorabilia, to place in your Family History Book. You'll treasure the results just as you treasure your school or wedding pictures.

But once you've gone that far it's difficult to stop. You'll find yourself wanting to go beyond the memories of living relatives and family mementos to discover more of your ancestral lines. In the next chapter, I'll show you a fast way to get a lot of already researched family history.

5

FINDING YOUR ROOTS WITH THE HELP OF THE WORLD'S GREATEST GENEALOGY COLLECTION

Deep inside massive vaults blasted out of the Rocky Mountains near Salt Lake City is the greatest treasure of genealogical information ever assembled. Here 1.5 million microfilm rolls, equivalent to more than 1.8 billion book pages, line six rockbound chambers. Visitors are not allowed inside because dust particles on their shoes, hair, or clothing might contaminate the film. Filtered, humidified air circulates constantly in the artificial light, for these microfilms can never see the destructive light of day. This huge underground storehouse, constructed in 1965 at a cost of $2 million, is built to withstand any disaster—it is hoped, even a nuclear holocaust. More protected than the crown jewels of England, here are the records of 2 billion of our ancestors, gathered from 126 different countries by over 150 microfilming crews filming religious, local, and national "people" records all over the world. The sponsor of this mammoth effort? The LDS (Mormon) church.

Why does the LDS church (short for The Church of Jesus Christ of Latter-day Saints) have the largest collection of genealogical material in the world? For

LDS church members, genealogy is a vital activity and filled with religious significance. Simply stated, genealogy is the method by which the living LDS sanctify their dead.

In over 40 world temples—closed to all but the faithful—members are married for "time and eternity," and the children are "sealed" to their parents so the family will remain intact in the afterlife. This doctrine of the "exalted family" is also extended to ancestors who walked the earth long before the LDS church was started by Joseph Smith in the 1830s.

And the reason for the huge genealogical collection is that ancestors, who have been identified through a genealogical search, are baptized by proxy —with the descendants standing in for his or her forbear. (Since 1842, more than 95 million ancestors have been baptized, five million in 1987 alone.) LDS members believe their ancestors in the hereafter have the opportunity to accept or reject the baptism. But if they accept, then they will be reunited with all the baptized generations of their family after the resurrection.

If you're not an LDS member, you may wonder what use this genealogical collection is to you. The answer is that some of the 2 billion recorded ancestors the church has gone to so much trouble to find are probably yours. Whether or not you have ever had an LDS member in your ancestral family, there is a good chance that someone, as part of this religious belief, has compiled information on your forebears. Furthermore, this immense genealogical complex is open to everyone, not just LDS church members. The implications for all family historians are therefore staggering.

HOW YOU CAN USE THOSE
BURIED MICROFILMS

If you are ever on a vacation or business trip near Salt Lake City, it would be well worth your time to stop if only for a few hours, at the main LDS library which houses the microfilms. Almost any family historian could probably add new branches to his family tree during such a visit.

But if getting to Salt Lake is out of the question you can still take advantage of the records by simply going to the LDS Family History Center near you. There are over 1,000 such facilities, with more being added each year.

Although LDS centers are generally self-help, there are always volunteer genealogist-librarians who will assist you with just the source you need to carry on your ancestor search. And most centers conduct periodic classes and seminars that help you learn how best to use their collection and instruct you on the operation of the microfilm readers.

LDS family history centers come in all sizes. Some are small with minimal microfilm collections of their own. Others hold large numbers of microfilmed census records, reference books, and issues of genealogical, historical and family magazines.

These centers can order rare microfilmed records for you from Salt Lake City for a small postage fee. Please contact a family history center in your area for more information and costs involved. I recommend you visit, not write, the nearest local family history center, since they are not staffed to answer mail inquiries.

Using a family history center in my home town paid off for me. I was able to order records of my German immigrant great-great-grandfather, Jacob

Bigler, which contained information on three older generations of Biglers, back to 1705. In another case I traced a female ancestor, Elizabeth Arnold, my fourth great-grandmother, and received information on her five children and whom they married; I also got her father's name, which took me back to 1733. Not everyone gets this kind of help from two microfilms, but some get even more.

THE LDS SALT LAKE CITY
FAMILY HISTORY LIBRARY

I once met a professional genealogy researcher who spends four months a year in Salt Lake City studying the LDS British materials. "For years I went to England to track down ancestors for my clients, going from parish to parish, shire to shire," he said. "Now I come to Salt Lake City because all those English records are here in one place."

The LDS library in Salt Lake City is an impressive place. It is on five floors in a new 142,000 square feet building. Over 200 unfailingly courteous people, collectively fluent in thirty languages, work in the complex. In a year well over 700,000 ancestor hunters visit the library.

The first thing you notice is 500 microfilm readers whirring and flickering, singing of vital statistics, passenger lists, and war records. And the giant card catalog that used to occupy so much room when I started my family search is now completely computerized. The lives of our ancestors can be brought up on screen in a fraction of a second.

General reference works and LDS church records are also available on the main floor.

The second floor houses research materials for the United States and Canada, including North American Indians and black ancestral material. This collection is the most complete in the library and is very strong on Midwest, Southern, and New England material. For some states (Massachusetts, for example) they have just about every existing record.

The Correspondence Unit of the library receives more than 5,000 letters per month. Of course, they are not able to trace entire family trees, but they do try to answer specific questions and let people know how best to utilize their records. Sometimes they refer people to one of their nearest family history centers: sometimes they suggest hiring an accredited professional genealogist who knows the main collection well.

A complete listing of the LDS library holdings at Salt Lake City would fill many catalogs, and new material is being added all the time. For a general overview, you can consult Mary L. Brown's *Handy Index to the Holdings of the Genealogical Society of Utah*, available at any LDS family history center, but here is an abbreviated list of what you can expect to find:

—185,000 volumes of genealogy and history
—118 million name computerized index representing 12 countries
—Genealogical periodicals from around the world
—U.S. census records up to 1910
—American Loyalists' claims with the British Government
—Church registers (U.S. and foreign)
—Land grants and property deeds
—Marriage records
—Wills and other court records
—Tax and pension files
—Naturalization records
—Passenger ship lists
—Port of Hamburg passenger lists (surname index

for years 1856-1871), one of the two major European ports of embarkation.

Specific sections of the library are devoted to specific countries, nationalities, or ethnic groups, as follows:

Africa and Asia

This collection contains materials for all countries of the South Pacific, Asia, the Middle East, and Africa. The library has Taiwanese and Hong Kong records, and the People's Republic of China (mainland) has agreed recently to microfilm their records for the LDS library.

American Indian

If you have American Indian blood, you'll find helpful records on eastern as well as western tribes. Here's a partial listing:

—Lives of famous chiefs
—History, biography and genealogy of the Wampanoag tribe
—Handbook of American Indian languages
—Notes and monographs—Powhatan tribes of Virginia
—Early history and names of the Arapaho
—Report on Indians taxed and not taxed (1890)
—Abenakis of Vermont
—Census of the Bureau of Indian Affairs
—Census of Cherokee (1835)
—Iroquois anthropology at the mid-century (1850)
—Navajo
—Quinnipiock
—Ute tribal membership rolls and other tribe enrollments

—Sioux personal property claims
—Genealogy of Indian families of the Pima, Maricopa and Papagos
—Indian deeds of Rhode Island (1638)
—Indian letters, talks and treaties
—Shawnees in Kansas
—Confederate Indian soldiers
—Indian students (1826-1835)
—Yakimas

Blacks

The U.S. section contains black genealogical information, including black censuses taken by the Southern states during the last century. The church has also begun to microfilm records in the French colonies of Haiti and Martinique.

Britain

The British section has extensive material from England, Wales, Scotland, Channel Islands and Australia. They also have large microfilm collections for Northern Ireland, Ireland, New Zealand and the Republic of South Africa. The depth and breadth of this material is astounding.

Continental Europe

The Continental Europe collection contains records from both Europe and Asia. Some of the countries represented are: Poland, Germany (east and west), Romania, Czechoslovakia, Bulgaria, Yugoslavia, Albania, Hungary, Austria, Switzerland, Netherlands, Belgium, Luxembourg, France, Italy, Greece, Mediterranean Islands, Spain and Portugal. The LDS church has been doing a great deal of microfilming in Bulgaria, Poland and Yugoslavia, and has a number of Polish records, some filmed before the Second World War. However, they have few records for many countries including the Soviet Union since officials will not exchange information or allow their records to be filmed.

In many eastern European countries, even the so-called Iron Curtain countries, vital records come under the Minister of Culture and they seem to have an understanding of what the LDS church is trying to do. But in the U.S.S.R. all records are under the jurisdiction of police authorities, and their attitude is quite different. In addition, four-fifths of the Soviet National records were destroyed by revolution and war.

Latin America and Iberian Peninsula

Records are sectionalized under South America, Central America (South and Central American Indians), Faeroe Islands, and Greenland.

Other Collections

Smaller countries, islands, and groups of people are also indexed in the LDS library. For instance, if you needed information on an immigrant ancestor from Liechtenstein, the library has material on this tiny country. Add to this vast numbers of maps, books on heraldry, old newspapers and gazetteers and you can see the mountain of information available to you—information that could take you back to your roots.

REACHING BACKWARD: USING LDS FAMILY HISTORY CENTERS

Many people don't know the LDS Family History Library resources are open to all people searching for their roots. Hardly a week goes by that I don't surprise someone with the news that the source he or she is so diligently looking for is probably located at the LDS family history center just across town, or can be easily ordered from the main library in Salt Lake City.

The main LDS library is located at 35 North West Temple Street, Salt Lake City, Utah, 84150. To find the address of the family history center near you look in your telephone directory or write the main library in Salt Lake City. New local centers are being added all the time. Again, I urge you to visit rather than write them.

6

FINDING YOUR ROOTS WITH THE HELP OF PUBLIC LIBRARIES, SPECIALTY LIBRARIES, AND GENEALOGICAL SOCIETIES

The last chapter established an important principle—namely, see if you can find out if other people have already done your work for you. Obviously, you would feel tremendously frustrated if you found out a few weeks down the road that you'd been blazing a trail that had once been blazed by someone else and you didn't know it.

For this reason, I feel you should definitely take advantage of the LDS library's immense stockpile of family history. However, despite the fantastic energy of LDS members, they haven't traced every ancestor or searched every record. There are a lot more family records out there. So, after you've checked the LDS library you should try looking for records of your ancestors in the following, which we will discuss in this chapter:

1. Public libraries
2. Genealogical-historical societies and their publications

3. Private libraries with special genealogical collections
4. State libraries or archives

Though you might not think so at first, these sources are useful even if you're a second- or third-generation American.

Before I explain libraries and archives, let me help you set up a simple system of record-keeping and research procedures.

YOUR RECORD-KEEPING SYSTEM

A good, uncomplicated system will help you find a source or note when you need it. Here's how to do it:

1. You have some sort of workbook which you call your Family History Book.
2. Into this Family History Book put—in alphabetical order by surname—all your records for each generation and each ancestor within that generation. You may want to label each surname with a colored plastic tab.
3. As you fill in Pedigree Charts and Family Group Sheets place them in your Family History Book by family surname. I like to keep Family Group Sheets for a particular ancestor together with all his or her photos, copies of wills, deeds, biographical material and maps (several companies specialize in selling maps to family genealogists—see the appendix).
4. Whenever you add any new family discoveries to your Family History Book, document your additions by naming the source (and date) of each find. (Label undocumented material "family tradition.")
5. As you write up family migrations and biographical stories from local histories, verify each one by

listing the author, book, title, volume, publisher, date of publication, page, and library or genealogical society where you found it.

6. Keep a sheet in your workbook with the title "Negative Research." On it list all the sources you consulted that proved to be dead ends. By listing them, you won't be as apt to forget and look in these same sources again.

7. Write down *immediately* in your workbook anything you glean from a source—a relative, a librarian, a card catalog. Several times, in a hurry, I have found a bit of information (such as an intriguing mention of an ancestor in a history book or a unique interpretation of one of my family surnames), neglected to jot it down, and later was unable to find it.

8. Keep a research reminder list in your workbook of sources you would like to check for a particular forebear. When you accumulate enough for a library visit or a research trip you will be able to accomplish all you need to do from notes on this list.

PROCEDURES TO FOLLOW

The first thing you need to decide is which line or surname of the family you want to trace. The second thing is to determine what I call a "research locale."

After you conduct your oral history and mail interview with relatives, you will probably have some information about a number of your family lines. LDS research may provide more. Now, instead of striking out in all directions at once, I recommend you choose one line at a time and concentrate on it for as long as you can easily follow it. Most people, of course, want to trace their own surname first (women, their maiden names), but if you have too much trouble with *any* family line, drop it for a time and go on to another one.

After all, the idea is to make your search fun, not work.

Next, determine your "research locale." A research locale is simply the place where you're likely to find the most records about the family line you've chosen to research. If you know your Grandpa Henry was born in Lincoln, Nebraska, and you want to find out more about him and his forebears, then Lincoln (whether or not *you* live there) becomes your research locale, since it has all the vital records, such as birth certificates, that will give you the information you want.

Once you have determined the research locale, write to the research sources concerned with that locale— namely, as I said earlier, public libraries, genealogical-historical societies, private libraries with special genealogical collections, and state libraries or archives. The addresses for many of these sources are given in the appendix called "State-by-State Family History Help List" at the back of the book.

When you write them, do the following:

1. Ask specific questions. For example, "Can you tell me if the name Alexander Luther Eddy, who resided in Dayton, Ohio, from 1850 to 1915, appears in any local histories or family genealogies in your collection?"
2. Ask the librarian to check for a family history if you think your ancestor may have lived in the area for any length of time. The chances may be slim, but who knows, maybe a cousin has already written one and deposited it in the library.
3. Ask if there is a local history book in which your ancestor might possibly be mentioned.
4. Ask if the librarian can suggest others to contact. Often he or she can direct you to people who are involved in local genealogical or historical research and might have unpublished information on your ancestor.
5. As a courtesy, enclose a stamped, self-addressed envelope. Offer to pay for any photocopying expense.

6. Don't mail librarians Pedigree Charts to complete or expect them to wade through page after page of family stories.

That's the basic program for extending your ancestor hunt to libraries and archives. The rest of this chapter describes the principal institutions to which to write. If you plan on visiting rather than writing to a library, see the box (p. 78), which tells you about things to look for.

PUBLIC LIBRARIES

Almost every public library, no matter how small, has a genealogy and local history section; some have large collections. Here are a few that are valuable not only to ancestor hunters living or searching in their locale but, because of the depth of their collections, to family historians all over the country.

Ft. Wayne (Indiana) Public Library

The Ft. Wayne library has an impressive holding of over 100,000 books, microfilms, and other genealogical records on Midwest forebears, including collections of records from England, Scotland, Ireland, and Canada. Some professional genealogists think this rapidly growing library will soon rival the Newberry (Chicago's famous private family history resource, to be discussed). You can write to the Historical Genealogy Collection, Ft. Wayne Public Library, 900 Webster Street, Ft. Wayne, Indiana 46802.

Free Library of Philadelphia

Philadelphia, which calls its library by its original eighteenth-century name, has records of immigration showing arrivals at the port of Philadelphia during the

HOW TO USE LOCAL LIBRARIES

If you aren't as familiar with a library as you used to be, ask a librarian to give you a short tour, so that you'll be able to find things for yourself. He or she knows the collections and can unravel a research puzzle that has you up a tree (but not family tree).

Get acquainted with the card catalog, which lists every book in the library alphabetically three ways —by author, title, and subject. You will find cards for all the books on genealogy in one place.

The card catalog will list related subjects on a "See Also" card which will lead you to other sources the library has for you. If you're in the research locale in which the ancestor you're hunting for lived, check the card file for a book under your family name; it may even be a family history. Next try to find a book about the history of the locality or state. Look for a card with the name of the state or county and the subheading "History" or "Genealogy." You just might find your ancestral name mentioned in such histories.

Go to the section of your library shelves numbered 929 (in Dewey Decimal System) and browse; this is where you will find how-to books on genealogy and biography, books on surnames, nobility, and heraldry. (Also see the bibliography at the back of this book.)

Nearby, in the 970 section, you will come across general United States history, as well as state, county, and local histories.

Ask your librarian if they have microfilmed census records. For example, the Atlanta Public Library has all Georgia census records on file, which could save having to write a letter to the National Archives in Washington, D.C. (see Chapter 8).

If you need to search further or you haven't found what you are looking for to fill in the empty spaces of your research, be sure to ask the librarian whether there are photo or clipping files or other books you should consult in the library. Because of their value, many one-of-a-kind family history books and rare reference works are not kept on the shelves, but will be made available to you if you ask.

period of 1728 to 1808, lists of German immigrants, naturalization records for the years 1740 to 1773, early Pennsylvania land grants, vital statistics (births, marriages, and deaths) prior to 1885, census records, and 138 volumes of the Pennsylvania and Colonial archives. Write to Free Library of Philadelphia, Logan Square, Philadelphia, Pennsylvania 19141.

Los Angeles Public Library

The Los Angeles city library system really caters to family historians in a big way. Over 40,000 books, magazines, microfilm rolls, and manuscripts deal with county, city, and family history, published vital records, military rosters, and books on surnames. While you are there, trained library assistants will help you find and use the library's materials and suggest other sources when you run into dead ends. Contact Los Angeles Public Library, 630 West Fifth Street, Los Angeles, California 90017.

New Orleans Public Library

This city library has developed an extensive collection full of fascinating local history—for example, 30,000 microfilmed photographs, Louisiana census schedules, Mardi Gras memorabilia, and civil court records dating back to 1769. You may address your questions to the Genealogy Section, New Orleans Public Library, 219 Loyola Avenue, New Orleans, Louisiana 70140.

New York City Public Library

The 39,000 volumes here include many vital birth, marriage, and death records, city directories, bibliographies, indexes, genealogical reference works, and surname dictionaries. As you might suspect, this library is strong on New York sources.

Some specific items in the library that could be useful to you are:

—New York area newspapers on microfilm
—791 genealogy and historical publications from the United States and Europe
—Local histories
—Scrapbooks and files of photographs of American towns during the past century
—International Card Index to scientists and aviators
—Index to New York probate and death notices
—83,000 biographies
—Many maps of New York state, county, and city

A unique aid to genealogists provided by the library is its "let's exchange" file, which encourages an information swap between family researchers. (If you are searching for a New York City ancestor, you should check this file to see if any other genealogist is already working on your family tree.) This is another way to keep from duplicating research someone else has already accomplished.

The library also maintains a file in which all its uncataloged family material is arranged alphabetically by name, such as letters and jottings not indexed elsewhere in the library.

Librarians will answer brief, specific questions you may have about any New York ancestors whose names are on file with them. Address these questions to the Local History and Genealogy Division, New York City Public Library, Fifth Avenue and 42nd Street, New York, New York 10018.

GENEALOGICAL-HISTORICAL SOCIETIES AND THEIR PUBLICATIONS

Family historians can reap several benefits by joining one of the several national genealogical societies. Two are the Genealogy Club of America (GCA) in Utah, and the National Genealogical Society (NGS) in Washington, D.C. The GCA, a grass-roots group, is probably more helpful to the beginner, while the NGS is more scholarly and attuned to the serious historian. Membership in these societies includes a subscription to their publication, which is the best way I know to keep up with new sources for genealogical research around the country. You may also wish to join your hometown genealogical group or one in your research locale. Addresses for many national and local groups can be found in the State-by-State Family History Help List at the back of this book.

Whether or not you decide to join a national or local genealogical-historical society, it can help you in your ancestor search. Many have established libraries which are absolute treasure troves, and some print well documented family histories as well as local histories and genealogical research forms. The most prestigious is the New England Historic Genealogical Society founded in 1845. Specializing in New England families and history, its library, one of the largest of its kind in the world, holds 200,000 books and two million manuscripts. Members may borrow books by mail, a month at a time, for a nominal fee to cover mailing costs.

Even the smallest genealogical society seeks to collect as many books for its members as possible, and most have ongoing research projects, such as copying courthouse, cemetery, and church records. And every genealogical society, no matter how small, generally publishes a magazine, if only a mimeographed one. The style of publication is no reflection on its contents. One beginning Nevada genealogist, trying to trace a family pioneer, joined the Rapid City (South Dakota) Society for Genealogical Research just to get a subscription to its publication, *The Black Hills Nuggets.* The small investment paid off in a big dividend when she found her great-great-grandmother in the magazine's listing of gravestone inscriptions.

Genealogical publications can provide extremely use-

ful information for the ancestor hunter. For instance,
most run a "quest" column which acts as a clearinghouse for people of the same surname who want to contact each other for help. *The New England Historic and
Genealogical Register* has printed passenger lists and
other records spanning oceans and covering literally
thousands of subjects over the past 130 years. *The
National Genealogical Society Quarterly* has reprinted
family histories and an invaluable alphabetical "Index
to Revolutionary War Pensioners." The point is that
such publications provide genealogical data that may
save you from having to do the work yourself. To
locate a genealogical library in your research locale,
look in the State-by-State Family History Help List at
the back of this book, or consult Mary Kay Meyer's
Directory of Genealogical Societies of the United States
in your library.

Often your genealogical search can be supplemented
by work already published by one of the 4,300 local
historical societies in the United States and Canada. In
these printed local histories you may find a wealth of
pure genealogical information as well as exciting stories
and biographies of your forebears.

If you have been unable to find a local history by
writing the public library in your research locale, look
in the *Directory of Historical Societies and Agencies
in the United States and Canada,* published by the American Association for State and Local History. You'll
find the address of the nearest historical society to your
research locale. For example, if I wanted to see if my
Barnes ancestors were mentioned in a local history (and
the public library could not help me), I'd write to the
Harrison County (West Virginia) Historical Society.
The *Directory* will also give you the addresses of specialized historical societies for racial, religious, and
ethnic groups—for instance, the American Jewish Historical Society, which publishes the *American Jewish
Historical Quarterly* (now in its sixty-sixth year) and
which has a large library containing almost everything

that has appeared in print on local Jewish communities in the United States.

PRIVATE LIBRARIES WITH SPECIAL GENEALOGICAL COLLECTIONS

There are private libraries in every state which have special genealogical collections. Many are listed in the State-by-State Family History Help List in the back. If one isn't listed for your research locale, check with the state library or archive for its location.

Of course, the largest private genealogical collection is the LDS library in Salt Lake City, but the next most important is the Newberry in Chicago, which has an outstanding private collection of family history. The Newberry records are strongest on the Midwest but contain some material on all regions of the United States and Canada as well. Here's a partial list of some of its 150,000 genealogical treasures:

—15,000 printed family histories
—Local county histories
—All major genealogical periodicals
—U.S. census records from 1790 to 1880
—Military records of the American Revolution, War of 1812, and Civil War

The Newberry also has some multivolume reference works usually found only in the largest public libraries, if at all, such as the *Dictionary of American Biography, Cyclopedia of American Biography,* and the *American Genealogical Index*. The library's own collection is a massive four-volume tome that was indexed in 1918, which, unfortunately, doesn't contain any item the library purchased after that year. Still it is worth consulting, particularly for nineteenth-century Chicago and Midwest records.

The Newberry Family History Room is staffed with
people who are interested in helping you identify and
locate materials that will help you find your ancestors,
and they also make a reasonable effort to answer specific mail inquiries. Keep your questions brief and to the
point, and expect to pay a small photocopying service
fee for material reproduced. Write the Newberry Library, 60 West Walton Street, Chicago, Illinois 60610.

STATE LIBRARIES AND ARCHIVES

Another source to be aware of is the state library or
archive in your research locale. (For addresses, see the
State-by-State Family History Help List in the back of
this book.) Such libraries, which concentrate on state
history can be invaluable in tracking down an early
forebear. For example, the Pacific Room of the state
library of Hawaii in Honolulu has the only collection
in the world on Hawaiian ancestry. The California Room
of the California state library in Sacramento maintains
a mountain of data on the early gold rush, on railroad-
ing, and on the Spanish colonial period. The Michigan
state library has over 30,000 historical books and microfilms and, in addition, publishes *Family Trails,* a
Michigan family history magazine. The Texas state library at Austin has a vast amount of material with special emphasis on the South and Southwest. This gener-
ous library will even take telephone (512-475-6727)
as well as mail requests for family information.

The point of this chapter has been that someone may
already have done a lot of your ancestor searching for
you, and the best way to find that out is through libraries and genealogical-historical societies. In the next
chapter I'll show you how to go beyond such secondary
research and get to the primary records themselves.

7

FINDING YOUR ROOTS THROUGH LOCAL PUBLIC RECORDS

There are two types of records useful to family historians—primary and secondary. In the last three chapters I described how to use secondary sources—either secondhand personal information such as oral history, or secondhand public information such as written histories. Now let me tell you how to find primary sources, principally local public records—birth, marriage, and death certificates; wills, probate documents and land deeds; and church and cemetery records.

Why should you be concerned with these? Three reasons:

First, you can use them to trace back another generation. Let's say you know your grandfather was born in Springfield, Missouri. By writing the courthouse there you could obtain copies of his birth certificate. This might provide *his* father's name, thus giving you another generation.

Second, you can use these records to authenticate information you aren't sure about—such as birthdate, residence, or wife's name. (Some people have even found they were heirs to money this way.)

Finally, such documents, often signed in your ancestor's own hand, are what make those long-dead forebears come alive for you. Imagine, for instance, coming across an old will in which a mother chastises her wayward son by leaving him 20 pounds, "to be paid him by my executors at such times as the overseers to this my will shal judge meet (that is to say) when he doth take good courses as to live orderly, & to follow the cordwainer's (shoemaker's) trade, & is clear of such debts as he now owes . . ." A will such as this gives clues to personalities, and will be one of the more valuable parts of your Family History Book.

VITAL RECORDS

"Vital records" is the name historians give to birth, marriage, and death certificates.

Birth certificates list the date, time, and place of birth, the sex of the baby, perhaps its name, and the names of the parents.

Marriage certificates list the woman's maiden name, residence, and place, date, and presiding minister or official.

Death certificates list name; age, date, place, and cause of death; and doctor's name.

With all such vital records, the originals remain in the custody of the town or county officials, but by law you are entitled to copies. Locating such certificates really isn't as difficult as it sounds.

Many such records have already been copied or extracted and published. Most libraries carry the WPA *List of Vital Statistical Records* published by the federal government in 1943. This is a state-by-state compilation of the whereabouts of marriage, birth, and death records which was put together by unemployed writers indexing vital records for the Works Progress Administration in the 1930s. It is a good place to start unless you are looking for vital records in Alaska, Connecticut, Delaware, Hawaii, Maine, Maryland, Ohio, Pennsylvania, South Carolina, or Vermont; for those you'll have to go to your specific research locale, following the procedures below, which are also not difficult.

Birth and Death Records

You can get booklets from the federal government explaining how and where to find birth and death certificates. Write the U.S. Government Printing Office, Superintendent of Documents, Washington, D.C. 20402, and ask for the pamphlet, "Where to Write for Birth and Death Certificates." (Or try your local library.) This lists the address, cost, and records available for each state and U.S. possession. With few exceptions those records date from the late 1800s.

For earlier birth and death records you should write directly to your ancestor's town or county. In New England, births and deaths were kept by the town or village clerk. In the South and West they were usually kept by the county (or parish, in Louisiana) clerk.

For information on records of U.S. citizens who were born or died outside the United States, write to the Health Resources Administration, National Center for Health Statistics, Rockville, Maryland 20852.

Marriage Records

For marriage records filed since 1900, send for the pamphlet "Where to Write for Marriage Records" (there's also one for "Where to Write for Divorce Records"), U.S. Government Printing Office, Superintendent of Documents, Washington, D.C. 20402.

Before 1800, marriages were often recorded differently from the way they are today. In many places, legal documents called "marriage banns" or "bonds of intentions" were posted by the suitor, usually with a stiff financial penalty if he defaulted—an interesting way of making a suitor's word as good as his bond. Such fascinating old legal documents can be found among city and county records. In addition, since almost all marriages then were also religious ceremonies,

they are also contained in church records, discussed
below.

LOCAL PUBLIC RECORDS: WILLS,
PROBATE DOCUMENTS, LAND DEEDS,
AND OTHERS

There are a lot of public records available in county
courthouses that are prime sources of ancestral information: wills, probate documents, land deeds, tax and
voting lists, and commissioners' records (showing locations of roads and mills).

Early land records with their grantor/grantee indexes and tract books showing time, place, and length
of residence are also real finds for the ancestor hunter.
Often, these records in the hands of the county recorder
also refer to a forebear's property ownership in other
areas at an earlier time, or even to unknown relatives.
Such information can mean extending your line back
another generation or even two.

A photostat of such records costs very little and can
be had by writing to the county clerk or clerk of the
probate court—these offices are generally located in
the county seat of your research locale. Or, if you can't
copy such a record in its entirety, you can get the
essence of it through a technique called *abstracting*.
Here's the information you should be sure to take or
ask for from your ancestor's last testament:

1. The name of the person making the will (or other
   document)
2. Any information about him, such as residence or
   health
3. All persons named in the document and their relationship to your ancestor
4. The essentials of bequests (if a will), including
   land and personal property descriptions

5. The names of executors and witnesses
6. A description of any signatures, marks, or seals (in the old days some people signed with special marks)

A thorough lesson in researching probate and other court documents for genealogical information is given in Norman E. Wright's *Building an American Pedigree*.

STATE AND TERRITORIAL PUBLIC RECORDS

Most of the original states and states with former territorial governments have published a manual or index as to what material is in their archives. If you had an ancestor who helped open the Oklahoma Indian Territory, for instance, you would have to check with Oklahoma state archives, or the state census, which most state libraries keep on microfilm. The same holds true for all states, and the documents preserved constitute a prime source of genealogical information.

Besides, the WPA *List of Vital Statistical Records*, another useful reference work is Jenkins and Hamick's *A Guide to Microfilm Collections of Early State Records*.

CHURCH RECORDS

When birth, marriage, and death certificates are not available to you from government records, you might find such information in church records, many of which have been published over the past century. For example, if you are researching an old American family, it is not unlikely that you have a Quaker ancestor on some branch of your family tree, since it was a large sect 200 years ago—and the Quakers kept meticulous records. If you find—or just suspect—that you have a Quaker forebear, you might check *The Encyclopedia of American Quaker Genealogy* by William Wade Hinshaw for your ancestor's surname. Many Quaker records have also been collected and indexed at the Friends Historical Library, Swarthmore College, Swarthmore, Pennsylvania 19081. The library contains 13,000 Quaker family names, genealogical charts, 20,000 books, and 1,000 volumes of original Quaker meeting records.

During the nineteenth century, back-country, circuit-riding preachers often kept a journal of the services, marriages, funerals, and baptisms they performed. Thus, if you are having trouble finding vital documents for an ancestor, some of these journals can be found today in the historical archives of most churches.

AMERICAN CHURCH ARCHIVES

American Baptist Historical Society
1100 South Goodman Street
Rochester, New York 14620

American Catholic Historical Association
Catholic University of America
Washington, D.C. 20017

Archives of the Greek Orthodox
Arch-Diocese of North America
10 East 79th Street
New York, New York 10021

Archives of the Mother Church
The First Church of Christ Scientist
107 Falmouth Street
Boston, Massachusetts 02110

Church of Jesus Christ of Latter-Day Saints
Genealogical Association
Suite 1006, 54 East South Temple St.
Salt Lake City, Utah 84111

Congregational Christian Historical Society
14 Beacon Street
Boston, Massachusetts 02108

Lutheran Ministerium of
Pennsylvania
Historical Society
Lutheran Theological
Seminary
7333 Germantown Avenue
Philadelphia, Pennsylvania
19119

Mennonite Historical
Library
Bluffton College
Bluffton, Ohio 45817

Moravian Archives
North Main at Elizabeth
Bethlehem, Pennsylvania
18015

Presbyterian & Reformed
Church
Historical Foundation
Assembly Drive
Montreat, North Carolina
28757

The Protestant Episcopal
Church
Church Historical Society
606 Rathervue Place
Austin, Texas 78700

The best way to research church records for an ancestor is to study the membership rolls and records at the original church, either by going there in person or by writing to them. There are also some major church archives listed on pp. 90–91, which contain valuable genealogical records.

Sometimes church records help to bring our ancestors and the times they lived into sharper focus. For instance, I researched the records from 1850 to 1900 for the St. Paul Baptist Church in Fairview, West Virginia, where my ancestor, Michael Eddy, was clerk for forty-nine years. One entry showed that Brother Eddy was paid the handsome amount of twenty bushels of corn for annually furnishing the meeting house with light and fuel. Another entry, written in his hand, reported that it was "moved and seconded that we as a church will exclude any member that will vend or retail ardent spirits."

SEARCHING CEMETERIES

Many people feel a fascination about old graveyards, and in recent times the art of making rubbings of decorative gravestones (see box next page) has become a popular pastime—one headstone in Old Deerfield, Massachusetts, for example, has had over 10,000 rubbings made of it. While such rubbings are too large to fit into your Family History Book, they can be framed and hung on a wall. Quite naturally you might not want to do this with a recent family monument, but the process of copying gravestones loses its morbid feeling when one is transcribing the sentiments of a tablet in an old Western ghost town, a 200-year-old cemetery in New England, or churchyard in Europe.

Most of the inscriptions on gravestones are straightforward or commonplace, but there are reports of discoveries of ones like the following:

Here lies Jane Smith, wife of Thomas Smith,
Marble cutter. This monument was erected
by her husband as a tribute to her memory
and a specimen of his handiwork.
Monuments of this style are fifty dollars.

Or this reproof above the grave of an unforgiving woman:

I told you I was sick.

More likely are inscriptions like the following found by a friend of mine of his ancestor in a Massachusetts cemetery:

Here lies interred ye Body of Deacon
Oliver Moor,
who deceased Dec. ye 23rd, A.D., 1774
Death is a Debt to Nature due,
Which I have paid & so must you.

Unless you know someone who lives in or is visiting the area of your research locale, you'll probably have to visit the cemetery yourself—especially if you want to photograph the gravestones or make rubbings—although many of the oldest tombstone inscriptions have been compiled and filed in nearby libraries. Some have even been published, such as *Gravestones of Early New England and the Men Who Made Them* by Harriette M. Forbes.

If you have the name of the cemetery, but can't find the location—a century ago there were many private cemeteries and it was not unusual for people to be buried on their own land—try going to the area's local library and asking for county maps and county atlases, which will show the site of most graveyards. If those maps don't show it, try the county surveyor's office,

---

PHOTOGRAPHING GRAVESTONES OR MAKING GRAVESTONE RUBBINGS

Making the inscriptions stand out enough to be photographed often requires some work. Use wire and bristle brushes to scrape off lichen, dirt, and moss. Then rub soft, white chalk into the inscriptions to make them easier to read and photograph.

As for making gravestone rubbings, the process is simple. Take an ordinary wax marking crayon, masking tape, and a sheet of tough pliable paper (like a good grade rice paper) to get started. Cut the paper to the size of the stone to be rubbed, stretch it flat, and tape it *securely* on all four sides (if the paper shifts, you will have a blurred inscription). Hold the wax crayon at a slight angle and rub gently, varying the pressure on the crayon, until the image or words appear. If you notice a part you would like to emphasize more, just go back over it with a firmer pressure on the crayon.

which will have aerial maps, or try county historians or long-time residents.

Once you have found the cemetery where your ancestors rest, be sure to go there with your workbook. Copy down the inscriptions *exactly* as you find them. (Don't correct any misspellings—they are part of the charm and the record.) One person I know copied down a gravestone inscription all in German in a Vermont cemetery which, when translated later, gave him his ancestor's origins in Germany, the date of his desertion as a Hessian mercenary soldier from the army of the British redcoats in America, and other facts about his later life.

Many older private (or even public) cemeteries have been ill-cared for, and you may find stones fallen over or tall weeds obscuring the epitaph. Having grass shears and a shovel in the trunk of the car helps.

That pretty much explains how to search public records at the local level. In the next chapter I'll show you how to find your forebears in federal records.

SPECIAL PUBLIC RECORD SOURCES

The above are the general guidelines for searching for your ancestor in primary public records and cemeteries. If you are an adoptee of any race—yes, even some adopted persons can trace their natural parents and natural forebears—or if you are black, Chinese-American, Mexican-American, or American Indian, there are other public records you will want to know about. These are described below.

Adoptees

There are over eight million adoptees in America excluded from the rewards of tracing their roots because many obviously do not know their own names. Some foreign countries (for example, England, Scotland, Israel, and Finland) open adoption records to adult adoptees. In the United States the system is more rigid. Except in Alabama, adoption files are forever sealed, not to be opened except by court order—an order rarely given.

Still, during the past decade some adult adoptees have been successfully finding their natural parents, using the techniques of genealogical research. For example, one young woman with only the surname Elliott and the information that her mother started college in 1940, wrote over 500 letters to New England colleges, inquiring about a young woman of that name who entered the freshman class of 1940. "I am searching the genealogy of the Elliott family," she wrote. Actually, this ruse masked her real purpose, which was to find out more about her natural mother's identity, information she could obtain in no other way. In this way, she was able to learn her mother's hometown and eventually trace her thirty years later to New York City.

Another adoptee, a college professor, found his mother after a ten-year search which included many visits with child-welfare officials, from whom he demanded more information. The officials, somewhat intimidated, yielded one or two small scraps of information each visit, information he eventually put together to find his mother.

Searching for natural parents has nothing to do with whether or not an adoptee loves his adopted parents. "A natural genealogical curiosity," says Los Angeles psychiatrist Arthur D. Sorosky, "is felt by even the most successful adoptee." Everyone wants to know all there is to know about himself. But adoption and government agencies have made finding an adoptee's natural parents difficult at best.

If you have any information *at all* about your birth identity, such as surname or birthplace, you can get some help from two reference books found in most libraries, which tell you where records are and how you can gain access to them. They are *Where's What* and *Protecting Your Right to Privacy,* the last a federal guidebook. In addition, Val D. Greenwood's *The Researcher's Guide to American Genealogy* (see bibliography) may be helpful because it is one of the few genealogical research books which deals with *twentieth century* records, specifically vital statistics.

The principal agency helping adoptees in their search is ALMA (Adoptees' Liberty Movement Association), P.O. Box 154, Washington Bridge Station, New York, New York 10033. Organized by adoptee Florence Fisher after her successful twenty-year-long search for her mother, ALMA helps natural parents and adoptees find each other.

It maintains a date of birth registry for relatives who do not know each other's current names or addresses, but who know the date of birth of the adoptee. Because both natural parents and adoptees use the service, some matches and subsequent reunions have occurred.

ALMA also acts as a clearinghouse for research tips. Hundreds of adoptees have discovered research methods that work, and have written to ALMA with their finds. These are disseminated to other ALMA members by mail, and passed along to members at monthly Search Workshops in New York City.

If you have some basic personal information, such as name and birthplace, you can use good genealogical records search techniques (outlined in this book) to find your natural parents, and from them go on to your ancestors. If you have been denied even the knowledge of your own name, you should contact ALMA for help.

American Indian

If you have American Indian ancestry, many tribal councils formed since 1934 have detailed enrollment records. These rolls usually give the Indian name, "English" name, age, and family relationship.

If your ancestor was a member of the so-called Five Civilized Tribes (Choctaw, Chickasaw, Creek, Seminole, and Cherokee), the Indian Archives of the Oklahoma Historical Society has a book of the *Final Rolls of the Citizens and Freedmen of the Five Civilized Tribes of Indian Territory,* which is a listing of the tribal members by name, age, sex, degree of blood, and census card number. Another good reference is Emmet Starr's *Old Cherokee Families,* which is indexed alphabetically by surname.

Numerous other Indian records are at the LDS library and still others are at the National Archives.

Church records are especially important if you have Indian ancestors because more often than not missionaries kept records of Indians they converted. Some church records, particularly the Spanish Catholic records, date from the early 1500s and detail christenings and births, marriages, deaths, and burials. Besides the essential vital statistics, these records often list clues to occupations and places of residence.

C. A. Weslager, professor of history at Brandywine College and an authority on the Delaware tribe, suggests in addition to knowing special records sources, that it is advisable to become familiar with the native customs of your ancestral tribe. However, even at that, he feels it is virtually impossible to trace lineage beyond the time English surnames were adopted—at least if you are looking in the 1700s beyond the reach of oral family-history traditions.

Dr. Weslager identifies naming practices as one of the two major problems in tracing Indian ancestors. The other is kinship systems. A family historian with an Indian line should determine tribal kinship terminology before attempting a records search. In some tribes, the words for "brother" or "sister" could also mean "cousin"; the words for "father" or "mother" also meant "uncle" or "aunt."

A good guide to repositories of Indian records is *Reference Encyclopedia of the American Indian* published by A. Klein of New York City in 1967. It lists reservations, regional agencies, libraries, museums, and schools. You can find it in many libraries.

Blacks

Although Alex Haley with his monumental work *Roots* has brought black genealogy into sharp focus today, he is not the first black to be highly conscious of his family's past. For example, W. E. B. DuBois, founder of the National Association for the Advancement of Colored People (NAACP), traced his genealogy back to the seventeenth century in his autobiography *Dusk of Dawn*. The poet James Weldon Johnson traced his ancestors back to uprisings in the West Indies in the late 1700s in his book *Along This Way*. Robert Russa Moton, former president of Tuskegee Institute, in his autobiography *Finding a Way Out*, writes with deep sensitivity of his grandfather, a proud African chieftain engaged in slaving, who fell victim to the trade himself.

Although more and more libraries are collecting works on the 15 million black Africans brought to America, the major library for black family historians (outside of the National Archives—discussed in the next chapter) is the Schomburg Center for Research in Black Culture, 103 West 135th Street, New York, New York 10030. The center has a number of useful tools, including a complete set of the federal population censuses from 1790 to 1890, which, most importantly, includes the slave schedules. It also has valuable papers, pictures, and other memorabilia of prominent black families, the ten-volume encyclopedia *The Negro Heritage Library,* and extensive church and military records valuable to black ancestor hunters. In addition, it has specialized histories such as *The Negroes of South Carolina,* a half-century of black periodicals, and the Harry A. Williamson collection of *Negro Masonry*.

The Schomburg Center will act as a repository for any family histories black ancestor hunters compile. If you decide to deposit a copy of your research with the center, you will know that your work has helped to illuminate what historian Wyatt Tee Walker has called the "cultural blackout" for the black in America.

In the South, state archives, probate court records (which house wills) and county records are good places to look for the "owner" of black slave ancestors. Plantation owners' wills, especially, listed slaves by specific names (something the federal census did not do until 1870) and often contained bits of narrative about slaves' personalities. A deed to the slave (who was considered property) was filed by the owner at the county courthouse.

Because many slaves were not able to read and write (indeed, were forbidden to learn), most slave records in the South are owners' property records. A great collection of these—plantation daybooks, auctioneers' sales charts, slave registrations, and even insurance policies on slaves—can be found in the state archives of many Southern states, and at Louisiana State University, Department of Archives, Baton Rouge, Louisiana 70803.

As a general rule black family historians with Northern ancestors will find a number of published records, particularly in Philadelphia, the city that had the highest concentration of black population prior to 1900. Early Philadelphia newspapers published marriage, birth, and death notices of "free people of colour." The obituaries are, as usual, the best source for mining family genealogical detail.

Other Philadelphia records are listed in Jane Aitken's *Census Directory for 1811,* the first census to enumerate blacks: Lebanon Cemetery records for the earliest chartered black cemetery; voting lists prior to the disfranchisement of free blacks by the Pennsylvania legislature in 1838. A final separate black census in Philadelphia was taken in 1838 by Benjamin Bacon and Charles Gardner and included intriguing material on occupations, religious affiliations, and even family life.

The Historical Society of Pennsylvania has early material considered by many to be one of the most important sources for the black family historian. A full list is available in its printed catalog *Afro-Americana, 1553–1906*. Some of the rare records include:

—An extensive collection of manumissions (freedom papers) and indentures (extremely valuable because they contain information on African background)
—Papers of the Pennsylvania Abolition Society
—Collection of the American Negro Historical Society
—Letters, pamphlets, books by blacks and abolitionists from 1500s to Civil War
—Records of the first (founded in Philadelphia) Bethel African Methodist-Episcopal Church

Chinese-Americans

For Chinese ancestors who landed in California during the last century, the best information is contained in Thomas W. Chinn's *Genealogical Sources of Chinese Immigrants*. This paper may be ordered from the LDS library in Salt Lake City.

For other records (and even complete family genealogies), you should contact the Columbia University East Asian Library, 116th Street and Broadway, New York, New York 10027, and Harvard University's Yenching Institute, Cambridge, Massachusetts 02138.

The Chinese in Hawaii have an active genealogical organization in the Hawaii Chinese History Center, 111 North King Street, Room 410, Honolulu 96817. This group has put together a number of locally published booklets which are invaluable guides for the Chinese-American family historian. The best one is Jean Bergen Ohai's *Chinese Genealogy and Family Book Guide*.

A special record source for Hawaiians of Chinese and Polynesian ancestry is the Aloha Chapter Memorial Library (Daughters of the American Revolution), 1914 Makiki Heights Drive, Honolulu 96822. Many Hawaiians have New England bloodlines reaching back to the

Mayflower, owing to the presence on the islands of early whalers and missionaries.

Mexican-Americans

Consult the following extra sources for early Mexican ancestors.

1. Special state censuses for Arizona, 1864, 1866, 1867, 1869, and for New Mexico and Colorado in 1885, at the Arizona State Department Archives, Phoenix, Arizona 85007.
2. Three population censuses for New Mexico, now in the custody of the Historical Services Division, State Records Center and Archives, 404 Montezuma Street, Santa Fe, New Mexico 87501:
   a. Spanish Colonial Census of 1790
   b. Mexican Colonial Census of 1823
   c. Mexican Colonial Census of 1845
3. Texas census schedules for 1829–1836. The originals are in the Lorenzo De Zavala State Archives and Library Building, Box 12927, Capitol Station, Austin, Texas 78711.
4. Printed work entitled *Origins of New Mexico Families in the Spanish Colonial Period,* by Angelico Chavez, a Catholic priest.
5. Roman Catholic church records in the Southwest, primarily registers of baptisms, marriages, and deaths.
6. The California State Library, Sacramento, California 95814, for data on early Spanish-Mexican colonial families.

8

FINDING YOUR ROOTS THROUGH FEDERAL RECORDS

"The heritage of the Past is the seed that brings forth the Harvest of the Future." That is the inscription on the Pennsylvania Avenue side of the National Archives in Washington, D.C. And indeed it is true for the family historian; the incredibly rich store of data in the federal government can give you a harvest of information about who you are and where you come from.

Here in the nation's capital is a wealth of census records: military records, veterans' pensions, and veterans' bounty land grants; ships' passenger lists and naturalization records; and other materials. These are available not only through the National Archives but also from the Immigration and Naturalization Service, the Veterans Administration, the Library of Congress, and the Smithsonian organizations, several of which are headquartered in Washington.

Thus, if you want to find out about an ancestor and everyone who was living in his household, whether he homesteaded, what his military record was, and when he immigrated to America and from where, Washington is the place to look. Let's start showing you what's in the National Archives—the central depository for U.S. Records.

THE NATIONAL ARCHIVES

The National Archives is a colonnaded Greco-Roman building not far from the Capitol. Here, under a seventy-five-foot dome and enclosed in helium-filled brass cases are housed the Declaration of Independence along with the Constitution and the Bill of Rights, the Louisiana Purchase, the Homestead Act, the Monroe Doctrine and similar historical documents. Here also are field dispatches from General George Washington, written as hundreds of Revolutionary War soldiers, among them my great-great-great-grandfather, Corporal Peter Righter, were dying of battle wounds. Here also are the surrender papers from Appomattox, signed while my Confederate great-grandfather, Henry Jones, and many others were escaping into the West Virginia mountains.

As you view such documents you clearly see that the history of this country is really the history of countless average families, and that we are, all of us, part of it.

After looking over the original records for the United States in the National Archives building, you will be ready to go ahead with the search for your own history.

Enter the Pennsylvania Avenue side of the National Archives, sign in with the guard, and go to room 200-B, where you will be asked to complete an application and are given a researcher's identification card (good for one year) and a kit of pamphlets about the archives' genealogical records and their uses. An experienced staff will direct you to proper sources in the reading rooms.

If you can't get to Washington, see if you can get to (or write to) one of the following eleven regional branches:

Atlanta Federal Archives
and Records Center
1557 St. Joseph Avenue
East Point, Georgia 30344
*Records for Alabama,
Georgia, Florida,
Kentucky, Mississippi,
North Carolina, South
Carolina, and Tennessee*

Boston Federal Archives
and Records Center
380 Trapelo Road
Waltham, Massachusetts
02154
*Records for Connecticut,
Maine, Massachusetts,
New Hampshire, Rhode
Island, and Vermont*

Chicago Federal Archives
and Records Center
7358 South Pulaski Road
Chicago, Illinois 60629
*Records for Illinois,
Indiana, Michigan,
Minnesota, Ohio, and
Wisconsin*

Denver Federal Archives
and Records Center
Building 48, Denver
Federal Center
Denver, Colorado 80225
*Records for Colorado,
Montana, North Dakota,
South Dakota, Utah,
and Wyoming*

Fort Worth Federal
Archives and Records
Center
4900 Hemphill Street
Fort Worth, Texas 76115

*Records for Arkansas,
Louisiana, New Mexico,
Oklahoma, and Texas.
Includes special collec-
tions of Indian records.*

Kansas City Federal
Archives and Records
Center
2306 East Bannister Road
Kansas City, Missouri
64131
*Records for Iowa, Kansas,
Missouri, and Nebraska*

Los Angeles Federal
Archives and Records
Center
24000 Avila Road
Laguna Niguel, California
92677
*Records for Arizona,
Southern California, and
Clark County, Nevada*

New York Federal
Archives and Records
Center
Building 22—MOT
Bayonne
Bayonne, New Jersey
07002
*Records for New Jersey,
New York, Puerto Rico,
and Virgin Islands*

Philadelphia Federal
Archives and Records
Center
5000 Wissahickon Avenue
Philadelphia, Pennsylvania
19144
*Records for Delaware,
Pennsylvania, District of*

Columbia, Maryland,
Virginia, and West
Virginia

San Francisco Federal
    Archives and Records
    Center
1000 Commodore Drive
San Bruno, California
    94066
Records for Northern
    California, Hawaii,

Nevada (except Clark
    County), and territories
    in the Pacific. Includes
    special material pertain-
    ing to American Samoa.

Seattle Federal Archives
    and Records Center
6125 Sand Point Way NE
Seattle, Washington 98115
Records for Alaska, Idaho,
    Oregon, and Washington

Each branch is building a library of National
Archives microfilm rolls, and all have the federal
population census schedules, a basic reference library,
microfilm readers, and document reproducing machines.
Material common to most of the branches are records
of U.S. District Courts and Courts of Appeals, records
of the Bureau of Customs and the Office of Engineers
for their districts.

Each branch serves a certain area, and will answer
mail inquiries about the documents in their control if
given specific information to help with their records
search.

For more detailed information about them, write the
National Archives in Washington, D.C. for the free
pamphlet "Regional Branches of the National Archives."

What can you expect to find in the National Archives
in Washington? As a brand new researcher you are entitled to a consultation with a staff research aide (the
three I talked with had a cumulative experience of over
100 years at the Archives), who will direct you to
the proper sources in the reading rooms.

You will be in good company. Barbara Tuchman
worked there on her biography of General Stilwell,
retired Senator Sam Ervin loved looking through
Revolutionary War records, film star Robert Redford
boned up on the Old West there, and author Bruce

Catton often researches Civil War material in the reading rooms.

Alex Haley also first conceived the idea for *Roots* there. He visited the archives out of curiosity about the names of some slaves his grandmother had mentioned. Too embarrassed to ask about them, however, he just took a cursory look through the census records and, finding nothing, decided to leave. On his way out, he passed through the main reading room. "I was struck by all those people intently scrutinizing old documents," he wrote. "It occurred to me that they were really trying to find out *who* they were." He went back to the microfilms and, after hours of searching, finally found the entry for his great-grandfather, "Tom Murray—black."

MAKING SENSE OUT OF THE CENSUS

Haley's breakthrough came while searching census schedules—something nearly every ancestor hunter can find gold in. The census, which first began in 1790 and for which records are available to you up to 1900 (the ones afterward are kept confidential by the restrictions of the 1974 Privacy Act), can give you a great deal of information, such as the following:

1. Your ancestors' occupations
2. Their immigration or migratory patterns—something you can put on a map and place in your Family History Book
3. The property—land and farms—they owned, and its whereabouts
4. The increase or decrease in your family from decade to decade
5. Which people died and at what ages
6. Whether someone remarried and had two distinct families in one household

You might even be able to trace your family back one more generation if you have not been able to do so from local and family records. For instance, say you know an ancestor was forty years old in 1880 and lived in a particular county, but you don't know his parents' names. By looking for his surname in the 1850 census (when he would have been ten years old), you might then be able to find the names of the people heading the household he lived in—his parents. With such information you can flesh out the bones of information you have acquired elsewhere.

If you know the county and state in which an ancestor was living during the year a census was taken, you can obtain census information about him (up to 1900) in several ways:

1. Through the LDS library and its branches, which give you access to the census up to 1890.
2. Through regional branches of the National Archives which have most census microfilm rolls, including the 1900 census. They can give you the number of the microfilm roll containing information about your forebear, and you can then try to arrange to borrow that roll from the National Archives branch.
3. Through state libraries, which often have copies of the federal censuses for their states.
4. By buying the exact census microfilm roll you want and finding a local library with a microfilm reader (which should not be too difficult). The way you do this is to first determine the roll number of the census you want by checking the National Archives booklet "Federal Population Censuses, 1790–1890" (a catalog of microfilm copies of the schedules). You will find order blanks in the back of this booklet.

A good reference on the federal census is Caroll D. Wright's *The History and Growth of the United States Census, 1790–1890*. (Write to the National Archives and Records Service, Publications Sales Branch, Washington, D.C. 20408 for a copy and their price list for other publications valuable to ancestor hunters.)

Here are the ways to go through census records:

1. Start with the most recent census—in this case the one for 1900—and follow your family back through the earlier censuses as far as you can.

2. For every census available, there are genealogical census worksheets, which will make it easier for you to take information off the census microfilms. (You may order them from the Genealogy Club of America.) Or you can copy the information off onto a Family Group Sheet and place it directly into your Family History Book.

3. To get an idea of the changes in your family line's structure during the censuses from 1790 to 1900—assuming you are tracing a family line that extends back into this period in America—use a United States Census Summary Chart like that provided by the Genealogy Club of America, or something like it. (See Figure 6, p. 110.)

4. Take down *all* census data listed about your ancestral family whether you can use it now or not. Later some stray fact could be important.

5. Watch for different surname spellings. It could change every ten years, since census takers weren't always careful about spelling.

6. Since prior to 1900, America was full of small towns where people of the same surname might well be related to each other, when searching census rolls you should extract all information for different families with your surname. It's not unusual to find a family connection.

7. Do not assume all children listed in one household in the censuses of 1850, 1860, and 1870 were necessarily members of the same family. They might have been nephews, cousins, even servants. It was not until 1880 that census takers

listed all members by their relationship to the head of the household.

8. Finally, allow for some error factors. In the early days, heads of households thought census takers were tax collectors in disguise. The census takers may thus have written down erroneous information from neighbors, failed to count people too difficult to reach, and even invented people— a practice that was especially prevalent when census takers were paid by the number of families they canvassed. In short, census information is not necessarily conclusive.

Mortality schedules—which are a census extract— taken from the 1850 through the 1880 censuses are particularly valuable aids to the family historian because they answer the question of who died within the twelve months preceding the taking of the census. This helps you pinpoint a death date which can lead you to other records, such as cemetery and the records of the probate court, discussed in Chapter 7. You can discover just how these mortality schedules were taken for your research locale, in "The Mortality Schedules," *National Genealogical Society Quarterly,* June 1943, a publication found in libraries with genealogical collections. See Figure 7 for information contained on the federal census schedules.

The Censuses from 1790 to the Present—in Reverse Order

The Present. The federal Privacy Act of 1974 forbids the release of federal records if they are less than seventy-five years old. Thus, if your parents or grandparents immigrated to the United States after 1900, you should write for a census search to the Bureau of the Census, Pittsburg, Kansas 66762. You will be sent a form to complete (the government doesn't do anything without a form, of course), and asked for an advance fee of $4. For this fee, the bureau staff will

FIGURE 6. Example of United States Census Summary Chart.

Name of Family_____

	1790	1800	1810	1820	1830	1840	1850	1860	1870	1880	1900
Husband's name:											
Wife's name:											
Children's names:											

Summary of Where Family Resided When Census Taken

Date Census	Where Taken
1790	
1800	
1810	
1820	
1830	
1840	
1850	
1860	
1870	
1880*	
1900	

*1890 census destroyed by fire

copy the personal information from your ancestor's census records, such as age, place of birth, and citizenship.

1900. The 1900 census, released in 1976 from most of the restrictions imposed under the Privacy Act, was a source most genealogists had been waiting for, since it was the first census to give *exact month and year of birth* of every person in the United States. You will find this census completely indexed by state and surname, a project of the WPA from the 1930s.

1890. This census was almost completely destroyed in 1921 by a fire in the basement of the Commerce Department building. An index at the National Archives lists the names of householders in the few surviving schedules. Also escaping the fire was a portion of the 1890 census dealing with Union Civil War veterans and their widows. This special census answers such questions as veteran's rank, company, regiment or vessel, dates of enlistment and discharge, length of service, disability, and assumed name if the veteran enlisted under one.

1880. This census was the first to give the relationship of family member to the head of the household, as well as the birthplace of the parents of each person listed. Such information can often push one's family history back another generation, to his immigrant ancestor's foreign birthplace. The 1880 census is also indexed alphabetically by family name (if that family had children ten years or younger) under the Soundex system, a method of indexing which uses the sound of the surname as well as the first letter.

1870. This was the first federal decennial census to list blacks, Chinese, and American Indians by name. This census also shows the month of birth of all citizens born within the year and month of marriage, if married within the year.

FIGURE 7. Information contained on federal population census schedules.

Question	1790	1800	1810	1820	1830	1840	1850	1860	1870	1880*	1900
1. Name of head of family	X	X	X	X	X	X	X	X	X	X	X
2. Number of free white males	X	X	X	X	X	X					
3. Number of free white females	X	X	X	X	X	X					
4. Place of residence	X	X	X	X	X	X	X	X	X	X	X
5. Number of foreigners, not naturalized				X	X						
6. Name of each family member							X	X	X	X	X
7. Age of each family member							X	X	X	X	X
8. Month and year of birth											X
9. Sex of each family member							X	X	X	X	X
10. Value of real estate							X	X	X		
11. Whether married within the year							X	X	X	X	
12. Whether deaf, dumb, blind, insane					X	X	X	X	X	X	
13. Whether a pauper or convict							X	X	X	X	
14. Whether attended school							X	X	X	X	X
15. Whether read or write						X	X	X	X	X	X
16. Whether father or mother of foreign birth										X	X
17. Month of birth, if born within year									X	X	
18. Relationship to head of family										X	X
19. Marital status										X	X

20. Birthplace of mother and father
21. Number of months unemployed in year
22. Occupation
23. Whether sick or temporarily disabled
24. Whether permanently disabled
25. Color of each family member
26. Number of years married
27. Mother of how many children
28. How many children living
29. Year of immigration to U.S.
30. Whether speak English
31. Ownership of home

* The 1890 census was destroyed by fire.

1860 and 1850. The information on the 1860 census was much the same as in 1850, which was considerably broadened in scope over prior censuses. Here for each *free* person in a household—not just the head of the house, as in earlier censuses—there was the name, postal address, age, sex, color (white, black, or mulatto), occupation (if the person was over fifteen years of age), value of real estate owned, place of birth, and whether or not the person was married within the year. For each slave an entry gave the name of the owner, the age, sex, and color (but not the name) of the slave, and whether or not he was a fugitive. There was also information on the number of slaves freed by each owner. The 1850 census has recently been computerized by the LDS genealogical library, and is available through LDS branches in book form, indexed by name—a tremendously important tool, making the work of family historians much easier.

1840. In 1840 questions about military pensioners (especially of the Revolutionary War) were added to the census and printed separately by the Department of State in *A Census of Pensioners for Revolutionary or Military Services.* This is available through the LDS library and its branches.

1830. The 1830 census shows family members broken down by five-year age groups for those under twenty years old, and ten-year age groups for those over twenty.

1820. In 1820 householders were asked about aliens in the family unit.

1810, 1800, 1790. The 1790 census was the first census, and the next two censuses were much the same. If you have traced any line back to before 1800, you have a good chance of finding your ancestor among the four million people counted in the 1790 census. It is indexed by surname and state and published in book form, and is available at the National Archives and in most libraries with genealogical collections. Only the heads of families are actually named, but all other free white males and females and slaves are counted. Unfortunately, the schedules for much of Virginia, Delaware, Georgia, Kentucky, New Jersey, and Tennessee were lost when the British burned Washington, D.C. during the War of 1812. Parts of these schedules were later reconstructed from state tax lists.

An invaluable aid in researching 1790 census records is E. Kay Kirkham's *Research in American Genealogy,* which reproduces Bureau of the Census maps for that period. Kirkham also computed the frequency with which your family name appears in the 1790 census, so you can tell at a glance how many families in what states comprised your 1790 family tree.

MILITARY RECORDS, VETERANS' PENSIONS, AND BOUNTY LAND GRANTS

Finding your ancestor's military record will add to your family history in two ways. First, it is often a good way to locate male ancestors if you cannot locate deeds, wills, or census records. (This is especially true if they were of military age during a major war.) Second, military records can include accounts of your forebear's military exploits, which help make your Family History Book more colorful and valuable to you.

If you want a copy of your ancestor's military service record for your Family History Book or to fulfill requirements for joining a patriotic organization, this is what you should do:

1. Write to the National Archives, Washington, D.C. 20408 for a copy of GSA Form 6751.
2. Complete the form with the name of the veteran,

war in which he fought (if Civil War, whether Union or Confederate), and state from which he enlisted. (Don't despair if you have few facts to go on. The National Archives audiovisual specialists have been able to compare the uniform in the photo of a Civil War veteran with others on file and come up with the exact military unit and the veteran's complete service record.)

3. Add any other information that will help the National Archives locate your ancestor's file— for example, his unit (regiment, company, ship); birthdate; date and place of death; and whether he claimed bounty land or a military pension.

National Archives staff members will make a reasonable search of their files and furnish photocopies of your ancestor's records for a small fee. (They will bill you—never more than a few dollars—for copying what they find.)

For more facts on the military records in the National Archives, write for their free pamphlet, "Military Service Records in the National Archives of the United States." For records of military service after 1914, write to the National Personnel Record Center in St. Louis, Missouri. (You must, however, be the veteran or next of kin.)

Although the Archives' military records contain everything from Matthew Brady's Civil War photos to Admiral Perry's reports on the opening of Japan for trade to George Washington's Revolutionary War expense accounts, chances are you will have to dig deep for records of older military ancestors, since fires in Washington destroyed many Revolutionary War records. But the archives has some remaining military records dating from 1775 to 1800, with the majority dating from 1800 to 1912. Many Union and Confederate veterans also have their service records in the National Archives, which list rank, age, place of enlistment, and often complete service. Other files on veterans of the Confederacy can be located in state archives and Southern state historical societies.

A partial list of National Archives military records is given in the box.

If you have traced a military veteran ancestor, a pension or land-grant file could very well offer the high point of your whole search. Many of these records are literally crammed with affidavits from relatives, old comrades-in-arms, and even whole pages torn from family Bibles—all material needed to justify the veteran's claims. The birth dates, marriage dates, birthplaces, lists of children, and other scraps of family history buried in these files can even provide you with a nearly complete genealogy of two or three key generations.

Pensions and land-grant applications after military service in the early days of the country contain the most genealogical information of all military records in the National Archives. The National Archives has millions of pension records for the period from the Revolutionary War through the Indian wars of the late 1880s.

Bounty land claims were based on military service between 1776 and 1855. Originally these land grants were made by land-rich but money-poor state governments as a way of paying off their militia after the Revolutionary War. Colonels got up to 500 acres and privates 100 acres of prime western wilderness—a method of payment which quickly filled the back country of Virginia, North Carolina, Pennsylvania, and New York.

Both pension and bounty land-warrant application files usually show name, rank, and military unit of the veteran, plus his place of residence and often a detailed explanation of his battlefield service.

To obtain a copy of your ancestor's pension or bounty land-grant files (or to check to see if your ancestor, his widow, or dependents filed any such claims) write to the National Archives, Washington, D.C. 20408 for GSA Form 6751. When you receive this form, fill

PARTIAL LIST OF MILITARY
RECORDS AT THE NATIONAL ARCHIVES

- Regular Army service records, 1800–1912
- Commissioned Army officer records, 1805–1917
- Commissioned Navy officer records, 1794–1930
- Marine officer records, 1798–1941
- Army officer correspondence to the Adjutant General's office, 1805–1917
- Army muster rolls, 1784–1912
- Register of Army commissions, 1792–1899
- Civil War staff officers
- Military histories of officers, 1789–1903
- United States Military Academy records, 1805–1917
- Records of Annapolis appointees, 1862–1922
- Army enlistment papers for enlisted men, 1800–1922
- Marine enlisted service records, 1798–1895
- Navy service record for enlisted men, 1798–1919
- Books, manuscripts, and photostats relating to soldiers, wagon masters, and others, 1775–1798
- Pay records
- Payrolls of vessels, 1798–1844
- Military service records of volunteers
- Records of the War of 1812
- Records of the Indian wars, 1817–1858
- Records of the Mexican War, 1846–1848
- Records of naval apprentices, boys aged thirteen to eighteen, 1837–1889
- Records of the Civil War, 1861–1865
- Records of the Spanish-American War, 1899–1901
- Records of the Philippine Insurrection, 1899–1903
- Prisoner of war records
- Civil War draft records
- Burial records of soldiers, 1862–1939
- Service files for Revenue Cutter and Life-Savings Services and the Bureau of Lighthouses (which became Coast Guard in 1915), 1791–1929

it in and send it back with a letter stating, "If complete
file is not copied, how much will it cost to copy entire
file on veteran?" There is a good reason for this extra
letter. The National Archives will copy about nine
pages of any military, pension, or land-grant file. Usually
that is more than enough, but not always. One family
historian received nine pages of what was clearly an
incomplete file. He wrote asking how much it would
cost to reproduce the entire record, never dreaming the
answer would be $54 for photocopying or $12 for
microfilming. Opting for the microfilm, this ancestor
hunter discovered he had a Revolutionary War hero
for an ancestor with a filé thick with valuable family
documents which had been gathering dust in Washington, D.C. for 150 years.

But before you spend more than a few dollars for
your ancestor's Revolutionary War pension records, you
may want to check microfilms of these pension files
through the LDS library or its branches. You can then
decide if the material is worth ordering for your Family History Book. If you see the file has an account of
your ancestor's war experiences (for any war) in his
own handwriting—remember this was before type-
writers were invented—you can ask the National Archives specifically for this often fascinating document.

A full listing of pension, bounty-land, and homestead (land grants after 1862) records can be found
in the National Archives publication, "Guide to Genealogical Records in the National Archives," available
for a small charge.

SHIPS' PASSENGER LISTS AND
NATURALIZATION RECORDS

Passenger lists are a means of determining when
your ancestors came to this country and, in some cases,
include their native countries. As you can imagine, for

a nation with the massive, long-term flow of immigration of the United States, these lists are far from complete.

The National Archives has passenger-arrival lists for ninety-five Atlantic and Gulf of Mexico ports. Some of the lists date back to 1798, but most of them are for the years 1820 to 1945. There are many gaps—indeed whole decades are missing from some of these lists. And many lists do not have complete information concerning passengers—names are illegible, occupations are omitted, and so on—but they remain a major source for family historians looking for immigrant ancestors.

The original lists were prepared on board ship by the captain of the vessel and filed later with the collector of customs when the ship reached port. You will find the following information in them: names of vessel, master, and port of embarkation; date and port of arrival; name of passenger, age, sex, and occupation; name of country or countries from which he came, and country to which he was going. If he died en route, the date and circumstances of his death were recorded.

Fewer than 1 percent of passenger records from 1790 to 1820 survived. For a bibliography of early passenger lists, you should look at A. Harold Lancour's *Passenger Lists of Ships Coming to North America, 1538–1825*, which can be consulted at the New York City Public Library. (A few of the most easily accessible lists for early immigrants can be found at the end of the book.) From 1820 to 1919, the National Archives has many, if incomplete, ships' passenger lists. Most passenger records dating after 1919 are located in the Department of Immigration and Naturalization.

The National Archives will search their passenger-list indexes for you if you can give them the passenger's full name, port of arrival, approximate date of arrival, and name of the vessel (helpful but not necessary if you have the other three facts).

For detailed information about East Coast and Gulf

ports lists, consult the National Archives publication, "Guide to Genealogical Records in the National Archives." (Some of the major ports of entry for immigrants and the extant passenger lists are given at the end of this book.)

The ships arriving in San Francisco during gold rush days came from the East Coast, from Panama, and directly from European and Chinese ports. Although these San Francisco passenger lists were destroyed by fire, San Francisco historian Louis J. Rasmussen has undertaken the monumental task of recreating them from old San Francisco newspapers and other sources. Four volumes of his fifteen-volume effort have so far been published by San Francisco Historic Records under the title *San Francisco Ship Passenger Lists*. The entire work covers the period 1850 to 1975, and lists both passengers and cargoes. The big help for family historians here is that Rasmussen has fully indexed the volumes by subject and surname, making it relatively easy to locate your ancestor. Rasmussen is also publishing an eighteen-volume work of passenger lists entitled *Railway Passenger Lists of Overland Trains to San Francisco and the West*, covering the period 1870 to 1890; it is indexed by train passengers' names.

If you are able to obtain ships' passenger information from the National Archives or any other source, you will have sufficient data to write to the Immigration and Naturalization Service, 119 D Street, N.W., Washington, D.C. 20536. Return the form N-585 they send you, and you will receive a copy of your immigrant ancestor's naturalization petition. It will contain a wealth of family information such as birthplace and parents' names (be sure and ask for the entire file), and should lead you directly back to the ancestral homeland.

For more information about how naturalization records can help you in your ancestor search, see *Locating Your Immigrant Ancestor: A Guide to Naturalization Records* by James C. Neagles and Lila Lee.

OTHER GOVERNMENT AIDS:
THE LIBRARY OF CONGRESS,
SMITHSONIAN, AND SERVICES FOR
ETHNIC GROUPS

The National Archives hosts an annual genealogical seminar for advanced family historians with specialized classes taught by authorities in such fields as census records, legal records, military service, colonial handwriting, cartography, migration patterns, oral genealogy, and Spanish and French colonists. As with everything else it does, its archive classes are well worth the trouble of attending.

But the National Archives is not the only source of information. Within walking distance of its Washington headquarters are the Library of Congress and the Smithsonian Institute.

The Library of Congress has a Local History and Genealogy Room on the fifth floor of the annex building which has the largest collection of published family histories in the country—about 30,000 volumes in all, arranged on the shelves by family name. In addition, it has some 90,000 works on local American history, which give a great deal of information on early settlers, churches, and communities. Although the library cannot undertake involved searches for family or heraldic information, consultants can point you in the right direction.

If you are unable to visit the Library of Congress in person, you can discover whether it has a history of your family surname by writing to its Science and Technology Division, Washington, D.C. 20540. If you want them to photocopy your family history—it may be the only one of its kind—an unbound Xerox copy of a 200-page book is $25, with mailing extra. While some family histories run to less than 200 pages, others run a great deal more. (My own "Eddy Family in America"

WHEN AND HOW TO HIRE A PRO

There are four occasions when you may want to consider hiring a professional genealogist:

1. When you seek research from a distant public institution or library and need an expert in the area.
2. When you wish to join a lineage society.
3. When you are ready to publish your family history and want to fill in some obscure or difficult lines.
4. When you don't have time to or don't wish to do your own research.

You can hire a professional genealogist by writing to the following: (a) The Board of Certification of Genealogists, 1307 New Hampshire Avenue, N.W., Washington, D.C. 20036, (b) The Genealogical Society of the Church of Jesus Christ of Latter Day Saints, Suite 1006, 54 East South Temple St., Salt Lake City, Utah 84111, (c) Libraries or genealogical societies in your research locale for a list of people familiar with their collection.

The Board for Certification of Genealogists licenses American professional researchers for a five-year period. Applicants take an exhaustive examination. The LDS Genealogical Society certifies professional genealogists after equally comprehensive examinations for specific areas of the United States and for foreign countries in which they have a proven language ability. When you contact the accrediting agencies, they will send you (for a small fee) a list of names, addresses, and the specialties of all the professional genealogists currently on their rolls. Cost of professional genealogical services vary widely, the average (according to my own 1977 survey of fifty professionals) being $6.50 per hour.

Choose a researcher in your research locale. If you are searching for early Virginians, for example, one with a specialty in records of the South will be the

WHEN AND HOW TO HIRE A PRO
(continued)

best selection. In your initial letter tell him or her what work you want done, and ask these questions:

1. Can you handle this assignment?
2. When can you begin work?
3. How often will you make reports?
4. What are your fees?
5. Are there ever extra charges? For what?
6. Do you require a deposit?

Most professional genealogists complain that queries are too vague. Here is what you should give them:

1. A precise statement of your objective. (For example, "I want to find the parents of Elizabeth Booher.") Or, if you have a general objective, such as tracing one line back as far as possible, be sure to send Pedigree Charts and Family Group Sheets. Send every known fact you can, including a record of any negative research so you won't have to pay twice for it.
2. Immediately reply to all correspondence from him or her. (Keep a carbon copy so that you will have a record of your part of the transaction.)
3. Prompt payment of fees.

As the client, here is what you should expect:

1. A full, written report, citing sources of all new information.
2. Photostats or photocopies of marriage records, wills, birth certificates, and deeds.
3. An accounting of how your money was spent.
4. Report of any additional records found and an estimate of the cost of searching them.

Most professionals are honest and will usually give more than a fair return for their wages, but if you believe you have been the victim of shoddy practice, you should report the incident to the source from which you received the name.

In the wake of the astounding popularity of Alex Haley's *Roots*, persons and agencies involved in other lines of work—finding missing persons, skip tracers, and the like—have been trying to cash in on the genealogy boom. Caveat emptor.

No professional can *guarantee* positive results. It's probably rare, but you may pay to find out there is nothing to find out. However, at least this will release your energies to search in some other directions.

contains over 1,000 pages plus supplements.) You may want to consider hiring a certified professional genealogist, who could go to the library himself and extract just the information you need for your ancestral line. (Or try an antiquarian bookseller to see if he can locate your family history at a more reasonable price. Write the Antiquarian Booksellers Association of America, Shop 2, Concourse, 630 Fifth Avenue, New York, New York 10020, for a dealer near you.)

Two Library of Congress publications are available (at no cost) to help you in your ancestor hunting: "The Library of Congress Guides to Genealogical Research Reference Services and Facilities of the Local History and Genealogy Room" and "Out of Print Materials and Reprinted Publications."

The Library of Congress does not have the staff to handle pages of names or other lengthy requests, but it can give general information. It can search a family name. It can provide a number of family histories— Japanese, Burmese, Danish, or any other country. If you want to know the genealogical information it has on, say, Japan, it will photocopy all the cards in its catalog under the heading "Japan—Genealogy." And the same for every other country.

A recent bibliography, "Genealogies in the Library of Congress," by Marion J. Kaminkow, is worth looking at to see if your family history was placed in the Library of Congress prior to 1972.

The Smithsonian Institute, really a complex of seven museums, does not contain genealogical information so much as samples of the actual tools, clothing, and weapons your ancestors may have used. When you look at a wooden plow covered with straps of iron, or a rigid pair of shoes (each shoe made to fit either foot), a lovingly carved bride's chest, ungainly rifles, and delicate silver spoons, they give your picture of your forebears a sense of reality. If you can't get to Washington, the book *A Nation of Nations* is a Smithsonian catalog that will give you the feel of the everyday objects immigrant ancestors brought with them to America and the ones they found when they arrived. Two other Smithsonian publications containing family traditions, anecdotes, old sayings, and biographical sketches, prepared for the Bicentennial Celebration in 1976, are "Your Own American Experience" and "I'd Like to Think They Were Pirates . . ."

SOME OTHER SPECIAL GOVERNMENT SOURCES

Blacks, Chinese-Americans, Japanese-Americans, Mexican-Americans, and American Indians should take note of specific kinds of information.

American Indians

Because of their special status as wards of the federal government, American Indians have available to them a great many government records with which to trace their forebears.

Indeed, this kind of ancestor hunting might even provide a financial return. A $29.1 million government settlement went to satisfy the claims of Yurok, Wintu, and other northern California Indians, and the Mesquakie Indians in the Midwest were awarded $6.6 million in 1976.

The National Archives is particularly strong on records of American Indians who kept their tribal affiliations. Here is a general (but by no means complete) listing of tribal records in the Washington archives:

- Removal records, 1815–1850 (mostly of the Five Civilized Tribes—Cherokee, Chickasaw, Choctaw, Creek, and Seminole)
- Tribal enrollment records, 1827–present
- Annuity rolls, 1841–1959
- Land allotment records, 1856–1935
- Census rolls, 1884–1940 (arranged alphabetically by Indian agency, tribe, year, and name)
- Probate records (heirship papers, 1907–present, and wills, 1906–1921)
- Carlisle Indian school reports, 1879–1918
- School census records, 1912–1939

Most of these records are full of family history details such as both Indian and "English" name, sex, degree of Indian blood, names of family or guardian, tribal and "band" affiliation, residence, and occupation.

Any American Indian who fought with federal troops may also have a record of veteran's benefits. The National Archives has in its military records section a separate alphabetical file for each Indian veteran who served prior to 1870.

One of the largest single collections of American Indian genealogical material is located in the National Archives branch at 4900 Hemphill Street, Fort Worth, Texas. (A full list of their holdings can be obtained by writing Chief, Archives Branch, Federal Archives and Records Center, P.O. Box 6216, Fort Worth, Texas 76115.) Some of their material is microfilmed and available through interlibrary loan. In other words, the film could be borrowed by your local library for examination by you. A few of the documents valuable to Indian family historians at this branch are the following:

* Records of the Bureau of Indian Affairs, 1856–1952
* Kiowa Agency records, 1881–1952 (contains records for Kiowa, Comanche, Wichita, Apache, Delaware, and Caddo Indians)
* Chilocco Indian school, 1890–1952
* Concho Agency, 1891–1952 (contains records for Cheyenne and Arapaho)
* Miami Agency, 1870–1952 (contains records for Seneca, Eastern Shawnee, Quapaw, Ottawa, Peoria, and Miami Wyandot; also for Captain Jack's band after the Modoc war and Chief Joseph's band of Nez Percé)
* Osage Agency, 1858–1952
* Pawnee Agency, 1870–1952 (contains records for Pawnee, Otoe, Kansa, Ponca, Kaw, and Tonkawa)
* Shawnee Agency, 1870–1952 (contains records for the Sac and Fox Indians)

Other published material the Indian family biographer will want to read are "American Indian Genealogical Research" by Jimmy B. Parker in the *National Genealogical Society Quarterly,* March 1975; "American Indian Records in the National Archives" by Edward E. Hill, a long paper presented at the 1969 World Conference on Records and available in most genealogical collections and at the LDS Library or its branches. This booklet will also give you a good, basic understanding of the major changes in federal policies toward Indians over the years.

Blacks

The National Archives has published "A Guide to Documents in the National Archives for Negro Studies," which encompasses black history in the United States, the West Indies, and Latin America.

There are also a number of plantation and slave sale records, a list of free black heads of families mentioned in the 1790 census, and the federal census schedules for 1870 and after. If you are searching for slave ancestors, the 1880 census may lead you to owner's locations through parent's birthplace and thus to even earlier generations.

Chinese-Americans

Chinese ancestry can be traced to the 1870 census, when Chinese-Americans were listed for the first time.

Japanese-Americans

With the recent opening of the 1900 census, Japanese-Americans can gain useful genealogical information including place of origin in Japan if this is unknown to you.

Mexican-Americans

Of special value are the census schedules for Arizona, California, Colorado, New Mexico, and Texas, beginning with the 1850 census.

THE PATRIOTIC LINEAGE ORGANIZATIONS

Membership records of patriotic heritage societies are sometimes an excellent source of genealogical information. If you have military forebears, most of these organizations keep files and pedigree information on members by surname, and can be a source for adding to your family history. In order to join these societies, whose aims are primarily educational and heritage preservation, an applicant must submit documented proof of descendance. To join the Daughters of the American Revolution, for instance, one must provide evidence that a forebear was a Revolutionary War soldier, sailor, or prominent patriot (man or woman).

Today the D.A.R. and other lineage societies demand good genealogical proof before admitting applicants to membership, but such was not always the case. In earlier days, slipshod research got into D.A.R. lineage books, and this earlier research is of little value to conscientious family historians today. For instance, Gilbert Doane, author of the respected *Searching for Your Ancestors*, tells the amusing story of a certain lady, prominent in her own city, who became a member of the D.A.R. based on papers showing the service on one Hezekiah Royce. "Now it happened," Doane says, "that there were two Hezekiah Royces, one of whom was a notorious Tory and the other a brave young man who marched to the defense of Bennington in 1777. The lady's ancestor was actually the Tory Hezekiah."

It is doubtful that such a mistake could slip past the scrutiny of experienced genealogists who pass on D.A.R. pedigrees today. Application papers must be accompanied by certified Bible or civil records and detailed data for each generation leading back to the Revolutionary War participant. Indeed, the D.A.R. and other patriotic societies have done much in recent years to raise the standard of genealogical research to its present height.

The D.A.R. and S.A.R. (Sons of the American Revolution) maintain genealogical reference libraries in Washington, D.C., and will answer mail queries, especially if you express an interest in membership.

Some patriotic and lineage societies you could consider as sources for your family-tree research are as follows:

Aztec Club of 1847
5225 Westpath Way
Washington, D.C. 20036
For descendants of
servicemen of the
Mexican War

Descendants of the Signers
of the Declaration of
Independence
1300 Locust Street
Philadelphia, Pennsylvania
19107

Ladies of the Grand Army
of the Republic
90 Conestoga Boulevard
Lancaster, Pennsylvania
17602
For female descendants of
Union soldiers

National Society,
Daughters of the
American Revolution
1776 D Street, N.W.
Washington, D.C. 20006
For female descendants
of Revolutionary War
patriots

National Society, Sons of
the American Revolution
2412 Massachusetts
Avenue, N.W.
Washington, D.C. 20008
For male descendants of

Revolutionary War
patriots

National Society, United
States Daughters of 1812
1461 Rhode Island Avenue,
N.W.
Washington, D.C. 20005

The Society of the
Cincinnati
2118 Massachusetts
Avenue, N.W.
Washington, D.C. 20008
For male descendants of
officers in the
Revolutionary Army

Sons of Confederate
Veterans
Southern Station, Box 1
Hattiesburg, Mississippi
39401

Spanish War Veterans
United
810 Vermont Avenue,
N.W., Box 1915
Washington, D.C. 20013
For descendants of veterans
of Spanish-American
War, 1898–1899

United Daughters of the
Confederacy
328 North Boulevard
Richmond, Virginia

By now you have a good working knowledge of all the family history resources you can search in this country. To what has it all been leading? The mother country, of course—tracing your ancestors back to their native land, where your family forebears lived for centuries. In the next chapter, I'll show you how you can extend your search for roots beyond the borders of the United States.

9

FINDING YOUR ROOTS
ABROAD:
SOURCES IN YOUR
ANCESTRAL HOMELAND

It is nearly impossible to describe the emotions one has when he or she returns to the land of one's ancestors. It does not matter what country or which generation of your forebears left it—the feeling is the same.

"When I first arrived in that tiny town, I was seized with a peculiar elemental feeling," said one friend of mine who returned to her ancestral home on a vacation visit. "It was as though I were coming back to my own personal cradle of civilization. I thought if nothing else happens beyond this, the feeling alone is worth the trip."

Something else could well happen. One could turn up relatives to visit and to correspond with for a lifetime. After another friend of mine searched out his cousins and uncles in Budapest, he went on to Rotterdam and stayed with second cousins there. "Even though there were language problems," he said, "there was a natural kind of communication, because we were all family. It's hard to describe how that trip made me feel—like I belonged to more of the world than just the United States."

Still another friend of mine, a thirteenth-generation descendant of an English rector, wrote to me about visiting her ancestral town. "Today Mr. Luckett, the present vicar, showed me the old church registry. All the entries had been written in William's own hand in a parchment book; it's a beautiful work and has artistic decorations. I saw the baptismal entries for his children, and I discovered to my surprise that he had a daughter with the very same name as mine."

To find a sample of your ancestor's own handwriting and get to know the place where he lived is to return to your roots. And this is what genealogy is all about.

FINDING THE HOMES OF YOUR FOREBEARS

Before you go beyond the U.S. borders, you should make every effort to gather all the facts you can collect about your immigrant forebears. Whether your heritage is European, Asian, Latin-American, or any other, the procedure is very much the same: you will need (1) your ancestor's name, (2) the locality in the old country from which he originally came, and (3) the date (at least approximate) of his migration. Without this minimal amount of information, you will not find your family beginnings—at least for this one line. (But remember, if you have trouble locating one immigrant ancestor, you can always try tracing another branch of your family tree.)

After getting all the facts you can about your progenitor on your own, make sure to search through the LDS foreign records in Salt Lake City—or through one of their branch libraries—before you undertake further research that involves an overseas trip or even extensive correspondence with officials of a foreign country. In some cases—in England, Germany, and Denmark, for example—LDS genealogists have microfilmed many of the available civil and church records. And they have quantities of filmed records available to the public on most other countries that have supplied America with immigrants.

Foreign research can be undertaken by mail, and even with a language barrier can be just as fruitful as doing research in person. The general procedures are the same as doing research in the United States. You will find many similarities among the records of every country in the world. Nearly all governments, after all, have found it necessary to gather census data; keep military records; certify births, deaths, and marriages; and tax their citizens. These activities have formed a body of records which vary little from country to country. Of course, some countries (England, for example) have much more information for family historians than do others, particularly Iron Curtain countries that do not encourage genealogy.

It is a good idea for any ancestor hunter to study the history of the country and locality of his ancestral home. Knowledge of the general history of your country of origin may give you clues to what records were kept in the past, where they may be found now, what language they were written in, and what authority (civil, military, or church) initiated them. For instance, if your ancestors emigrated from Alsace-Lorraine, a territory that was alternately governed by Germany and France, you will be able to chart a much better search campaign with a general knowledge of the area's history.

It is always a good idea to write for advice to the genealogical society nearest your foreign research locale. And, by all means, drop in when you get there. Societies' members are people with your same interests, plus a knowledge of their country's records. They may even be able to put you on to a local family historian working on your line. And, of course, if you run into language barriers (as you may, especially if your search takes you to small towns away from the metropolitan areas), a local genealogical society can help you hire a native genealogist who speaks English. Many such societies are listed in this chapter.

There are two courtesies to observe when writing to foreign countries:

1. Send International Postal Reply Coupons (you can purchase them at any post office) when you expect an answer to your questions. Two coupons will cover airmail costs, so you won't have to wait weeks for surface mail.
2. When paying fees or sending search deposits, send American Express money orders or go to your bank and get a draft in the money of the country.

A word about maps, which can be an important part of your search. Maps of the immediate locale of your ancestral homes (for the eighteenth and nineteenth centuries) are available for Europe, from Ireland to Western Russia, from Karta Europa, 7212 4th Street, N.W., Seattle, Washington 98117. Often they are so detailed that they show individual farmhouses, and thus could pinpoint the exact site of an ancestral cottage. To provide these maps, Karta Europa needs three pieces of information:

1. The name (or names) of your ancestral hometown, or the nearest town or city. Include all the various spellings you know, since what you may believe to be an unusual spelling here in America may be the preferred spelling in Europe. (Although some villages have disappeared in the wars that have swept back and forth over Europe, the number is surprisingly small. In most cases, villages have been absorbed into expanding neighboring cities.)
2. The name of the state, shire, province, or county of the particular country in which your town is located. (There are dozens of towns named Neudorf and Holzhausen in Germany, for instance.)
3. Any descriptive information you may have about

your ancestor's home, such as its geographical location (near a certain large city, hill, or castle; on a river or lake; on the coast), or a feature peculiar to it (the village was famous for glass or bell making, for example).

In this chapter I have tried to include the mother countries of most of our immigrant ancestors, but it is impossible to cover the entire world's records, especially when boundaries have shifted so radically since our forefathers lived there. If you don't find your ancestor's country of origin listed here, the best and easiest way to find out where to write is to contact the LDS library in Salt Lake City. On the rare occasions they can't help you, write to that country's Washington, D.C. embassy. (A reference librarian can give you the address.)

There are times when embassies write back saying they know of no genealogical interest in their country. Don't believe it. Cultural attachés don't know everything. In that case, simply get the address (from a library) of the American embassy in your ancestor's country and write to them about your problem. If it's a record of birth, death, or marriage, often they can get it for you or tell you how to proceed. If it's a question about genealogical research in that country, they may be able to direct you to the national archives or some native family history expert.

The countries and origins discussed in this chapter are as follows:

Africa (including Gambia, Ghana, Guinea, Ivory Coast, Liberia, Senegal, Sierra Leone, and Togo)
Australia
British Isles (including England and Wales, Northern Ireland, and Scotland)
Canada
China, Peoples Republic of
Czechoslovakia
Denmark
France
German Democratic Republic (East Germany)
German Federal Republic (West Germany)
Greece
Ireland, Republic of

Italy
Japan
Jewish Ancestors
Mexico
Norway
Philippines, Republic of the
Poland

Spain
Sweden
Switzerland
Yugoslavia, Federal Peoples
  Republic of
Union of Soviet Socialist
  Republics

AFRICA

So far only about a dozen Americans descending from black African slaves have been able to trace their ancestors back across the sea. Author Alex Haley, of course, is one; tennis champion Arthur Ashe, a member of the Blackwell family on his maternal side, is another. But in the years to come, many more black Americans will accomplish it.

The key to unlocking the puzzle is often a family oral-history tradition of Africanisms—words or place names that can be traced to present-day African countries. Haley, for instance, was able to track ancestor Kunta Kinte to the Mandingo people of Gambia because his family had a tradition of using African expressions containing "k" sounds, which he discovered to be common in the Mandinka language of the present-day Mandingos. There is often a lack of paper documentation, for Africans have been a people whose history has been transmitted from generation to generation by word of mouth. As a result, it is said in Africa, "every elderly person who dies is a book that disappears forever."

Below is a list of West African embassies and other information about these countries, from whose territory most of the black slaves originally came.

The Gambia

Write to Office of the Consulate General, 300 East 56th Street, New York City, New York 10018.

Ghana

Write to Office of the Embassy, 2460 16th Street, Washington, D.C. 20009.

You may also contact the following sources if you think you may have been of Ghanaian descent:

1. President
   African Descendants Association Foundation
   P.O. Box 2024
   Accra, Ghana
2. Institute of African Studies
   University of Ghana
   Legon, Ghana
3. The Bureau Director
   Bureau of Ghana Languages
   P.O. Box 1851
   Accra, Ghana

In addition, historians at the University of Ghana history department in Legon may be able to give help and advice.

Guinea

Write to Office of the Embassy, 2112 Leroy Place, Washington, D.C. 20008.

Ivory Coast

Write to Office of the Embassy, 2424 Massachusetts Avenue, Washington, D.C. 20008.

You may also want to contact an expert on the African oral tradition, Professor Georges Bouah Niangoran, Université Nationale d'Abidjan, Abidjan (République de Côte d'Ivoire), West Africa.

Liberia

Write to Office of the Embassy, 5201 16th Street, Washington, D.C. 20011.

Senegal

Write to Office of the Embassy, 2121 Wyoming Avenue, Washington, D.C. 20008.

Sierra Leone

Write to Office of the Embassy, 1701 19th Street, Washington, D.C. 20009.

Togo

Write to Office of the Embassy, 2208 Massachusetts Avenue, Washington, D.C., 20008.

AUSTRALIA

Early emigrants to America, Canada, and Australia from Britain tend to be from the same stock, and so all have many ancestors in common.

Each of the six states of Australia has its own registration authority. In addition, there is the Australian Capital Territory and the Northern Territory. Thus there are eight separate authorities to be considered when undertaking family research.

Birth, Marriage, and Death Records. Applications for copies of birth, marriage, and death certificates should be addressed to the following:

1. *Australian Capital Territory.* The Registrar, Birth,

Death and Marriage Registry, Canberra, ACT, 2601.
2. *New South Wales*. The Registrar-General, Births, Deaths and Marriages Branch, Prince Albert Road, Sydney, NSW, 2000.
3. *Northern Territory*. The Registrar-General, Births, Deaths and Marriages Branch, P.O. Box 367, Darwin, NT, 5794.
4. *Queensland*. The Registrar-General, Treasury Buildings, Brisbane, B7, Queensland, 4000.
5. *South Australia*. The Principal Registrar, Box 1351H, GPO Adelaide, SA, 5001.
6. *Tasmania*. The Registrar-General, Box 875J, Hobart, Tasmania, 7001.
7. *Victoria*. The Government Statist, 295 Queen Street, Melbourne, Victoria, 3000.
8. *Western Australia*. The Registrar-General, Oakleigh Building, 22 St. George's Terrace, Perth, WA, 6000.

Immigration Records. At some time in your Australian research, it will become necessary to check to see when the emigrant you are looking for arrived in the country. Some of the lists refer to the parish in Britain from which the ancestor originated. You can check shipping lists at the following libraries:

1. *New South Wales*. The Senior Archivist, Archives Office of NSW, Public Library Building, Macquarie Street, Sydney, NSW, 2000.
2. *Queensland*. The Archivist, Commonwealth Archives Office, Wynnum Road, Cannon Hill, Brisbane, Queensland, 4000.
3. *South Australia*. The Principal Librarian, State Library of SA, Archives Department, North Terrace, Adelaide, SA, 5000.
4. *Tasmania*. The State Librarian, State Library of Tasmania, Archives Department, 91 Murray Street, Hobart, Tasmania, 7000.
5. *Victoria*. The Chief Librarian, State Library of

Victoria, Archives Division, 304–324 Swanston Street, Melbourne, Victoria, 3000.

6. *Western Australia.* The State Librarian, The J. S. Battye Library, State Library of WA, 3 Francis Street, Perth, WA, 6000.

Miscellaneous Sources. If you run into a problem in Australian research, try writing to Secretary, Genealogical society of Victoria, Room 1, 1st Floor, 98 Elizabeth St., Melbourne, Victoria 3000. The society also publishes a book, *Ancestors for Australians,* which contains all the genealogical information you would need for a successful search. The book costs $3 Australian or $3.75 U.S.

BRITISH ISLES

England and Wales

Start your quest by visiting or writing the Society of Genealogists, 37 Harrington Gardens, Kensington, London SW7 4JX. If your research objective is well defined, the staff there can advise you on how best to proceed.

Birth, Marriage, and Death Records. All civil registration in England and Wales started in 1837, and these certificates are deposited at St. Catherine's House, 10 Kingsway, London WC2B 6JB. You may have access to the indexes but not to the certificate records themselves. Copies are made for a fee and usually require about twenty-four hours to prepare.

Probate Records. Copies of wills filed since 1958 can be obtained from the Principal Probate Registry, Somerset House, Strand, London, WC2. Earlier wills can be located in the regional courts. Some of the records go far back in history (for example, the probate records for York commence in 1389).

Census Records. The 1841, 1851, 1861, and 1871 census records are kept at the Public Record Office, Somerset House, where clerks will undertake short searches for you on request. (The 1841 through 1861 censuses are on microfilm at the LDS library in Salt Lake City, and are available through its branches.) The 1851 census is the first to give the birthplace of each member of the household, a fact that will lead you to church records (see below). Census returns from 1881, 1891, and 1901 are considered confidential, but some information will be provided. No information will be released from the 1911 census.

Church Records. The most valuable genealogical information for the years before 1837 can be found in the 14,000 parish church registers throughout England and Wales. Many go back as far as 1538 and have been copied for the library of the Society of Genealogists in London, where you should check first. For a small fee, you can search the society's general index of more than 4,000 registers containing three million names. If you do not have the time to search, professional genealogists on duty at the library will search for you for a fee.

For American genealogists, the chance that their ancestors were outside the established Church of England is rather high. If you have Quaker ancestry, check with the Religious Society of Friends, Friends House, Euston Road, London; if Catholic, check Catholic Record Society, St. Edward's, Sutton Park, Guildford, Surrey; or if Huguenot, The Huguenot Society, 67 Victoria Road, London, WC1A ILH.

Miscellaneous Sources. The College of Arms on Queen Victoria Street in London (discussed at length in Chapter 10) has more than the records of English heraldry. It is possible to find an authenticated family tree deposited there by a distant relative who was once looking for his coat of arms. The college has a vast number of unpublished pedigrees, stretching back centuries. Searches can be made (although usually these take more time than you may have on a vacation) for about $15.

If you are unable to find what you are looking for in London, you may want to go directly to a local record office in your search area. A full list of *Record Repositories in Great Britain* has been prepared by the British Records Association and the Historical Manuscripts Commission, The Charterhouse, London EC1.

Before starting your research in England and Wales, it is a good idea to consult *Genealogical Research in England and Wales* by Frank Smith and David Gardner, a four-volume work that covers the records of England in great genealogical detail. Volume I details vital records, the census, and church records. Volume II offers research planning advice plus military record information. Volume III is helpful to anyone planning a great deal of research in parish registers, where he will encounter Latin abbreviations and Old English handwriting. Volume IV describes apprentice and school records and township and country records. You can find these reference volumes in most genealogical libraries.

There is no professional genealogist's certification agency in England, but a list of qualified searchers can be obtained from the Association of Genealogists, 2 Burnhill Road, Walton on Thames, Surrey, England.

A publication printed in the United States for Americans interested in English genealogical research is the *English Genealogist,* a quarterly put out by the Augustan Society, 1617 West 261st Street, Harbor City, California 90710. Subscription is $6 per year. Also, the British Tourist Authority has issued an authoritative pamphlet called "Tracing Your Ancestors" for Americans looking for their English forebears. You can obtain a free copy by writing the BTA at 680 Fifth Avenue, New York 10019.

Northern Ireland

There is some crossover of record keeping between Northern Ireland and the Republic of Ireland. You should try both authorities if the first does not yield a record. (See also The Republic of Ireland, pp. 165–167.)

Birth, Marriage, and Death Records. In Northern Ireland, Protestant marriages have been recorded since 1845, births, deaths, and Catholic marriages since 1864. The original certificates are in the custody of the registrar of each district in which the event took place. Since 1922, central record keeping has been under the jurisdiction of the General Register Office, Fermanagh House, Ormeau Avenue, Belfast, which also maintains an index.

Probate Records. Many old wills were destroyed by fire in Dublin during 1922, but copies and extracts from thousands of Ulster wills are preserved in the Public Record Office for Northern Ireland, Law Courts Building, May Street, Belfast.

Church Records. Parish records for Northern Ireland were also largely destroyed by fire in 1922, but some do remain in the custody of individual parish clergymen. Most of them do not go back beyond the 1700s.

Presbyterian records for forty-three congregations are located with the Presbyterian Historical Society, Church House, Fisherwick Place, Belfast.

Miscellaneous Sources. There are two aids Americans with Northern Irish ancestry should not overlook:

1. Information about Ulster forebears can be obtained by contacting the Ulster-Scot Historical

Foundation, 66 Bilmoral Avenue, Belfast, 66 16 21.

2. You should write for the free pamphlet entitled "Tracing Your Ancestry in Ulster," issued by the Northern Ireland Tourist Board, River House, 48 High Street, Belfast, BT 12DS.

Scotland

Unlike England and Ireland, the Scots have gathered together all their parish registers in one place—a great help to ancestor hunters.

Birth, Marriage, and Death Records. Compulsory registration of vital statistics began in 1855, and contains such complete family information that genealogists consider it superior to almost any other country's system. You can have these records searched by accredited genealogists, a list of which can be obtained from the Registrar General. For more information you should contact The Registrar General, New Register House, Princes Street, Edinburgh, EH1 3YT. The fee for a copy of a certificate from New Register House is $1.25, plus postage. (The LDS genealogical library in Salt Lake City has microfilm copies of certificates from 1855 through 1875 and 1881 through 1891.)

Church Records. The Registrar General also has 4,000 old parish registers (few of them indexed), some dating from the 1500s. The established church in Scotland is the Church of Scotland, or the Presbyterian Church. Baptismal records are unusually (and, for the family historian, beautifully) complete.

Most registers for nonconformist denominations, Catholics, and Jews are in the custody of the local minister. (Some are on microfilm at the Salt Lake City LDS library.)

Probate Records. At the Scottish Record Office, H. M. Register House, Princes Street, Edinburgh, EH1

3YX are indexes of wills, deeds, and other legal documents that may be extracted for a fee.

Census Records. Census returns for the years 1841, 1851, 1861, 1871, 1881 and 1891 are available for genealogical researchers. Application forms can be obtained from the Registrar General, New Register House, Edinburgh, EH1 3YT.

Miscellaneous Sources. For further aids in hunting your Scottish forebears you should contact the Scots Ancestry Research Society (20 York Place, Edinburgh, EH1 3EP), a nonprofit organization that will help you with your research for a fee. The maximum charge for tracing one line is about $40. The Society also publishes a quarterly, *The Scottish Genealogist,* and maintains a list of knowledgeable genealogists who will research your family in Scotland.

If you can trace your ancestry back to a Highland clan, you may wish to know more about the tartan identified with your family. You should write the Scottish Tartans Society (Museum of Scottish Tartans, Comvie, Perthshire, Scotland) which will send you information about your tartan from their collection—which is the world's largest—for a small fee, usually less than $2. Also check with the society to see when your clan will gather next. You would certainly want to try to plan your visit to Scotland to coincide with such an event.

If you have many Scottish lines or one that is particularly important to you, you may want to subscribe to the *Scottish Genealogical Helper,* four issues for $6 from the Augustan Society, 1510 Cravens Avenue, Torrence, CA 90501.

It is particularly important to get Scottish place names right when attempting research in Scotland by mail. The *Genealogical Gazetteer of Scotland* from the Everton Publishers, P.O. Box 368, Logan, Utah 84321, contains locations of places, with a map of each Scottish county to facilitate area searches.

CANADA

There was a great deal of traveling back and forth between the United States and Canada in the early days of the republic. There were no border guards, no formalities to observe, so it is highly possible that many ancestors of today's Americans simply got on their horses and rode from Canada to their new home.

Research in Canada is not difficult. The Public Archives of Canada in Ottawa, Ontario, corresponds to the National Archives in Washington, only the Canadian archives were founded much earlier, in 1872. The services offered by the Canadian Public Archives are similar in nature to those of the National Archives in that they will do a limited amount of research on request and make copies (photocopy or microfilm) for a small fee. They also have a list of capable professional genealogists who will undertake research too extensive for the archives' staff.

Census Records. Census returns from 1851 through 1871 list each person individually with his or her country or province of birth—very helpful information for any family historian. The archives has published checklists of census records. These lists are set up geographically. The archives also has on microfilm some early census rolls dating from 1671.

Birth, Marriage, and Death Records. The following provincial registrars are in charge of civil registration (vital records):

1. *Newfoundland.* Registrar of Vital Statistics, Department of Health, St. John's.
2. *Nova Scotia.* The Registrar General, Department of Public Health, Halifax.
3. *Prince Edward Island.* Division of Vital Statistics, Department of Health, Charlottetown.

4. *New Brunswick*. The Registrar General, Department of Health, Fredericton.
5. *Quebec*. Registrar General, Population Register, Department of Social Affairs, Québec City.
6. *Ontario*. Deputy Registrar General, Macdonald Block, Queen's Park, Toronto.
7. *Manitoba*. The Recorder, Division of Vital Statistics, Department of Health and Social Development, Winnipeg.
8. *Saskatchewan*. Director of Vital Statistics, Department of Public Health, Regina.
9. *Alberta*. Director of Vital Statistics, Department of Health and Social Development, Edmonton.
10. *British Columbia*. Division of Vital Statistics, Department of Health Services and Hospital Insurance, Victoria.
11. *Yukon*. Registrar of Vital Statistics, Whitehorse.
12. *North West Territories*. Registrar General of Vital Statistics, Yellowknife.

Louisiana genealogists will be happy to know that there is a source for Acadian genealogy, called "Gaudet's Notes," at the Public Archives. These give birth, marriage, and death dates of early Acadian citizens.

Church Records. The Public Archives has some original parish registers but not a comprehensive number. They have prepared *A Check-List of Parish Registers*, listing the churches for which they have material on file.

Property Records. The Public Archives has records relating to land titles of crown lands dating back to 1764, plus a list of holdings in each province.

Military Records. According to archival sources, detailed personnel records for Canadian soldiers were not kept until after 1900. Records of some British regular units and Canadian militia (including some Loyalist units from the Revolutionary War) exist, but most of them date from 1812.

Immigration Records. Canada does not have extensive passenger-list records. Those they do have date from 1865 for the port cities of Québec and Halifax.

Miscellaneous Sources. The Public Archives has on file valuable genealogical information relating to United Empire Loyalists (Americans who remained loyal to England during the Revolutionary War), including Loyalist claims for losses sustained during the Revolution.

For additional information on the holdings of the Public Archives of Canada, write to Roger Duhamel, Queen's Printer and Controller of Stationery, Ottawa, Canada, enclosing 60 cents, and ask for a copy of the pamphlet "Tracing Your Ancestors in Canada."

If you have many Canadian lines, you may want to study the specific of Canadian genealogy in more detail. A good place to start is Eunice Ruiter Baker's paperback book, *Searching for Your Ancestors in Canada* (try Books Canada, 33 East Tupper Street, Buffalo, New York 14203).

Two genealogical societies are particularly recommended to ancestor-hunting Americans. One is the Ontario Genealogical Society, Box 66, Station Q, Toronto, Ontario M4T 2L7. The other is the Alberta Genealogical Society, Box 3151, Station A, Edmonton, Alberta T5J 2G7.

PEOPLES REPUBLIC OF CHINA

The Peoples Republic of China, unlike some Eastern European Communist countries, encourages visits to ancestral villages and contacts with relatives and clansmen in mainland China.

If you plan a trip to China, you are advised by

Chinese genealogists to write to relatives well in advance of your trip, outlining your desire to learn more about your family history.

There will be several possibilities for advancing your personal genealogy in China. Although conditions vary from one district to another, it is possible to locate cemeteries and ancestral tablets in your clan temple or ancestral hall. Each of these tablets contains from three to five generations of male lineage.

Thus far, Chinese-American genealogists attempting to gain access to written records under the jurisdiction of the Peoples Republic of China have not been successful. Perhaps with increased interest and further cultural exchange this situation will change for the better.

Although a great deal of early Chinese genealogical material remains in libraries and genealogical collections, many priceless manuscripts and ancient genealogies were burned between 1950 and 1955 during an effort to eradicate "publications characteristic of reactionary thought of bourgeois society and feudal ideology."

Nevertheless, there is a continuing publication of clan and family genealogies in Taiwan. For information about these works (and for inquiries about family histories that were removed from the mainland in 1949) contact the Chief Librarian of the National Central Library in Taipei, Taiwan.

The definitive work on the current status of Chinese genealogy was written by Professor Hsiang-lin Lo, entitled "The Extent and Preservation of Genealogical Records in China." This pamphlet was published by the World Conference on Records in 1969 and can be located in any LDS branch library or ordered from the main library in Salt Lake City. The monograph contains an extensive bibliography of recently published material.

Other research papers that can be ordered from the main LDS library which might help Chinese-American family historians are *The Content and Use of Chinese*

Local History, by Tsun Leng, and *History and Arrangement of Chinese Clan Genealogies,* by Hsiang-lin Lo.

CZECHOSLOVAKIA

Although church registers go back as far as the 1600s, civil registration of births, marriages, and deaths did not begin until 1918, when Czechoslovakia (Bohemia, Moravia, Slovakia, Croatia, Serbia) was created as a nation. Parish registers (almost 7,000 of them) for both Catholic and Protestant churches remain in the local parish jurisdiction.

For permission to conduct research, the Czechoslovakian government prefers all first inquiries be directed to the Consular Division, Czechoslovakian Embassy, 3900 Linnean Avenue, N.W., Washington, D.C. 20008.

Miscellaneous Sources. For additional information about Czech records you should contact Československý ústav zahraniční, Karmelitská 25, Prague 1.

For more information about Slovakian records you should write or visit Maticá Slovenská, Nositerka Radu Republicky, Oddelenie pre zahraničných Slovákov, Pugačevova 2, Bratislava 1. According to Anna Ištvančinova, chief of the Department for Slovaks Abroad, her library is eager to cooperate with Americans researching their family tree.

The Matica Slovenská is a large library with genealogical material and is located at Martin-Hostihora, Národná Knižnica.

Zdenka Kucera, Czechoslovakian genealogist, reports that genealogical records inside the country are quite good, and that a well-stated and precise letter should bring positive results.

DENMARK

Before working with Danish records in Denmark or at the LDS library in Salt Lake City or through one of the LDS branches, it is a good idea to learn a bit about Danish history. Off and on throughout its history, parts of Denmark were governed by Germany and Norway, which makes a difference in the kinds of records you will find.

Birth, Marriage, and Death Records. Many parish registers were ill-kept before 1814, when each parish was issued a printed book so that all information included would be uniform from parish to parish. The Danish provincial archives (Landsarkivet) are the most important sources for parish registers belonging to the Lutheran National Church and all other denominations. Some parish registers go back to 1660. Following is a list of regional archives:

1. Landsarkivet, 10 Jagtvej, DK 2200, Copenhagen N (for Sjaelland m.m.).
2. Landsarkivet, 36 Jerbanegade, DK 5000, Odense (for Fyn).
3. Landsarkivet, 5L1. Sct. Hansgade, DK 8800, Viborg (for Norrejylland).
4. Landsarkivet, 45 Haderslevvej, DK 6200, Abenra (for de sønderjyske Landsdele).

Census Records. The Danish National Archives (Rigsarkivet), 9 Rigsdagsgården, DK 1218, Copenhagen K, are the genealogical source for census forms dating from 1787. From 1845 onward these rolls contain information about birthplaces.

Military Records. The draft register located at the National Archives (see above for address) goes back

to 1788, when all peasants' sons were registered for
the draft from birth.

Property Records. The Landsarkivets, or regional
archives, also contain land registers that can yield information about land tenants back as far as the early
1700s. The regional archives also have the burgess rolls
of towns in their area. These rolls contain professional
information and descending genealogy of citizens.

Immigration Records. The Danes Worldwide Archives (Udvandrerarkivet), 2 Konvalvej, DK 9000
Ålborg, has copies of the original immigrant lists compiled by the commissioner of the Copenhagen police.
These archives will also advise on genealogical problems, if you can furnish enough detail.

For further information about genealogical research
in Denmark, you should write for "Tracing Your Danish Ancestors and Relatives," a free fact sheet published by the Department of the Ministry of Foreign
Affairs of Denmark, 2 Stormgade, DK-1470 Copenhagen K.

FRANCE

In France, there is a vast storehouse of genealogical
information in some of the earliest records of Europe,
dating back to the eleventh century. The key to successful family historical research in France, just as in
every European country, is to know where (village or
city) your ancestor was born. In this way the National
Archives of France can help you determine the *département,* which will lead you to the proper regional archives.

Birth, Marriage, and Death Records. From 1539 to
1792 and during the French Revolution, vital records
were kept in registers by the parish priest. After that

time, these became civil records kept by the state. The older registers are now in the regional *(département)* archives.

Census Records. Some early census records go back as far as 1590, but modern census rolls begin with 1836. They have been taken every five years to the present time. You can find them in the regional archives for your ancestral home.

Immigration Records. Passenger lists from 1686 to the present are located at the National Archives or Archives Nationales de France, 60 rue des Francs-Bourgeois, 75141 Paris CEDEX 03.

Military Records. Army and navy personal files (mostly of officers), with name, birth date, place of birth, address, and physical description, are preserved from about 1600 to the present. Army records can be located in the National Archives, navy records at the Ministère de la Marine, 3 Avenue Octave Grenard, 75 Paris 07.

Church Records. You can locate some Protestant registers by contacting Bibliothèque de la Société d'histoire du Protestantisme Français, 54 rue des Saint-Pierres, 75 Paris 07.

Probate and Property Records. Land and property records and wills from 1300 to today can be researched at the office of local notaries for more recent records, and at the National Archives for ancient ones.

Miscellaneous Sources. Feudal and allegiance records from 1050 to 1700, containing names of lords, serfs, taxpayers, lists of men owing allegiance to lords, and dates of feudal contracts can be seen at the National Archives.

Jean Favier, Director General of the Archives of France, suggests Americans of French descent read the following books: *Les Archives* by Jean Favier, *La Généalogie* by Pierre Duryé, *Guide des Sources de l'Histoire des Etats-Unis dans les Archives Françaises*, and *A la Recherche de vos Ancêtres, Guide du Généaalogiste Amateur* by Yann Grandeau. In addition, *Guide des Recherches Généalogiques aux Archives Nationales* by Jacques Meurgey de Tupigny can be helpful.

It is possible to buy inventories and printed index lists published by the Archives of France by writing to the Documentation Française, 29-31 Quai Voltaire, 75340 Paris CEDEX 07, and, for a certain number of inventories out of print, to Kraus Reprint, a Division of Kraus-Thomson Organization Ltd., F1. 9491 Nendeln, Liechtenstein.

The National Archives of France will undertake to answer a specific question by mail, such as "What was the birthplace of Jean Favier who emigrated to the United States in 1896 from Le Havre?" They will not, however, do any pedigree or genealogical work beyond that.

If you are unable to find any of the books listed above in your library, you should write to the National Archives of France, asking for the name of the publisher of the book that most interests you. (All are in French.)

If you have a French ancestor who emigrated early in this country's history, or if you think you might have noble ancestry, write to Les Vieux Noms de France, 12 rue Caumartin, Paris 9 eme, France.

GERMAN DEMOCRATIC REPUBLIC (EAST GERMANY)

Although West Germans are the most genealogically active of all Europeans, this is not the case with East

Germans. The Kulturbund (League of Culture) in East
Berlin reports that there is very little interest in things
genealogic in the DDR (Deutschen Demokratischen
Republik). Nevertheless, there is a collection of family
history records at the Berlin State Library which might
prove helpful to Americans of East German descent.
Write Berlin State Library, 1086 Berlin, Unter Den
Linden 8, East Germany.

GERMAN FEDERAL REPUBLIC
(WEST GERMANY)

One out of every six Americans today is of German
descent. Outside of the British Commonwealth, most
Americans heading for overseas reunions with their
ancestral beginnings are Germans.

German genealogical research is a special science in
itself. According to Dr. Heinz F. Friederichs, an expert
on German ancestor hunting, the best way to find your
ancestors in Germany is to get in touch with the genealogical society in your research area and get some help
from them.

The biggest problem you will have with German
research is German history. During the last century,
when most civil record keeping started, Germany had
thirty different independent states, all with their own
record systems. Today, for instance, some church parish registers are collected into state archives *(Staatsarchiv)*, some remain in the original parish, and still
others (in former French communities on the west side
of the Rhine) are located in the mayor's office.

It would be impossible to list here the variations of
record keeping for West Germany. Your best bet (if
you want to do your own searching) is to locate the
regional archives from the following list and write
them, asking for the whereabouts of the information
you need. They will refer you to a town archive or

town genealogical society. (You can also find them in
the LDS library or one of its branches.)

State Archives

Baden:
1. Generallandesarchiv, D 7500 Karlsruhe, Nördliche Hilda-Promenade 2
2. Staatsarchiv, D 7800 Freiburg, Colombistr. 4

Bayern (Bavaria):
1. Hauptstaatsarchiv I, D 8000 München, Arcisstr. 12
2. Staatsarchiv für Coburg: D 8630 Coburg, Schloss
3. Staatsarchiv für Mittelfranken: D 85 Nürnberg, Archivstr. 17
4. Staatsarchiv für Niederbayern: D 8300 Landshut, Burg Trausnitz
5. Staatsarchiv für Oberbayern: Hauptstaatsarchiv V, D 8000 München, Schönfeldstr. 3
6. Staatsarchiv für Oberfranken: D 8600 Bamberg, Hainstr. 39
7. Staatsarchiv für Oberpfalz: D 8450 Amberg, Archivstr. 3
8. Staatsarchiv für Schwaben: D 8858 Neuberg a.d.D., Schloss
9. Staatsarchiv für Unterfranken: D 8700 Würzburg, Residenz

Berlin:
1. Staatsarchiv, D 1000 Berlin 33, Archivstr. 12–14
2. Landesarchiv, D 1000 Berlin 12, Strasse d. 17. Juni

Brandenburg:
1. Deutsches Zentralarchiv, DDR 15 Potsdam, Berliner Str. 98–101
2. Staatsarchiv, DDR 15 Potsdam, Sanssouci-Orangerie

Bremen:
    Staatsarchiv, D 2800 Bremen, Präsident-Kennedy-Platz 2

Hamburg:
    Staatsarchiv, D 2000 Hamburg, Rathaus

Hessen:
1. Hauptstaatsarchiv (für Nassau): D 6200 Wiesbaden, Mainzer Str. 80
2. Staatsarchiv für Hessen-Darmstadt: D 6100 Darmstadt, Schloss
3. Staatsarchiv für Hessen-Kassel: D 3550 Marburg, Friedrichsplatz 15

Mecklenburg:
    Staatsarchiv, DDR 27 Schwerin, Graf-Schack-Allee 2

Niedersachsen (Lower Saxony):
1. Staatsarchiv für Hannover: D 3000 Hannover, Am Archive 1
2. Staatsarchiv für Braunschweig: D 3340 Wolfenbüttel, Forstweg 2
3. Staatsarchiv für Bückeburg: D 4967 Bückeburg, Schloss
4. Staatsarchiv für Niedersachsen: D 2160 Stade, Sand
5. Staatsarchiv für Oldenburg: D 2900 Oldenburg, Damm 43
6. Staatsarchiv für Osnabrück: D 4500 Osnabrück, Schlossstr. 29
7. Staatsarchiv für Ostfriesland: D 2960 Aurich, Georgstr. 50

Pfalz (Palatinate):
    Staatsarchiv, D 6720 Speyer, Domplatz 6

Pommern (Pomerania):
    Staatsarchiv, DDR 22 Greifswald, Dreishaus

Rheinland (Rhenania):

1. Personenstandsarchiv für Kirchenbücher und Zivilstandsregister, D 5040 Brühl, Schloss
2. Hauptstaatsarchiv (für das nördliche Rheinland), D 4000 Düsseldorf, Prinz-Georg-Str. 78
3. Staatsarchiv (für das südliche Rheinland), D 5400 Koblenz, Karmeliterstr. 1–3

Saarland:

Landesarchiv, D 6600 Saarbrücken, Am Ludwigsplatz 7

Sachsen (Saxony):

1. Staatsarchiv, DDR 806 Dresden, Archivstr. 14
2. Staatsarchiv, DDR 701 Leipzig, Georgi-Dimitroff-Platz 1
3. Staatsarchiv, DDR 86 Bautzen, Ortenburg

Sachsen-Anhalt:

1. Staatsarchiv, DDR 30 Magdeburg, Hegelstr. 25
2. Staatsarchiv, DDR 37 Wernigerode (Harz)

Schleswig-Holstein:

Landesarchiv, D 2380 Schleswig, Schloss Gottorf

Thüringen (Thuringia):

1. Staatsarchiv, DDR 58 Gotha, Schloss
2. Staatsarchiv, DDR 66 Greiz, Oberes Schloss
3. Staatsarchiv, DDR 61 Meiningen, Schloss Bibrabau
4. Staatsarchiv, DDR 682 Rudolstadt, Schloss Heidecksburg
5. Staatsarchiv, DDR 53 Weimar, Beethovenplatz 3

Westfalen:

1. Personenstandsarchiv für Kirchenbücher und Zivilstandsregister, D 4930 Detmold, Willi-Hofmann-Str. 2
2. Staatsarchiv, D 4400 Münster, Bohlweg 2

3. Staatsarchiv, D 4930 Detmold, Willi-Hofmann-Str. 2

Württemberg:
1. Hauptstaatsarchiv, D 7000 Stuttgart, Gutenberg-str. 109
2. Staatsarchiv, D 7140 Ludwigsburg, Schloss
3. Staatsarchiv, D 7480 Sigmaringen, Karlstr. 3

National Genealogical Societies. The national archives are:
1. Deutsche Arbeitsgemeinschaft genealogischer Verbande, E.V. 7000, Stuttgart 1, Fichtetstrasse 18.
2. Zentralstelle für Personen- und Familiengeschichte, 6000 Frankfurt 50, Dehnhardstr. 32.
3. Bund der Familienverbande, 6000 Frankfurt 50, Dehnhardstr. 32.

Regional Genealogical Societies. Germans love the hobby of genealogy, and so there are literally dozens of regional and local genealogical societies you can contact for expert advice and professional assistance. Check the following list for a society near your research locale. (When making inquiry, be sure to give complete details of the research you need and the research already done. Do not forget to include International Postal Reply Coupons.)

Baden-Württemberg:
1. Verein für Familien- und Wappenkunde in Württemberg und Baden, 7000 Stuttgart, Hasenbergstr. 18
2. Landesverein Badische Heimat, Ausschuss für Familienforschung 7528 Bretten, Heilbronner Str. 3

Bayern:
Bayerischer Landesverein für Familienkunde, 8000 München 13, Winzerer Str. 68

Berlin:

Verein zur Förderung der Zentralstelle für Personen- und Familiengeschichte, 1000 Berlin 33, Archivstr. 12-14

Bremen:

"Die Maus," Gesellschaft für Familienforschung, 2800 Bremen 1, Präsident Kennedy-Platz 2 (Staatsarchiv)

Franken:

Gesellschaft für Familienkunde in Franken, 8500 Nürnberg, Archivstr. 17

Hamburg:

Geneaiogische Gesellschaft, 2000 Hamburg 36, Postfach 239

Hessen:

1. Hessische Familiengeschichtliche Vereinigung, 6100 Darmstadt, Schloss Gesellschaft für Familienkunde in Kurhessen und Waldeck, 3500 Kassel-Wilhelmshöhe, Wilhelmshöher Allee 306
2. Familienkundliche Gesellschaft für Nassau und Frankfurt, 6370 Oberursel, Hopfengarten 19
3. Vereinigung für Familien- und Wappenkunde zu Fulda, 6400 Fulda, Beethoven-Str. 27

Mitteldeutschland (Sachsen, Thüringen, Sachsen-Anhalt, Brandenburg, Mecklenburg):

Arbeitsgemeinschaft für mitteldeutsche Familienforschung, 3500 Kassel, Emilienstr. 1

Niedersachsen:

1. Niedersächsischer Landesverein für Familienkunde, 3000 Hannover, Köbelinger-Str. 59
2. Genealogisch-Heraldische Gesellschaft, 3400 Göttingen, Theaterplatz 5
3. Familienkundliche Kommission für Niedersach-

sen und Bremen sowie Angrenzende ostfälische
Gebiete, 3 Hannover, Appelstr. 9

Oldenburg:
> Oldenburgische Gesellschaft für Familienkunde,
> 2900 Oldenburg, Stargardter Weg 6

*Ostdeutschland (Pommern, Ost- und Westpreussen,
Schlesien, Südetenland, deutsche Sprachgebiete ausserhalb der alten Reichsgrenzen):*
1. Arbeitsgemeinschaft ostdeutscher Familienforscher, 4330 Mülheim a. d. Ruhr-Saarn, Eibenkamp 23/25
2. Vereinigung südetendeutscher Familienforscher, 3501 Fuldatal 2, Hauffstrasse 10

Ostfriesland:
> Ostfriesische Landschaft, Arbeitsgruppe Familienkunde u. Heraldik, 2690 Aurich, Bürgermeister-Müller-Platz 2

Ost- und Westpreussen (see also Ostdeutschland):
1. Verein für Familienforschung in Ost- und Westpreussen, 2000 Hamburg 62, Postfach 126
2. Forschungsstelle Westpreussen (Helmut Stehlau) 48 Bielefeld/Westfalen Hartlagerweg 76

Pfalz:
> Arbeitsgemeinschaft für Pfälzisch-Rheinische Familienkunde, 6700 Ludwigshafen/Rh, Carl-Bosch-Str. 195

Pommern: See Ostdeutschland

Rheinland:
1. Westdeutsche Gesellschaft für Familienkunde, 5302 Beuel, Rheinallee 34
2. Arbeitsgemeinschaft für Pfälzisch-Rheinische Familienkunde, 6700 Ludwigshafen/Rh, Carl-Bosch-Str. 195

Saarland:

> Arbeitsgemeinschaft für saarländische Familienkunde, 6600 Saarbrücken 2, Neunkircher Str. 98

Schlesien: See Ostdeutschland

Schleswig-Holstein:

> Schleswig-Holsteinische Gesellschaft für Familienkunde und Wappenkunde, 2300 Kiel 1, Gartenstr. 12

Südetenland: See Ostdeutschland

Westfalen:

> Westfälische Gesellschaft für Genealogie und Familienforschung, 4400 Münster, Warendorfer Str. 25

Westpreussen: See Ost- und Westpreussen

Württemberg: See Baden

Miscellaneous Sources. There is another source in Germany you should not overlook; it may give you just the background help you need. The Verlag Degener & Company, D 8530 Neustadt A.D. (Aisch), is the principal genealogical publisher in West Germany. They will send you a free copy of their catalog, which lists all their publications in English and German.

Are you descended from one of the many Germans who migrated to Russia during the years 1763 to 1862 and thence to the United States? If so, you should contact The American Historical Society of Germans from Russia, 615 D. Street, Lincoln, Nebraska 68502.

You may also wish to subscribe to the *Germanic Genealogist,* published by the Augustan Society at 1617 West 261st Street, Harbor City, California 90710. Subscription price for four issues is $6.

An extraordinary source book on the subject of

German family trees is the *Encyclopedia of German-American Genealogical Research* by Clifford Neal Smith and Anna Piszczan-Czaja Smith, published by R. R. Bowker Company, 1180 Avenue of the Americas, New York City 11036. Sections include information on church records, vital records, census and military records, along with passenger lists of emigrants and muster rolls of German mercenaries in the American Revolution.

GREECE

If you know the name and birthplace of your Greek ancestor, you should have no trouble locating him or her. In each Greek community the birth records of males and females have been kept since 1833 in a town archive. The registrar is usually the mayor.

Church Records. Church registers have been kept traditionally in all parishes, usually in three separate books, one each for marriages, births and baptisms, and deaths.

Probate Records. In Greece there are three kinds of wills: handwritten, secret, and public. These are held by the notary public drawing up the will until the death of the testator. Then the will is forwarded to the Secretary of the Court of the First Instance in Athens. The court will issue information on your ancestor's will on request.

THE REPUBLIC OF IRELAND

Written records in Ireland have suffered much from the unsettled history of that country. You will find most of the record sources of genealogical information are maintained in Dublin.

Birth, Marriage, and Death Records. These vital records are written in Latin and go back to 1864. They are kept in the office of the Registrar-General, The Custom House, Dublin 1.

Property Records. Property leases, sales, and mortgages dating from 1708 are kept at the Registry of Deeds, Henrietta Street, Dublin 1.

Church Records. Roman Catholic registers, which usually start around 1800, are under the jurisdiction of local parish priests. However, the National Library in Dublin has many of these registers on microfilm.

Census Records. Most of the early census records of Ireland were destroyed and are incomplete until 1901. (Many of the census fragments still available are on microfilm at the LDS library in Salt Lake City.)

Miscellaneous Sources. If you plan a vacation in Ireland, you will want to spend some time at the National Library, Kildare Street, Dublin 2. It has a giant collection of family histories, historical journals, newspapers, and a manuscript collection of deeds, letters, rentals, and other papers relating to Irish families, all card-indexed.

The Genealogical Office, Dublin Castle, Dublin 2, is part of the National Library, but it has its own extensive collection of pedigrees, armorial registers, wills, abstracts, family histories, and other material valuable to a genealogist. The Genealogical Office can be commissioned by mail to make searches of its records for about $4 an hour. A normal search takes from four to six hours. (Many of the records in the Genealogical Office are on microfilm and can be searched in the LDS library at Salt Lake City.)

If you have enough ancestral information to search near your family's original home, you should not overlook local libraries, even in the smallest cities. Irish libraries often have much information to offer on local families.

Some aids to Irish genealogical research can be found in the quarterly publication *Irish Genealogical Helper,* published for $6 per year by the Augustan Society, 1617 West 261st Street, Harbor City, California 90710.

An Irish publication you may wish to see is the *Irish Ancestor—An Illustrated Journal,* two issues yearly by subscription, $9 by sea mail and $11.50 by airmail. For more information write to Miss Rosemary Folliott, Pirton House, Sydenham Villas, Dundrum, Dublin 14.

There are two books every family historian of Irish ancestry should consult. One is *Handbook on Irish Genealogy,* published by Heraldic Artists Ltd., Trinity College, College Green, Dublin 2. The other is *Irish Family Names, with Origins, Meanings, Clans, Arms, Crests, and Mottoes* by Captain Patrick Kelly, republished recently by Gale Research Company, Book Tower, Detroit, Michigan 48226.

Because of England's long association with Ireland, don't forget to check with the Irish Genealogical Research Society, 82 Eaton Square, London, SW 1.

ITALY

Italian research is the most straightforward of any in Europe. If you know the town of origin of your ancestor, you are likely to be able to compile a full and authenticated pedigree without going much further.

There has been little or no centralization of records in Italy. Most civil registers, which were started in 1869, remain in the hometown, or *frazoni,* the smallest civil division of government in Italy. The registers are kept in bound books on printed forms, and the information is unusually complete. Often the names of the paternal and the maternal grandfather appear on the record, because so many surnames are alike in one town. For example, in one northern Italian village with a population of 1,400 today, 850 people bear one surname. In another town in Sicily with a population of 6,000, 80 percent of the population share only seven surnames between them. Fortunately, for Italian ancestor hunters, the civil registers provide more than enough information to link each record to the right pedigree.

Census Records. The hometown archive contains a record called the *Anagrafe,* which is like a town census. The earliest of these dates from about 1885.

Probate Records. Wills filed within the past century will be lodged with the local notary, a job that is often hereditary in Italy. For wills older than 100 years you should write for information to Archivio Notarile, Ispettatore Generale, Via Flaminia 160, Roma.

Church Records. For early birth, marriage, and death records, the parish priest in your ancestor's hometown is the person to contact. In many cases, it will be difficult to get information without searching it out yourself (and you'll need to know Latin) or hiring a professional to do it for you. (In some places it is advisable to get permission of the Vicar-General of the diocese and arrive at the parish church with a letter of permission in hand.) The difficulty does not lie with the priest himself but with the inaccessibility of the records, which may be hidden away in musty old lofts and which may be badly weathered or even destroyed by mice.

Immigration Records. There are very few immigration records in Italy, because quite a bit of the pre–World War I immigration was clandestine.

Miscellaneous Sources. There are nine *Archivio di Stato* (state archives), in Rome, Naples, Palermo, Venice, Turin, Milan, Genoa, Florence, and Bologna, which have gathered some records of genealogical interest, in particular the *Leva,* or military conscription rolls of the nineteenth century. Contact the archives in the city which represents the province where your ancestor was born for these records.

Luigi Amaduzzi of the Italian Embassy in Washington, D.C. suggests the following sources for Americans hunting ancestors in Italy:

1. Istituto di Genealogia
   e Araldico
   Via Antonio Cerasi 5-A
   Roma
2. Istituto Araldico Coccia
   Borgo Santa Croce 6
   50122 Firenze
3. Istituto Genealogico
   Araldico
   Guelfi Camaiani

   Via Torta 14
   50122 Firenze
4. Studio Araldico Scorza
   Via Caffaro 3
   16124 Genova
5. Araldico
   Istituto Genealogico
   Italiano
   Largo Chigi 19
   00187 Roma

JAPAN

Because of the more recent immigration of most Japanese-Americans (since 1900), preliminary information from parents, grandparents, and relatives should help ancestor hunters pinpoint the ancestral hometown.

Birth, Marriage, and Death Records. When you have determined the home village, town, or city of your immigrant forebear, you should write for a copy of the household registration record *(Koseki)* for your family. It can be found in the *Mura-yakusho* (village office), *Gun-yakusho* (county office), or *Shi-yakusho* (city office).

If you find your ancestral village no longer in existence, the LDS library in Salt Lake City can help you discover into what city the village was consolidated. (Because Japan is becoming a highly urbanized country this process is happening more frequently.) You will need, if at all possible, to supply the library with transliteration or *Romaji* and also *Kanji* characters for the village place name. For people who have difficulty writing Kanji characters, the library does have available a Japanese form of request.

When writing for *Koseki,* enclose about 300 yen per household record. An international money order, which may be purchased at a post office, is acceptable to Japanese public offices.

Miscellaneous Sources. For general information about Japanese national records you should address your inquiries to the National Diet Library, 1-10-1 Nagatacho, Chiyoda-ku, Tokyo 100.

There are two genealogical societies in Japan which can give a great deal of help. One is Nihon Kakei Kyokai (Japan Genealogical Association), 8-4, 3-chome, Ginza, Chuo-ku, Tokyo. The other is Nihon Keifu Gakkai (Genealogical Society of Japan), 3, 2-chome, Nakatsu Hondori, Oyodo-ku, Osaka.

JEWISH ANCESTORS

While Israel is a Jewish "nation," the Jews are not, of course, from this one country. If records of your Jewish forebears exist, they can often be found in the country of ancestral origin by using the same methods as a genealogist of any other origin. Despite the attempt by the Nazis to wipe out not only the Jews but all records of Jewish historical existence, there are still many records of Jewish communities in Europe that survived. Some of the oldest are in Vienna, where in some cases Jewish pedigrees can be traced back to the 1500s. If your ancestors came from Austria, write to the Jewish Historical and Religious Record Center, Schottenring 25, Vienna I.

In Germany, particularly in the state of Württemberg (see address for Württemberg archives in the section on Germany in this chapter), Jewish family registers were kept from 1810, with genealogical information going back to 1750.

In Poland, surviving Jewish synagogue records for the years between 1810 and 1870 have been placed on microfilm and are available at the LDS library in Salt Lake City.

In France, Jewish records containing such genealogical data as name changes, census, biographies, and circumcision records can be found at the Alliance Israelite Universelle, 45 rue La Bruyère, 75 Paris 09.

Some of the oldest Jewish cemeteries in Europe are a fabulous hunting ground for genealogical information. The Halnlein-Alsback cemetery in the German state of Hesse served twenty-nine Jewish communities; the Prague Jewish cemetery in Czechoslovakia is the oldest in Europe.

The state of Israel is attempting to piece together European Jewish records. The following agencies, according to the Embassy of Israel in Washington, D.C., have agreed to respond to genealogical queries:

1. "Yad Vashem"
   Remembrance Authority
   P.O. Box 84
   Jerusalem, Israel
2. Institute for
   Contemporary Jewry
   The Hebrew University
   Givat Ram
   Jerusalem, Israel
3. Ben-Zvi Institute for
   Research on Jewish
   Communities in the
   East

The Hebrew University
Givat Ram
Jerusalem, Israel
4. The Diaspora Research
   Institute
   Tel Aviv University
   Ramat-Aviv, Israel
5. Institute for Research on
   Jewish Families and
   Communities
   Tel Aviv, Israel

Some Jewish family historians may think there is little chance of tracing ancestry beyond their immigrant forebear. This is not necessarily true.

A few years ago, an American woman visited Israel and placed small newspaper ads seeking relatives of her

Russian-Jewish family named Shkolnik. Before she left to return home, she received a call and an invitation to tea from her cousin Levi, who had changed his family name to Eshkol—and was prime minister of Israel.

For further help with the special problems of tracing Jewish ancestors in Europe, contact the American Jewish Historical Society, Two Thornton Road, Waltham, Massachusetts 02154.

MEXICO

Don't head for Mexico ancestor hunting unless you have thoroughly checked the LDS library in Salt Lake City. Its staff has filmed many of Mexico's civil and church records, and may have just what you need. Even if you do go to Mexico, do not overlook the LDS branch libraries in that country. They will advise you how to proceed to solve your particular research problem. (For their location, contact the main headquarters in Salt Lake City.)

Birth, Marriage, and Death Records. Local parishes have baptismal, confirmation, marriage, and death records from 1524 to the present. Mandatory civil registration has been the law since 1859 and includes the same general information as parish registers, with the exception that marriage certificates record the grandparents' names. These records are located in the Office of the Civil Registrar in each municipality.

Census Records. A special early census was taken (Spaniards only) in 1689, which listed name, birthplace, parents, grandparents, rank, and orders of chivalry bestowed. This census is located in the Archivo General de la Nación, Palacio Nacional, Mexico City 2, D.F. Modern census rolls exist from 1842 to the present, and include standard census data plus religion, race, and Indian dialect. These census rolls are located in La Casa Amarilla, Mexico City.

Property and Tax Records. Property-tax records for the years 1542 to 1825 include the name, residence address, date of payments, and spouse's name. They can be found in the Archivo General de la Nación in Mexico City. Land records from 1524 to the present are also at the Archivo General.

Military Records. Historical military records from 1524 to 1700 are at the Archivo de Indias in Seville, Spain. These documents usually contain names of parents, dates of commissions, and biographies. Modern military and some historical military records dating from 1600 to 1650 are at the Archivo General in Mexico City.

Immigration Records. Immigration records from 1519 to 1820 are located in the Archivo Histórico de Hacienda. Records from 1917 to the present are at the Archivo des Ex-Ayuna-Miento. Both are in Mexico City. Immigration records for the period 1820 to 1850, during the expulsion of the Spanish, are at the Archivo General.

Other immigration reports, called land entry records, are particularly valuable to Mexican-Americans. From 1903 to 1952 the names, ages, birthplace, and last permanent address were recorded for 1,500,000 immigrants at the El Paso, Texas, port of entry. For information on these lists, write to the Immigration and Naturalization Office, P.O. Box 9398, El Paso, Texas 79984. (These lists have also been microfilmed by the LDS library.)

Miscellaneous Sources. Mexican Indian records are the oldest records in Mexico, dating from 900 to the present time, including the *Mayan Chronicles.* (In this country, you can find the chronicles at Brigham Young University in Provo, Utah.)

Other records, such as land and property grants to Indians from 1574 to 1700, are recorded in the Archivo General.

The Academia Mexicana de Genealogía y Heráldica in Mexico City has many family histories, with biographical and pedigree data, plus proofs of nobility.

NORWAY

About three million Americans descend from Norwegian Viking ancestors, most of whom emigrated from Norway after 1825, with the peak year in 1883. This means that most of your progenitors do not reach back beyond Norway's modern records, so it should be fairly simple to pick up the trail.

Birth, Marriage, and Death Records. Registers of vital statistics were first made compulsory in 1946, so most of the data for genealogical purposes must be gathered from parish registers.

Church Records. Norwegian parish registers record birth, baptism, marriage, and death, and in some instances movements into and out of the parish. Some registers date from 1600, but most are from 1700. According to law, parish registers are transferred to regional archives eighty years after the last entry. Here is a list of regional archives with the regions they serve:

1. *Statsarkivet i Oslo,* Prinsens gate 7-9, Oslo 1 (for Østfold, Akershus, Oslo, Buskerud, Vestfold, and Telemark fylker)
2. *Statsarkivet i Hamar,* Strandgata 71, N-2300 Hamar (for Hedmark and Oppland fylker)
3. *Statsarkivet i Kristiansand,* Vesterveien 4, N-4600

Kristiansand S (for Aust-Agder and Vest-Agder fylker)
4. *Statsarkivet i Stavanger,* Domkirkeplassen 1, N-4000 Stavanger (for Rogaland fylker)
5. *Statsarkivet i Bergen,* Arstadveien 22, N-5000 Bergen (for Hordaland, including Bergen, and Sogn og Fjordane fylker)
6. *Statsarkivet i Trondheim,* Høgskoleveien 12, N-7000, Trondheim (for Møre og Romsdal, Sor-Trøndelag, Nord-Trøndelag, Nordland, Troms, and Finmark fylker)
7. *Statsarkivkontoret i Tromso,* Peterborggata 21-29, N-9000, Tromso (for principal records of Troms and Finmark)

Census Records. Norway has one of the oldest population rolls in Europe, dated 1664. These cover the rural districts only and list just men and boys or women engaged in farming. These early rolls and later official censuses from 1769 to 1900 are kept in the National Archives: Riksarkivet, Bankplassen 3, Oslo 1.

Probate Records. Probate registers going back to about 1660 are preserved in the regional archives (see addresses above) and show the registration, valuation, and division of real estate and property of all kinds left by the deceased. In recent years many have been indexed on cards.

Property Records. Property deeds back to about 1720 can be located in regional archives. Real estate books called *matrikler* will give you the names of owners of farms from 1665 to 1723 and are in the National Archives. Some older records from the Middle Ages have been printed.

Immigration Records. Emigrant lists kept by the police of a number of districts are located in the regional archives. They show the name, home address, date of departure, destination, and name of ship. These lists may often prove to be the best starting point for genealogical inquiries.

Military Records. Those dating from 1650 are kept partly in the National Archives and partly in the regional archives, especially those in Bergen and Trondheim. The early ones are sketchy, but the later ones give much detailed personal information you are unlikely to find in any other source.

Miscellaneous Sources. For a free copy of "How to Trace Your Ancestors in Norway" and a huge packet of travel material, write to the Norwegian National Tourist Office, 75 Rockefeller Plaza, New York, New York 10019, well in advance of your trip.

According to Norwegian authorities, the LDS genealogical library in Salt Lake City possesses film copies of all the principal family history records of Norway.

Other sources in the United States you can check with for help in locating your Norwegian ancestry are the Supreme Lodge of the Sons of Norway, 1312 West Lake Street, Minneapolis, Minnesota 55408, and the Norwegian-American Historical Association, St. Olaf College, Northfield, Minnesota 55057.

Finally, there is a strong literary heritage left by descendants of Scandinavian immigrants. Norwegian-Americans, in particular, can learn what the early days were like by reading O. E. Rolvaag's *Giants in the Earth.*

You may be able to trace living relatives in Norway through the Salvation Army. If you have tried every other approach and failed, they may be able to help with their Missing Persons Department. You can write to them in Norway at Frelsesarmeen Ettersokelseskontoret, Pilestredet 22, Oslo 1. (They do not undertake genealogical research; they are a missing persons bureau for the living only.)

REPUBLIC OF THE PHILIPPINES

For helpful information regarding Philippine ancestors write to Luis G. Cordero, Department of General Services, Bureau of Records Management, San Luis Street, Manila.

POLAND

It has been estimated that about 30 percent of Americans can trace at least one of their ancestral lines into Poland.

The best way to approach genealogical research in Poland is to get in touch with the two central archives in Warsaw. One is for old records, the other for modern records (post-1945).

1. Old records: Archiwum Glowne Akt Dawnych, Warsaw, Dluga 7
2. New records: Archiwum Akt Nowych, Warsaw, Dluga 7

The National Library (Biblioteka Narodowa) in Warsaw is a good source to ask where the particular records you seek are located.

Polish archives provide a unique service for Americans with Polish ancestry. For a $10 entrance fee the Naczelna Dyrekcja Archiwów Pánstwowych in Warsaw will research all Polish records for you and provide photocopies of all documents found. The total fee can amount to more than $100, so this is not a step to be taken until other sources have been tried.

If you are interested in this service, send the $10 entry fee together with your request for information to Narodowy Bank Polski, V Oddzial Miejski, 1052-882 rachunek srodkow specjalnych, typ 33, Naczelna Dyrekcja Archiwów Pánstwowvch, Warszaw, ul. Długa 6. Give them the fullest possible data on your ancestor and his or her family members, such as names, birth and death dates, marriages, spouses' names, and parents' names. The more you can give them, the less it will cost for the search. Correspondence in the Polish language is preferred, but English is accepted.

Birth, Marriage, and Death Records. The United States Embassy in Warsaw will, for a $2 fee, obtain birth, marriage, or death certificates for the period since 1870. Include the full name of the individual plus the date and place of the event and given names of parents.

Miscellaneous Sources. The Polish Embassy in Washington, D.C. suggests that genealogists needing special help with problems of Polish ancestry, contact Dyr. Hieronim Kubiak, Uniwersytet Jagiellonski, Instytut Badan Polonijnych, ul. Straszewskiego 27, 31-101 Kraków.

The LDS church has microfilmed archival records (about 6,000 rolls) in Poland, and Protestant church registers as well. However, Catholic church records remain in their individual parishes and thus far have not been released for microfilming. The Salt Lake City library and its more than 200 branches have a film valuable to Polish ancestor hunters which gives many of Poland's place names and how they have changed since World War II. The film is of the book *Slownik nazw Geograficznych Polski.*

There are two printed sources you should consult. One is the article "Polish-American Genealogical Research," in *Michigan Family Trails,* vol. 4, no. 1 (Summer 1972), published by the Michigan Department of Education, State Library Services, 735 E. Michigan Avenue, Lansing, Michigan 48913. The other is "Some Sources for Polish Genealogy," in *The Genealogist's Magazine* (December 1969), which can be found in any library with a genealogical collection.

SPAIN

There is not one but four principal national archives in Spain, each holding material of specific interest to American family historians of Spanish ancestry. The four archives are:

1. *Archives of Simancas in Valladolid.* Here are military, naval, royal, and judicial records dating back to 1545. Of particular interest is a tax list of residents of Castilla during 1752, giving surnames of parents and grandparents.
2. *National Historical Archives in Madrid.* Founded in 1866, these archives are the most valuable for genealogical study. Many historical records have three to five generations referenced; also documents of the Court of the Holy Inquisition from 1400 through 1800. The records are indexed.
3. *Archives of the Crown of Aragon in Barcelona.* These archives have cataloged some of the earliest legal, royal, and church documents in Spain, reaching back to the 1000s.
4. *Archives of the Indies in Seville.* These have a massive collection of 14 million reports on military and early land discoveries in the New World, and are very valuable records for tracing early Spanish-Mexican ancestry.

Church Records. For early church parish records for Spain's 19,000 parishes it is best to consult *The Guidebook of the Spanish Church,* published by the General Office of Information and Statistics of the Church in 1954. The book lists all of the parishes of Spain and their dioceses, with the date of their earliest known document. The most ancient church register in Spain is in the parish of Verdu and dates from 1394.

Miscellaneous Sources. Manual Carrion Gutiez, the

Secretary General of the *Biblioteca Naciónal* in Madrid, suggests these sources for Spanish genealogical research:

1. Instituto Internaciónal de Genealógia y Heráldica, C/Atocha 94, Madrid
2. Instituto Salazar y Castro, Consejo Superior de Investigaciónes Científicas, Duque de Medinaceli, 4 Madrid
3. Asociación de Hidalgos, C/Atocha, 94, Madrid

Both Spanish and Mexican ancestor hunters may find the *Spanish Genealogical Helper* worth reading. It is published quarterly by the Augustan Society, 1617 West 261st Street, Harbor City, California 90710. Subscription price is $6 per year.

SWEDEN

Finn A. Thomsen, an authority on Scandinavian research, points out two interesting challenges to the Swedish-American ancestor hunter. First, many of the records made prior to 1875 were written in a gothic script. Thus, you will have to learn to read in a new way, since some of the characters are completely different from the Roman alphabet. Second, there are some interesting surname customs. More than 40 percent of the current population share twenty names, all of which end in "son." Johansson, alone, accounts for one out of every fifteen Swedes. This means that it is very difficult for you to trace your Swedish ancestors by name. As you might guess, multiple sources are a must.

But the rewards are great for the 12 million American descendants of Swedish ancestors who want to find living family still in Sweden. About half (or four million) of Sweden's population are related to Americans.

Birth, Marriage, and Death Records. In Sweden keeping vital statistics has been the duty of the church. Every parish maintains these records whether or not the person sets foot in the church itself. Since the late 1600s, the parish clergyman kept not only records of births, marriages, deaths, and confirmations but also records of arrivals and removals from the parish. Each parish also has records called *husförhörslängder,* or household rolls, which are similar to a parish census.

Although some of these records remain in the parishes, most of the records more than 100 years old were transferred from their *län* (equivalent to our state) to regional archives called *landsarkiv.* A few cities have established their own archives called *stadsarkiv.* All are listed below with the areas they serve:

1. *Landsarkivet,* S-751 04 Uppsala (for the *län* of Stockholm, Uppsala, Södermanland, Örebro, Västmanland, and Kopparberg)
2. *Landsarkivet,* S-592 00 Vadstena (for the *län* of Östergötland, Jönköping, Kronoberg, and Kalmar)
3. *Landsarkivet,* P. O. Box 142, S-621 00 Visby (for the *län* of Gotland)
4. *Landsarkivet,* Fack 2016, S-220 02 Lund (for the *län* of Blekinge, Kristianstad, Malmöhus, and Halland)
5. *Landsarkivet,* P.O. Box 3009, Geijersgatan 1, S-400 Göteborg (for the *län* of Göteborg and Bohus, Älvsborg, Skaraborg, and Värmland)
6. *Landsarkivet,* Nybrogatan 17, S-871 01 Härnösand (for the *län* of Gävleborg, Västernorrland, Västerbotten, and Norrbotten)
7. *Landsarkivet,* S-831 01 Östersund (for the *län* of Jämtland)
8. *Stadsarkivet,* P.O. Box 22063, Kungsklippan 6, S-104 22 Stockholm (for the city of Stockholm)
9. *Stadsarkivet,* St. Petrigången 7A, S-211 22 Malmö (for the city of Malmö)
10. *Stadsarkivet,* P.O. Box 851, S-501 15 Borås (for

the city of Borås, except for church records that
have been transferred to *Landsarkivet* in Göteborg)

11. *Stadsarkivet,* S-721 87 Västerås (for the city
    of Västerås, except for church records that have
    been transferred to *Landsarkivet* in Uppsala)

12. *Stadsarkivet,* Fack, S-701 01 Örebro (for the
    city of Örebro)

13. *Stadsarkivet,* Uppsala kommun, P.O. Box 216,
    S-751 04 Uppsala (for the city of Uppsala)

14. *Stadsarkivet,* Gävle centralarkiv, Stapeltorgsga-
    tan 5B, S-802 24 Gävle (for the city of Gävle)

15. *Stadsarkivet,* Stadshuset, Drottninggatan 32, S-
    652 25 Karlstad (for the city of Karlstad)

16. *Stadsarkivet,* Kriebsensgatan 4, S-632 00, Es-
    kilstuna (for the city of Eskilstuna)

17. *Stadsarkivet,* Norrköpings kommun, Stadsarki-
    vet, S-601 81 Norrköping (for the city of Nörr-
    koping).

Property and Tax Records. Material in the *Kam-
mararkivet* (the Cameral Archives), Fack, Fyrverkarbacken 13-17, S-100 26 Stockholm, dates back as far
as 1540.

Immigration Records. Beginning in 1867, the police
gathered complete information about passengers bound
for America, including the *destination* in America.
These records are indexed and available in the Göteborg *Landsarkivet,* the Emigrantinstitutet (Emigrant
Institute), P.O. Box 201, S-351 04 Växjö and the
Emigrantregistret (the Emigrant Register), P.O. Box
331, S:a Kyrkogatan 4, S-651 05 Karlstad.

Military Records. All military records are located at
the *Krigsarkivet* (the Royal Swedish Military Record
Office), Fack, Banérgatan 64, S-104 50 Stockholm.

Miscellaneous Sources. For general information about
Sweden's records you can contact *Riksarkivet* (the Na-

tional Swedish Record Office), Fack, Fyrverkarbacken 13-17, S-100 26, Stockholm. Or contact *Statistika centrabyrán* (the National Central Bureau of Statistics), Fack, Karlavägen 100, S-102 50 Stockholm.

A source book for Americans looking for Swedish ancestry, called *Cradled in Sweden,* has been written by Carl-Erik Johannson. It gives explicit directions for trans-Atlantic research in Sweden, including an alphabetical index of all parishes and the *län* in which they are located.

Two genealogical societies can help you with specific problems in Swedish research. The first, *Personhistorika samfundet, Riksarkivet,* Fack, S-100 26 Stockholm, publishes a magazine, *Personhistorisk tidskrift.* The second, *Genealogiska föreningen,* Arkvigatan 3, S-111 28 Stockholm, publishes *Släkt och hävd.*

For a free copy of "Tracing Your Swedish Ancestry" and an interesting history of Swedish emigration to America entitled "Americans from Sweden," write to the Royal Swedish Embassy, Watergate 600, 600 New Hampshire Avenue, N.W., Washington, D.C. 10037.

SWITZERLAND

If you are descended from Swiss ancestors and are under twenty-two, you may still be a Swiss citizen. The law in Switzerland states that persons of Swiss ancestry, even those living for generations in a foreign country, can report to any Swiss government agency in Switzerland or in any foreign country before they are twenty-two years old and reclaim their Swiss citizenship. They may at the same time retain dual citizenship in any other country.

Under Switzerland's unique citizenship laws every Swiss is first of all a citizen of a community (village or city), and only by right of this community citizenship is he also a citizen of a canton (state), and last of all a citizen of Switzerland.

Each Swiss community has a genealogical records center for all its citizens, even those who actually reside elsewhere in the country. Hometown citizenship is inherited like a surname, so no matter where a person moves within Switzerland, his vital records are channeled back to the place where he is a citizen and entered into *Buergerregisters.*

The civil registrar of the town will, on request, prepare a *Familienschein,* or family record. Some of these records (in the Canton of Bern, for example) go back to 1820, but most date from 1876, when such registration became law. Before 1876 the church maintained vital statistical records as in most other Western countries. Most of the church records date from 1600.

The National Archives for Switzerland is located at Archivstrasse 4, 3003 Bern. If you need some help to point your efforts in the right direction, contact that agency.

Because of the Swiss passion for record keeping from an early time, it is possible, especially in the case of noble families, to trace genealogies back to medieval times—even to Charlemagne. One of the exceptional genealogical achievements of all time is the pedigree charts of the Rubel-Blass family, prepared by Dr. W. H. Ruoff of Zurich. Dr. Ruoff traced the family back to the eighth century and documented 12,000 ancestors on 313 huge pedigree sheets.

You may want to contact the Swiss Society for Genealogical Studies. For general information address the Secretary, Lindenhofstrasse 4, 3048 Worblaufen. Sectional branches of the Society are as follows:

1. *Basel.* Kreuzackerweg 12, 4148 Pfefflingen
2. *Bern.* Hess-Strasse 8, 3097 Liebefeld
3. *Luzern.* Drelfindenstrasse 26, 6006 Luzern
4. *Neuchâtel.* rue des Beaux-Arts 3, 2000 Neuchâtel
5. *St. Gallen.* Landvogt-Waser-Strasse 70, 8405 Winterthur
6. *Zurich.* Eggwiesstrasse 26, 8332 Russikon

If you know from which Swiss community your ancestor emigrated, you should write directly to the civil registrar with your questions. If you do not know the community, you should consult the *Family Name Book of Switzerland (Familiennamenbuch der Schweiz),* which should be in most libraries with sizable genealogical collections. This multivolume work, the magic key to Swiss genealogical research, has all present-day Swiss family names listed, with reference to which cantons they appear and what date they first appeared. If you do not have access to the *Family Name Book,* contact the Agency for Civil Status *(Amt für Zivilstandswesen)* in Bern or the Director of the Swiss Society for Family Research *(Vorstand der Schweizerischen Gesellschaft für Familienforschung)* in Neuchâtel for help in locating your ancestral home.

FEDERAL PEOPLES REPUBLIC OF YUGOSLAVIA

Yugoslavia is a country composed of six federated republics—Serbia, Croatia, Bosnia and Herzegovina, Macedonia, Slovenia, Montenegro—and two autonomous provinces, Voivodina and Kosovo. Each of the republics represents a different ethnic group with unique customs and history.

Civil registration in Yugoslavia has been required only since 1946. Whatever records remain from the latter part of the nineteenth century and the early part of this century, when most emigration to America occurred, are located in regional archives. You should direct your questions to the archive in the region where your ancestor lived. If the staff cannot answer your question from their records, they will refer you to the appropriate source, free of charge.

1. *Arhiv Bosne I Hercegovine,* Sarajevo, Save Kovacevica 6 (Bosnia)

2. *Arhiv SR Crne gore,* Cetinje, Totov trg, (Montenegro)

3. *Arhiv Jrvatske,* Zagreb, Marulicev trag 21 (Croatia)

4. *Arhiv Makedonije,* Skopje (Macedonia)

5. *Arhiv Slovenije,* Ljubljana, levstikov trg 3 (Slovenia)

6. *Arhiv Srbije,* Beograd, Karnedzijeva 2 (Serbia, Belgrad)

7. *Istoriiski arhiv AP Voivodine,* Stremski Karlovci, Trga Branka Radicevica 8 (Historical Archive of Voivodina)

8. *Pikrajinski drzavni arhiv,* Pristina, Nikola Tedko 43 (Archive of Kosovo-Metohija in the city of Pristina)

Probate Records. There is very little information on wills being released from Yugoslavia. If a will is vital to your family history, check with the Lawyers' Association: Udruzenje Pravnika FNRJ, Belgrade, Proleterskih Brigada 74.

UNION OF SOVIET
SOCIALIST REPUBLICS

The U.S.S.R. is composed of the following Republics (and ethnic groups): Russia, Armenia, Azerbaidzhan, Estonia, Georgia, Karelia, Kirgiz, Latvia, Lithuania, Moldavia, Tadzhikistan, Turkistan, Turkmenistan, Ukraine, Uzbekistan, White Russia. At this time, the Soviet Embassy in Washington, D.C., does not respond to genealogical inquiries by private American citizens or by professional genealogists. That does not necessarily mean you should not continue to ask them for access to historical vital records for the purpose of tracing your Russian ancestry. There is some reason to hope, with the increasing exchange of cultural programs, that continuing interest and pressure on the part of American genealogists might cause the Soviets to change their position in the future.

Two organizations that might be able to help you with biographical and family history information from their 1,000-volume library are the Russian Historical and Genealogical Society and the Russian Nobility Association, both at 971 First Avenue, New York, New York 10022.

10

DOES YOUR FAMILY
HAVE A COAT OF ARMS?

One day a secretary at the Jomar Advertising Agency in Memphis, Tennessee, opened a letter addressed to "Jomar Adv. Agy."

"Good news for the Agy family!" it cried. "Did you know that the family name Agy has an exclusive and particularly beautiful coat of arms?"

The Agy family, the letter went on, could now have its arms exactingly reproduced with "regal red flocking."

Perhaps you, too, have received one of these "personal" computerized letters, for there are over a hundred mail-order arms companies flooding the country with them. While there is nothing wrong with having a mail-order wall plaque with your family name on it just for the fun of it, you should be aware of the fact that it is probably not authentic.

Still, a genealogist friend of mine has collected several family crests from ancestral lines he has researched, and though he realizes the chances are slim that these arms were actually granted to his ancestors, they still dramatically and decoratively reflect his interest in family history.

If you want to display arms on your wall for the fun of it, as my friend has, look up your surname in a book of arms (called an "armory") for your ancestral country (you'll find many armories in genealogical libraries), and copy the coat of arms on a piece of paper.

When your friends ask about this intriguing decoration, you can say, "Oh, those arms belonged to someone with my surname a long time ago." An honest answer and heraldically correct—caveat auditor.

Many countries have a heraldic tradition, but in most cases, coats of arms were issued to *individuals* rather than families. Under most heraldic rules, only first sons of first sons of the recipient of a coat of arms may legally bear their ancestor's arms. Younger sons may use a version of their fathers' arms, but the rules of heraldry are that they must be changed ("differenced"). If the possessor of a coat of arms (called an "armiger") dies without male heirs, his daughter may combine her father's arms with her husband's arms (called "impaling"). There are many more such ancient rules, but these give you the general idea.

HERALDRY FOR GENEALOGISTS

Greeks used distinguishing marks on their shields centuries before the Christian era, and African warriors painted hereditary designs on their hide-and-wood shields. But it was in medieval Europe that this form of military decoration reached the kind of flowering that has come to be known as heraldry.

Heraldry probably began among the English in the early 1100s and came about because, during the Crusades, men from many countries were thrown together and needed quick, nonverbal ways of identifying each other—a problem accentuated by the fact that armor had by then become so sophisticated that closed helmets prevented facial recognition during hand-to-hand combat. English knights gradually added other identifying marks to their armor, and their fashions were soon adopted by most of the rest of Europe. Distinguishing crests were placed atop helmets, because the shield was not always visible in battle; a cloth coat (surcoat) on

"KNYCHTHEDE IS A GREIT HONOUR"

What is all this fuss about knights and coats of arms? Who were these ancestors and what did all this mean to them? To answer these questions, here is a noble explanation of the meaning of knighthood, written in 1456 by a Scottish knight, Sir Gilbert of the Haye. If our ancestors lived up to a fraction of their code, they are worthy of our pride.

Knychthede is a greit honour. [he wrote—and hereafter I'll translate into 1980s English] married with a great servitude, that insomuch as a man has a noble creation and beginning, he has honor, insomuch as he is bound to be good and agreeable to God he is bound to him that does him honor. Unworthy is he to be lord and master that never knew what it was to be a servant.

The office of knighthood is to maintain and defend widows, maidens, fatherless and motherless children, poor miserable, pitiable persons, and to help the weak against the strong and the poor against the rich, for ofttimes such folk are despoiled and robbed and their goods taken and put to destruction for want of power and defense.

He that has none of these virtues is not a true knight and should not be accounted as one of the order of knighthood.

Where honor is not kept, order goes backward.

which the knight's arms were sewn was worn over the armor, becoming literally a coat of arms.

During the thirteenth and fourteenth centuries, coats of arms became more elaborate and numerous, so much so, in fact, that they created the need for heralds, experts who memorized the arms of each man. Heralds acted as "masters of ceremonies" during knightly tournaments and announced each contestant by name as he rode into the arena.

Of course, each knight tried to make his arms unique, but duplications inevitably occurred, resulting in court battles and some bloodier fights as well. By 1418 it was apparent that some kind of royal regulation was necessary. In 1419 Henry V of England forbade anyone to assume arms unless by right of ancestry or as a gift from the crown. Later in the century, Richard III sent the heralds, now royal authenticators of arms, into the shires on what were called "visitations." These visitations were held about once every generation for almost two centuries for the purpose of officially verifying, listing, or denying arms in use.

Heraldry early developed its own language—largely Norman French, the court language of the time—which is still in use. A description of a coat of arms is called a "blazon" and is written in the same way as it was 500 years ago.

For example, if your coat of arms has a silver horizontal dividing line on a red shield with three five-pointed stars and three gold lions' heads, your blazon reads: *Gules, on a fess argent between three lions' heads Or, three mullets of the first.* Even the most complicated blazon is usually only one sentence long, like this one.

Figure 8 is a simplified explanation of the different parts of a coat of arms. The main component is the shield *(escutcheon)* upon which certain decorative devices, called *charges,* are placed. On top of the shield is the *crest,* sometimes an animal; and as part of the crest, a helmet and mantle, a fancy representation of the protective cloth knights once wore. The last main element of a coat of arms is the *motto*—which may be in any language, but in England is usually in Latin.

There are about 100,000 English (including Wales and the six northern Irish counties) on the rolls of the Royal College of Arms in London today. Scottish heraldry is a separate institution and is governed by different traditions and rules. Although there is a continuing interest in heraldry in Germany, France, and

FIGURE 8. Heraldic components and "tinctures."

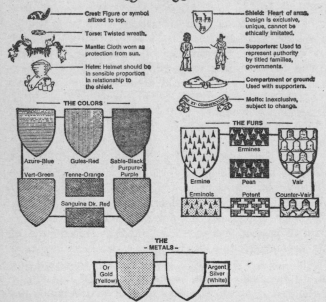

Crest: Figure or symbol affixed to top.

Torse: Twisted wreath.

Mantle: Cloth worn as protection from sun.

Helm: Helmet should be in sensible proportion in relationship to the shield.

Shield: Heart of arms, Design is exclusive, unique, cannot be ethically imitated.

Supporters: Used to represent authority by titled families, governments.

Compartment or ground: Used with supporters.

Motto: Inexclusive, subject to change.

THE COLORS

Azure-Blue Gules-Red Sable-Black

Vert-Green Tenne-Orange Purpure-Purple

Sanguine Dk. Red

THE FURS

Ermines

Ermine Pean Vair

Erminois Potent Counter-Vair

THE METALS

Or Gold (Yellow) Argent Silver (White)

Italy, there is no ongoing heraldic system, primarily because there has been no monarchy for some time. Spain is the exception. Although only recently a monarchy again, it has done a much better job of maintaining heraldic records.

A COAT OF ARMS, WITH OR WITHOUT A PRINCE IN YOUR PAST

If you are among the 82 percent of Americans with at least one line stretching back to England, Wales, Scotland, or Ireland, your ancestor, no matter how humble, may have had noble blood and may have had arms registered in his name. You may even have an ancient king concealed high in the branches of your family tree, like two of our former Presidents. Abraham Lincoln was descended from King Edward I of England. Ex-president Richard M. Nixon is actually twentieth in line of descent from King Edward III, who also had problems during his reign—the Hundred Years War and the Black Plague. Although this sounds like a very special pedigree, the truth is that there are over 100,000 persons of English background living today in England and the United States who are known descendants of Edward III, who in turn was related to most of the main royal lines of Europe in the Middle Ages.

The reason so many average Americans of English descent have such exalted pedigrees, according to British heraldic expert L. G. Pine, is that in continental Europe royal family circles kept very much to themselves, and formed a kind of marriage trade union. The same thing happened with the nobility, so that they would not be contaminated with commoner folk. In England and Scotland, however, these rules were not observed, so that from royalty to peasant, there were degrees of relationship over several generations. Consequently,

many distinguished connections turn up in families of
plain folk.

A kingly ancestor, therefore, is highly probable for
anyone with many English lines, and it can be a lot of
fun to find out. If you are of European descent, however, unless you have a family tradition that indicates
some title in your ancestry, there is not a great chance
you have a coat of arms. The European nobility and
royalty rarely intermarried with the commoner folk—
those who became the principal migrants to America.
Nevertheless, you may want to check out a family
rumor.

If your ancestors did not have royal blood, that does
not necessarily mean your forebears did not have a coat
of arms—at least not in England. If you find one with
the abbreviations Gent. or Esq. (for Gentleman and
Esquire) after his name, it is an indication he was a
bearer of arms.

Some printed sources for Americans with connec-
tions to English royal lines are *Burke's Presidential
Families of the United States of America, Ancestral
Roots of Sixty Colonists* by Weis and Sheppard, *The
Magna Charta Sureties* by Adams and Weis, and *Living
Descendants of Blood Royal* by Adams and d'Anger-
ville. National societies interested in proving royal an-
cestry for Americans are Descendants of the Illegitimate
Sons and Daughters of the Kings of Britain, c/o
Brainer T. Peck, Lakeside, Connecticut 06758; and the
Augustan Society, 1617 West 261st Street, Harbor City,
California 90710.

There is a way for Americans to have a coat of arms
other than through inheritance or grant from a foreign
power. Private U.S. heraldic institutions, which are busi-
nesses not chartered by the government, will design
heraldic devices in the ancient manner to order. Such
coats of arms may then be copyrighted to prevent them
from being used by others, and you have the modern
equivalent of a medieval grant of arms. If it all seems
a bit silly, it is no more so than the way arms were
originally granted by some European countries.

Coats of arms can be purchased for about $100 from The American College of Heraldry, Box 29347, New Orleans, Louisiana 70179. Another business that sells coats of arms to Americans is the Augustan Society, mentioned above.

These and other organizations are seeking to register the use of arms in this country, but unlike the College of Arms in England, they have no legal standing and are unable to enforce the registration of your arms.

HERALDIC INSTITUTIONS WORLDWIDE

In the rest of this chapter I have tried to describe the heraldic traditions of most of the countries that provided the United States with immigrants. But the fact is that the British Isles and Western Europe took heraldry far more seriously than did the rest of the world, establishing offices of heraldry which have survived the centuries. Other countries, which at one time had heraldic traditions, such as Hungary, Russia, Lithuania, and other so-called Iron Curtain countries, have legally banned such activities and very little information is available. If the heraldry of your mother country isn't described in this chapter and you are still determined to search for a coat of arms, try writing to the country's embassy in Washington, D.C. They may be able to direct you to a historian or university with an interest in heraldry.

Austria

There never was a central bureau in Austria expressly for the purpose of granting arms. After 1760, laws forbade anyone outside the nobility from bearing arms. Arms granted by the king or emperor are included in general genealogical records in Austrian state archives. In 1919, the official use of arms was forbidden.

Belgium

The Heraldic Council of Belgium, operating since 1844, verifies noble titles and coats of arms. Address your questions to Le Conseil Héraldique, 85 Rue du Prince Royal, Brussels.

British Isles: England, Wales, and Northern Ireland

All coats of arms in England, Wales, and the six northern countries of Ireland are granted through the Royal College of Arms in London. (Scotland has a separate registry, described later in this chapter.) The heralds at the college have original records of arms going back to the times of the visitations plus all the arms recorded in the nearly 500 years since then.

Unless you are going to be in England for an extended visit, there is little chance that you can have your ancestor's arms assigned to you (or new arms granted) during your vacation. It is best to get the investigation started well in advance of your trip. In any event, you will not be allowed to search in the College of Arms for your own records. These documents, most of them priceless, are considered the property of the heralds (officers of the Queen's Household).

If you are not planning a trip abroad, you can conduct all your business with the heralds through the mail by writing the Secretary to the Earl Marshal, The College of Arms, Queen Victoria Street, London EC4V 4BT.

There are three conditions under which you can be granted arms:

1. If you are one of those rare individuals who can document that you are a direct descendent from an armigerous ancestor in an unbroken succession of first sons (or heirs), you can have your ancestor's arms assigned to you.

2. If you can prove descent through any other son of an armigerous ancestor, you are entitled to "differenced" arms.
3. You can apply for (buy) an entirely new grant of arms if you are of English or Welsh descent. (Charges for searching records and granting arms range from a few dollars to several hundred.)

About fifty Americans every week visit or write to the College of Arms, curious to know whether they have a coat of arms. To familiarize yourself with the records at the college, you should take a look at *Records and Collections of the College of Arms* by Sir Anthony Wagner, a former herald. You can find this book in most large English libraries, and in the Library of Congress in Washington, D.C., the New York City Public Library, and the Newberry Library in Chicago.

The Heraldry Society at 28 Museum Street, London WC1A1LH, is a heraldic organization particularly friendly to Americans. Its quarterly magazine, *The Coat of Arms,* is well worth its price of $5 per year.

If you are interested in hiring an English professional to help you establish your right to arms, you should contact Achievements Ltd., Centre for Heraldic and Genealogical Research, Canterbury, England, or the well-known author of *Heraldry* and *Teach Yourself Heraldry and Genealogy,* L. G. Pine, Hall Lodge Cottage, Brettenham, Ipswich, Suffolk 1P7 7QP, England. (You should always include International Postal Reply Coupons when writing for a research quotation.)

Scotland

According to L. G. Pine, there are at least 50,000 spurious coats of arms in use in England today. Not so in Scotland. The system of heraldry in Scotland is probably the most simple and well governed in the world. Since 1672, the Lord Lyon (the name derived from the rampant lion on the arms of the royal line of Scotland) has had full legal control of all coats of arms. The willful use of a coat of arms not granted by the Lord Lyon can bring a jail sentence or fine today, just as it did 300 years ago. A Lyon Register that now fills some fifty volumes ensures that no person may legally use arms that have not been registered in his own name.

If you are a descendant of a Scottish armiger, you can petition the Lord Lyon for a grant of your ancestor's arms. If you do not have an ancestor who was granted arms in his lifetime, you must petition to obtain a grant of arms for *that ancestor*. Then you can apply for the reassignment of those arms to you, if you are an heir, or another version of the arms if you are descended from a younger son. This double procedure, which is more expensive, is often the only way Americans can obtain armorial bearings in Scotland where none had previously existed.

The Scottish system does not exclude women. Arms can be granted to appear on a lozenge (diamond-shaped shield) if the woman is an heiress of a chief of a clan or of noble family. After marriage, she may continue to use her own armorial design or have it impaled (combined) with her husband's arms.

To check on your Scottish coat of arms you should write or visit Court of the Lord Lyon, Lyon Office, H.M. New Register House, Edinburgh, EH1 3YT.

A former Lord Lyon, Sir Thomas Innes, has written what many consider to be the best book on Scottish heraldry, *Scots Heraldry,* which is in many major library and genealogical collections in this country.

For professional help in establishing rights to Scottish arms, write Donald Whyte, 4 Carmel Road, Kirkiston, West Lothian, Scotland. (Always include Postal Reply Coupons.)

Denmark

There is no central bureau in Denmark which corresponds to England's College of Arms. Arms are taken today only in conjunction with a high Danish award, such as the Order of Dannebrog. For ancient arms, the book *Danmarks Adels Aarbog* shows illustrations of coats of arms. To locate this book write to the Danish National Archives: Rigsarkivet, 9 Rigsdagsgården, DK 1218, Copenhagen K.

Finland

Coats of arms belong only to noble families who are members of the House of the Nobility. During Finland's troubled history, nobility was granted by Sweden, Russia, and even the Holy Roman Empire. Since 1919 no new nobles or arms have been created. You should address your questions on heraldry to the House of the Nobility, Riddarhusgenealogen, Riddarhuset, Helsinki.

France

France, like many republics, does not recognize heraldry except when it constitutes a seal for a town or a trademark for a product, such as a wine or an automobile. But, of course, France has a rich heraldic tradition from the Middle Ages. It was the French king Charles IV who established the world's first college of arms in 1406, an office now long defunct.

The major source of heraldry in France is the *Grand Armorial of France*, an encyclopedia of 40,000 coats of arms published by La Société du Grand Armorial de France, 179 Boulevard Haussman, Paris.

The principal heraldry society in France is Société Française d'Héraldique, 113 Rue de Courcelles, Paris.

Germany

For the records of German coats of arms, address Deutsches Wappenrol Bureau, Bonn, West Germany.

For information about an ancestor who was a member of the German nobility, write Deutsches Adelsarchiv, Schonstadt, West Germany. Also check with Der Herold, Verein fur Heraldik, 1000 Berlin 33, Archivstr. 12-14.

The records of the *Edda* (Iron Book of the German Nobility) are deposited in the above three archives.

For the complete story of German heraldry and nobility, consult the *Genealogisches Handbuch des Adels* by Forest E Barber in the Library of Congress.

Republic of Ireland

Although the office of the Chief Herald of Ireland dates from only 1943, all the surviving Irish heraldic records from the centuries of English occupation can be checked for your ancestral arms by addressing The Chief Herald of Ireland, Dublin Castle, Dublin 2. Some of these records date from the reign of the English King Richard II in the late · 1300s. Most of these ancient arms have been photostated for the College of Arms in London, since there are so many family ties between the two countries.

Irish arms, in a way, are family arms in that the Chief Herald will grant you the arms of the chief of your name if you can show that you are descended from him or one of his ancestors.

A publication of interest to Irish heraldists is *Heraldry Today,* 10 Beauchamp Place, London SW3, which issues a number of catalogs annually, including often rare Irish items.

Italy

Since the end of World War II, noble titles have not been recognized in Italy, although there is a continuing interest in the history of the nobility and in heraldry.

For information about your Italian ancestors who may have been entitled to arms write to Araldica, Istituto Genealogico Italiano, Largo Chigi 19, 00187 Roma.

For professional help in Italy write to Count Guelfo

Guelfi Camaiani, Istituto Genealogico Italiano, Via Torta, 14 (Palazzo Gondi), 50122 Firenze (Florence).

The Library of Congress contains several books on Italian heraldry which you may find helpful: *Bibliografia Araldica e genealogica d'Italia* by Guistino Colaneri; and *Dizionario storicoblasonico delle famiglie nobili e notabili italiana estinti e fiorenti* by Giovanni di Crollalanza.

Japan

In the Orient, Japan alone had a highly developed heraldry, starting in the eleventh century. Today, ancient family crests—plum flowers, bamboo leaves, cranes—are in use everywhere as trademarks on the products and shops of industrial Japan. (Mitsubishi, the airplane manufacturer, has a crest of three diamonds.)

As in Europe, Japanese heraldry had its root in the need for instant identification between military friends and foes. Gradually, however, the crests (called "mons") went home with these early warriors after battle and became family symbols.

For many years, the family crest was the prerogative of the nobility and high-ranking soldiers (Samurai), but about 1600, during a more peaceful era that lasted until the middle of the nineteenth century, commoners began to design and use family crests. At first they were used on soldiers' shields and ceremonial kimonos, then on lanterns and lacquerware, and today, not surprisingly, on shops and products. Of course, there were restrictions based on custom. The three-leafed hollyhock was reserved for the Tokugawa family and the sixteen-petal chrysanthemum was considered the exclusive property of the Imperial family.

There are 200 basic patterns of crests surviving today, with some 4,000 variations. Many are lovely representations of nature—three gingko leaves, wild cherry blossoms, Korin-style crane.

For help in locating your family crest write to National Diet Library, 1-10-1 Nagata-cho, Chiyoda-ku, Tokyo 100.

The Netherlands

Any individual may adopt a coat of arms in Holland. There is no regulation and no official registration.

Norway

There have been no titled families in Norway since 1814, and no registration of heraldic arms since 1821. Individual Norwegians may adopt a coat of arms at will, although there is no extensive history of heraldry in the country.

For heraldic information write Universitetsbiblioteket i Oslo, Drammensveien 42B, Oslo.

Poland

Many of Poland's records were destroyed during World War II. Those that survive are at the main historical archives: Archiwum Glowny Akt Dawnych, Warsaw, ul. Dluga #7.

Since nobility and heraldry are not politically popular in modern-day Poland, many Polish-Americans searching for their coat of arms get more help from Chev. Leonard J. Suligowski, Director of Heraldry, Polish Nobility Association, Villa Anneslie, 529 Dunkirk Road, Baltimore, Maryland 21212. Suligowski has put together a bibliography of all the known books still in print dealing with Polish heraldry. This list can be seen at the New York City Public Library and the Library of Congress, or ordered from the Polish Nobility Association for a fee. An additional book can be found in the Library of Congress under the title *Herbarz polski* by Kaspar Niesiecki.

Chevalier Suligowski, an expert on Polish heraldry, explains that Polish coats of arms, unlike European heraldry in general, can often represent a "clan" or tribe with more than one family in it. On the whole, he says, the rules of Polish heraldry were much less rigid than the rules on arms developed in Western Europe. As a result of the tribal system that influenced all the countries of the Polish Commonwealth, the nobility, consisting of more than 40,000 families, used about 7,000 arms.

Portugal

Few records of ancient Portuguese arms survived the devastating earthquake of 1755. Those that remain are at the National Archives. Address your queries to Arquivo Nacional da Tôrre do Tombo, Lisbon.

Spain

The archives of Spain, in spite of losses during the civil war of the 1930s, are marvelously full of information about the heritage of Spanish nobility and heraldry. Nevertheless, there is no central college of arms as in England. This makes hunting for your ancestor's arms more difficult. On the other hand, your search has a good chance of success. There were 500,000 noblemen (hidalgos) in Spain at the end of the 1700s, which means there are literally millions of their descendants entitled to display ancestral arms.

Manuel Carrion Gutiez, the secetary general of the *Biblioteca Naciónal* in Madrid suggests two sources other than his library for Americans of Spanish descent searching for their family's heraldic tradition. They are (1) Instituto Internaciónal de Genealogía y Heráldica, C/Atocha, 94, Madrid, and (2) Asociación de Hidalgos, same address.

The major source book of Spanish heraldry is *Heraldic and Genealogical Encyclopedia: Spanish-American* in the Library of Congress in Washington, D.C. It contains the arms and genealogies of many families in Spain and Latin America.

The principal heraldic publication in Spain is *Hidal-*

guia. For information about this publication write to
Vicente De Cadenas y Vicent, Cronista Rey de Armas,
Dirección y Administración, Calle de Atocha, 91,
Madrid.

One of Spain's foremost professional heraldic inves-
tigators, according to the Spanish embassy in Washington, D.C., is Jesús Casado, Apartado 461, Madrid.
Letters to him should be written in Spanish.

Sweden

The traditions of heraldry are governed in Sweden
by an official board called the Riddarhusdirektionen
(the Directorate of the House of the Nobility). This
group approves coats of arms for flags, towns and
individuals.

For heraldic information write Riksheraldiker, Riddarhuset, P.O. Box 2022, S-103 11, Stockholm.

Switzerland

Switzerland, where anyone may adopt arms at will,
has a long tradition of heraldry. Write for information
concerning your ancestor's arms to Archives Héraldique
Suisses, Chemin du Parc de Valency, 11, Lausanne.

Union of Soviet Socialist Republics

The Soviet Embassy in Washington, D.C. does not
respond to heraldic queries from private American
citizens or professional heraldists.

The major American sources for Russian heraldry
consist of these works in the Library of Congress: *De-
partament gerol'dii* (eighteen manuscript volumes) and
Alfavitnyi spisok familiiam, plus *Armorial de la no-
blesse de Russie* by Igor V. de Tretiakoff.

You might also want to contact the Russian Nobility
Association, 971 First Avenue, New York City, New
York 10022.

11

YOUR FAMILY
HEALTH HISTORY

A few years ago *The Times* of London ran a picture of
Lady Jane Howard, born in 1945, alongside a portrait
of her ancestor Queen Catherine Howard, born in
1521. The family resemblance was striking. *The Times*
also showed that Viscount Robert Devereux, born in
1932, was a dead ringer for an earlier Robert Devereux, born in 1566, who was reputed to be the lover
of Queen Elizabeth I.

Now, most of us do not have portraits of ancestors
five centuries back, but if we did we might find remark-
able resemblances caused by a family's dominant
genetic code being transferred from one generation to
another—great-grandma's nose, for instance, or great-
great-grandpa's blond hair. You might even inherit
webbed toes. But they are not the only things we inherit, and in this chapter we'll explore how investigating your background can help you understand something about your health, both physical and emotional.

CHARTING YOUR FAMILY MEDICAL
HISTORY

Over 1,500 genetically caused diseases have been
identified, including hemophilia, diabetes, Addison's

and Parkinson's disease, glaucoma, muscular dystrophy, and night and color blindness.

Inherited diseases can be transmitted through groups, as well as through family trees. The disease known as Tay-Sachs is peculiar to American Jewish children of Eastern European ancestry; sickle-cell anemia to blacks of West African heritage; cleft lip to Japanese; clubfoot to Maoris; and Cooley's anemia or thalassemia to Italians and other people of Mediterranean stock. (For a nontechnical and highly readable explanation of what genetics means to the individual, consult *The Human Pedigree* and *The Heredity Factor* by Dr. William L. Nepham.)

Why are genetically transmitted illnesses important to the genealogist? William H. Carlyon, director of health education for the American Medical Association, believes it is important not just to family historians but to everyone. It would be diagnostically valuable, he says, for every American to be concerned with his family history of illness. For instance, a healthy, athletic friend of mine was shocked to have his weak spells and extreme thirst diagnosed as diabetes. "There's no diabetes in my family," he insisted. When his doctor suggested he check with relatives, his mother confirmed that a grandfather had died of the disease.

If there were such a thing as a medical census, and the census taker asked you what your great-grandmother died of, would you know? Chances are you would not, because families tend to avoid such subjects. To take one unusual example, in *Jody*, newspaper writer Jerry Hulse's book about his wife's hereditary illness, doctors had to know whether Jody's parents had suffered from stroke or diabetes before they could perform a delicate, life-saving operation on her brain. Since Jody was adopted, she had no information about her natural family's medical history. The successful search for her mother provided vital medical clues that saved Jody's life. While few cases are so extreme, it could prove invaluable someday for you to know your family's medical history.

It is not too difficult to obtain medical history three generations back, and most of us can get some information for the fourth generation as well. That is over 100 years of your family's health history. Making a point to seek such information often gives insights into family "behavior."

A woman friend of mine had been warned by her mother never to lift anything heavy. "Something might break loose inside you," she said, "and it could kill you." My friend passed along the same advice to her daughter, without really understanding why. Later she researched her family medical history and found her great-great-aunt had seen a heavy carriage fall on her younger brother, and with strength born of desperation, had run and lifted it off him. He survived, but she died days later of internal hemorrhaging, leaving behind a health lesson for four generations of women in her family.

If, after compiling your family medical history, you find that heart attacks, cancer, or any hereditary diseases predominate, you should share this part of your genealogy with your doctor. One family researcher found three generations of cancer among the female members of her paternal line, which alerted her to be especially watchful for cancer signs in herself and to make sure to have an annual physical examination. Her husband, whose medical history showed a series of strokes for both male and female family members, modified his diet and made attempts to bring his blood pressure down.

If you make a point of collecting your family's medical history—long illnesses, causes of death—you will gain insights into your own health patterns. Certainly you will be able to deliver into your doctor's hands a valuable diagnostic tool.

CHARTING YOUR FAMILY
PSYCHOHISTORY

Have you ever wondered why you behave the way you do? If you would like to understand yourself better, perhaps you should take a close look at your family's emotional behavior patterns over the last few generations.

Very recently there has developed a new field of study called *psychohistory*. One of the experts in this field, Dr. Mary Matossian of the University of Maryland, explains that a family is an emotional system, with each member developing a pattern of behavior toward every other member of the family. If we examine these relationships back through many generations (five is preferred, but three is sufficient), we can often find patterns of behavior recurring. Your research should not become just a hunt for family faults and foibles; you should also try to uncover cases of accomplishment and perseverance in the face of disaster, for the qualities that led to such deeds are an important part of your genetic inheritance, too.

The signs of an emotionally successful family, according to Dr. Matossian, are as follows: (1) good ties with cousins, uncles, aunts, grandparents; (2) parent-child relationships that are warm and affectionate; (3) well-defined roles for individual family members; (4) families where strong, stable members come to the aid of those who need help; (5) families that keep track of each other, giving support and encouragement all through life.

Americans have long prided themselves on being a nation of rugged individualists, she points out, but the truth is, most of us have derived our strength from our families. Thus, the more we know about our forebears, the more we really know about ourselves.

What kind of family emotional patterns should you

look for? Here is a list of questions to ask to help chart your family's psychohistory. You will already know the answers to some of them from previous chats with your older family members. But for other questions, you may have to pry very gently for answers from those older relatives whom you know more intimately.

1. How did your grandmother get along with your mother, and her mother with her daughter?
2. How did your grandfather get along with his father and his father with his son?
3. Who was father's favorite child and which child did father discipline most?
4. How well does your generation get on with cousins, uncles, aunts, and grandparents?
5. What is the family's attitude toward its older members?
6. Does your family have a history of prodigal sons and scapegoats?
7. Are there bad-luck stories of fortunes nearly made?
8. Are there alliances and counteralliances between branches of your family tree?
9. Does your family have a long history of either dominant mothers or dominant fathers?
10. Does your family include an unusual number of marital separations, divorces, aggressive or violent individuals, or mental illness?
11. What types of family conflicts occurred and what was the family's response to them?
12. How were family members ranked in terms of family prestige—by sex, age, ability, profession, or money?
13. Did your family pull together and help each other in times of trouble?

After you have gathered sufficient information, you may want to try charting your family's emotional history, in the way that Dr. Matossian has charted the psychohistory of the royal English Tudor family. The Tudor chart (see Figure 9) reveals strong patterns of family ambivalence and conflict.

Here is a narrative key to Dr. Matossian's code:

1. Strong positive bond—strong feelings of love and admiration.
2. Distant relationship—between people who do not talk about any subject that might be anxiety provoking (they discuss the weather).
3. Positive bond—less intense love and admiration than item 1.
4. Imaginary bond—relationship between two people closely related by blood who know each other only slightly or not at all (or a relationship between a child and parent who died when the child was an infant).
5. Ambivalent bond—the simultaneous existence of conflicting emotions of love and hate.
6. Conflictual bond—relationship between people who fight a lot; but they get something out of fighting, since they keep at it; they are bound together.

Using this method of diagramming relationships, you will be able to draw a schematic of your own family's emotional system.

If you would like to see how a psychiatrist develops an individual's psychohistory, I recommend the book *In Search of Nixon: A Psychohistorical Inquiry* by Bruce Mazlish, a Massachusetts Institute of Technology professor who is also preparing a similar psychohistory on Henry Kissinger. You may be able to apply some of his techniques to your own family chart.

What does psychohistory mean to you? Until now you have been concerned with the questions, "Who am I?" and "Where did I come from?" Charting your family's psychohistory can answer an important third question: "Why am I the kind of person I am?" While this is not a question everyone wants to explore, I

FIGURE 9. The Tudors—an emotional system.

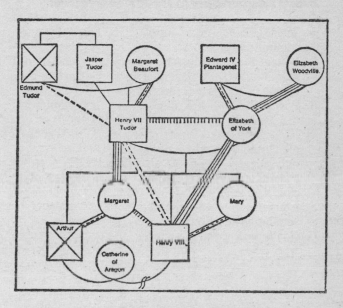

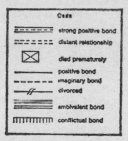

believe psychohistory can give today's family history a depth never known before. It will show you how your ancestors thought and felt, and it will help you challenge destructive family emotional patterns and shore up positive ones.

12

FAMILY GATHERING: HOW TO UNITE YOUR NEWFOUND FAMILY

One special reward of ancestor hunting is sharing a common blood bond with others in your extended family. After all, you are a part of them and they are part of you. While some people may simply not want to know their great uncles or second cousins, others will find their holidays, their vacations, and their lives in general given extra dimension and pleasure if they reunite with their extended families.

After you have been collecting family history for a while, you may want to try collecting—getting together—the family itself. You can start with brothers and sisters, parents and grandparents, aunts and uncles. Before you know it you'll have a family association—a group of many families of the same name joined together. In fact, there may already be a family association organized for your surname, for there are presently hundreds, perhaps thousands, of American families united in this way. For example, the Tolman branch of my family has 10,000 members and employs several of them as full-time family genealogists. At no cost (except for sending along a stamped, self-addressed envelope), you can obtain from the Genealogy Club of America a list of family associations, including their addresses and the names of their newsletters or you can check your library for the annual issue of the *Genea-*

logical Helper, a bimonthly magazine (P.O. Box 368, Logan, Utah 84321), which publishes a similar list. If you find your surname, by all means get in touch with your relatives. If you cannot find an already organized family association, you might want to consider starting one. (I'll show you how later in the chapter.)

GETTING TO KNOW YOUR EXTENDED FAMILY

The way to start getting to know your extended family is through a summer or holiday family reunion. It's a good idea to start planning the reunion well in advance—a year, if you can—and pick a place centrally located for most family members, with sufficient accommodations and children's play areas close by. Of course, it's even better if you can hold the gathering near an old homestead or other historical place associated with the family.

On the day of the reunion have Pedigree Charts and Family Group Sheets available (blank or filled out) and set out displays of family photographs, medals, or other family heirlooms. The program itself should include some get-acquainted time, a chance to tell family stories, an informal talk by someone on some aspect of the family history, and a reunion photograph.

Besides the fun and good feelings a family get-together can generate, reunions are a good place to enlist other relatives in your ancestor-hunting projects. You may also be able to solve some family history mysteries. Most relatives have terrific family stories that need only the stimulus of a story-telling session to pry loose. In addition, you can discover a great deal of family folklore, unique to your family and no other— traditions, favorite expressions, humorous and memorable incidents. Preserve them in writing. They will help you fill in the map of the past.

In America today there is a new sense of the importance of family relationships. Children, in particular, respond positively to family reunions because they receive the strong message that they are part of a family with heritage, a family that cares about itself.

HOW TO ORGANIZE A FAMILY ASSOCIATION AND PUBLISH A NEWSLETTER

If you cannot find an already organized family association (after checking the GCA list or the *Genealogical Helper*), why not start one? Just as your Pedigree Chart starts with you, so does your family organization.

How many generations back and how many names does the family association cover? It will follow only one surname line, probably at least back to the immigrant ancestor (called the "family progenitor"). If it is a not-so-common name like Eddy, it may well take in all the Eddys in the United States, and trace back to some ancestors overseas. If it is a more common name like Williams, you may want to establish your family association as "The Descendants of Jesse Williams" or whatever your immigrant forebear's name was.

With your own immediate family you already have the nucleus, and if you have been gathering your family's history from relatives you have probably got a good family address file already started. Visit every relative that lives close to you; personal contact is the best way to build enthusiasm, get their ideas, and solicit their support. Write to every family member you cannot talk to personally, and get the names and addresses of other relatives, no matter how distant. You will be surprised how fast your mailing list will expand.

Of course, in many of today's far-flung families, it is difficult to visit people, but a family association can still be started by telephone and correspondence. The Linder Family Association, according to its organizer, Shirley Linder Rad, was started entirely this way. The first family officers lived in Texas, New Mexico, and Utah, and did not meet until they held a national convention eighteen months after organizing. By this time the Linder Family Association had grown to over 100 members from thirty-seven states. Five years later, the Linders had collected more than 700 Family Group Sheets for its 2,000 members.

In the beginning, you may be all your family association's officers rolled into one. But just as soon as possible, the work should be divided and a governing board of sorts established. Communications should be opened with the rest of the family, money raised, and a family reunion planned. A family association history book should also be started to follow the surname line back to the immigrant ancestor.

To get in touch with as many family members as possible to tell them a family organization is being started, it is best to put out a newsletter—something more official-looking than the average letter—to let them know you're serious. (You can give it a fancy name such as *Carswell Chronicle* or *Sparkman Family Tree,* or a cute name such as *Koch Kith and Kin,* or *Long Line.*)

The main idea is to imbue your first few issues with your own enthusiasm so that others will be interested in organizing, working, and in making financial contributions to the family association. You should provide dues information and a clip-out coupon in each issue to make it easy for them to join.

Include stories of some of the goals of the new organization such as reunions, the collection of family history, anything you think will pique the interest of your cousins. Show family members right from the start that the publication will help them put together their own branch of the family tree. Publish a few photos of early forebears or of family heirlooms. Write a story about one of the family's common ancestors who turned up in your own research, or about the family coat of arms (if any), or the origins of the family name. In later editions invite other members to contribute family history stories; tell about births, deaths, marriages among the members; give reunion news and have a column that puts members working on their personal genealogy in touch with each other.

The biggest problem facing most new family associations is money. A common error is to set membership dues too low. It is difficult to publish and mail a newsletter four times a year (the usual number) for much less than $5 per subscriber, and $7.50 is safer. Even this price will do no more than take care of essentials and will not help you build the family treasury for ultimate publication of a family surname history. You may wish to study other family association newsletters for money-raising ideas.

In the final chapter I will show you how to complete your ancestor hunt in the most satisfying way—by writing and publishing a book about your family history.

13

HOW TO WRITE
AND PUBLISH A
FAMILY HISTORY

Most ancestor hunters sooner or later feel the urge to assemble their findings into a written history to pass on the record to succeeding generations. Although publishing a book of family history looks like a monumental job to most people, there are logical and really quite simple steps for doing it.

PULLING YOUR RESEARCH TOGETHER

Every family historian begins to compile a mass of ancestral notes, charts, photos, and documents right from the beginning of his search. Soon your one workbook becomes two and then three, and the material you transfer to your personal Family History Book begins to strain the loose-leaf binder. This will probably give you close to what approximates a book manuscript.

A good family history requires you to identify the exact sources of your information. Check through your material to make sure your findings have been carefully documented. If there are conflicts with the sources you have found, simply recognize them in your writing or footnotes and present your reason for resolving them the way you have.

Since no history is ever finished, one of the toughest decisions to make is when to stop collecting and start publishing. Look over your material. If it seems fairly well rounded and well documented, consider it ready.

Don't omit the renegades. Every face discovered—both good and bad—is part of your heritage. Did your ancestor sell horses by day and steal them back by night and was he hanged for it? Put him in! Did one of your forebears start West in a covered wagon and turn back at the first sight of Indians—as one of mine did? Put him in! A family history is a mirror of human lives. You are not supposed to fictionalize or to judge the past. So include the scalawags and the fainthearted as well as the saints.

BEGIN WITH YOUR OWN HISTORY

Include yourself in your Family History Book. Tell your story in a plain, direct, honest manner. A little humor helps.

Some newcomers to the mysteries of genealogy might consider a personal history unnecessary or downright vain. But think with what delight your descendants a hundred years from now will read about your life. Invite your spouse and children to add their personal histories also. A Family History Book should be a family project.

Write as much as you want—what you wish your ancestors had told you about themselves. Put in your vital statistics, your name in full (and nickname), the doctor's name who delivered you. Do the same with your parents and with your siblings and your spouse and your own children. Tell about how your parents earned a living, what your household was like, what the surrounding area was like. Tell about childhood and school memories: diseases, pets, how you earned money, classes, teachers, clubs. Tell about your young adulthood—early jobs, how you met your spouse, your in-laws, military experiences. Then tell about your life today—your work, home, religious and political affiliations, and so on. Make a list of ten things you'd like to accomplish in your lifetime. Make five predictions about what the world will be like in a hundred years. Writing your own personal history may look like a great deal of work, and it can be if you try to do it all at once. Just take it easy and have fun with it.

You might want to arrange your book something like this, since this is the form that many such books take:

1. Frontispiece—a coat of arms, heraldic description or blazon, photo or portrait of the family progenitor, the old homestead, a map of the travels of your family's immigrant ancestor
2. Title page—book title, author's name, printer, date, copyright
3. Foreword—a few pages explaining your numbering system and any unusual or amusing incidents that occurred while you were writing the history, acknowledgment of people who helped, and a dedication
4. Your personal history
5. Family lineage charts
6. Family name—its origin and meaning
7. Contents—the story of pre-American ancestry, the story of your immigrant ancestor, the family lineage of succeeding generations to the present
8. List of family sayings, recipes, other miscellaneous traditions
9. List of abbreviations used or a short dictionary of genealogical terms
10. Bibliography
11. Index of names included

Family histories can be arranged in different ways. The system favored by the New England Historical and Genealogical Society and most other genealogists is the *Register Plan,* which works as follows:

1. In the Contents section of your book, give your first known ancestor the number 1.
2. Give his children lowercase Roman numerals (i, ii, iii, and so on).
3. His sons are also given consecutive numbers (2, 3, 4), if they head their own family unit.
4. Write the personal history of each individual when he or she appears as head of a family; the personal history of children (both males and females) who, as adults, do not head family-surname units should be given when their names first appear.

PREPARING YOUR MANUSCRIPT

Once you have compiled your material, edit it for spelling errors, capitalization, and the like, and type the manuscript double-spaced, with large margins on all four sides. It is then ready for the printer. (See *A Manual of Style,* published by the University of Chicago Press and available in most bookstores, for stylistic matters.)

Some family historians are frankly only interested in a few copies (perhaps as few as ten) to give as Christmas presents to their immediate family. Others, especially those with family association contacts, may want hundreds of copies. I recommend a pre-order plan through the family association, in which members order and pay for a certain number of books so a definite amount can be ordered. For a few copies (any number less than fifty) consult two or three "instant print" shops in your community. They can give you a 100-page book printed on long-lasting paper and bound into binders (even have them imprinted with your title) for as little as $7.50 a book—not a bad price for a gift that will be treasured for generations to come.

If you want a larger number of books or want the

look of a typeset book, there are dozens of publishers around the country who solicit your business in genealogical publications. You might try two or three of them just to see how their bid price compares to printers in your own community. For an order of 500 books (100 pages each), expect to pay about $5 each for hard-covered books, and about $3.25 each for the same number of soft-covered books.

For more information about how to publish your family history book, read *Publish It Yourself* by Netti Scheiner-Yantis (Genealogical Books in Print), and *How to Get Your Book Published*, by John D. Hawkes (Hawkes Publishing, Inc., 156 West 2170 South, Salt Lake City, Utah 84115).

You will want to copyright your work. Print the proper notice on the title page of your book (for example, © *John Doe 1977*). Then obtain Class A, Form A from the Registrar of Copyright, Library of Congress, Washington, D.C. 20540, have it notarized, and send it along with $6 and two copies of your book to the Registrar.

A TOUCH OF IMMORTALITY

By the time your book is off the press, family members who may have contributed photos or biographical sketches will be clamoring for it. Be sure you advertise in your family association bulletin and in the publication of any genealogical society to which you belong. It is also a good idea to take out an ad in historical or genealogical publications in an area where your family originated.

You will want to see that your Family History Book survives and is available to genealogists and historical researchers. The way to ensure this is to send complimentary copies to your local library, the library in your ancestral hometown, and the LDS library in Salt Lake City. You may also want to make a gift of it to other important genealogical collections.

Carl Sandburg said, "When a society or a civilization perishes, one condition can always be found. They forgot where they came from." With a history of your family in hand, there is no forgetting, no sense of coming to an end. Because there is no end, there is only the sense of continuing.

SELECTED BIBLIOGRAPHY

Allcock, Hubert. *Heraldic Design.* New York: Tudor Publishing Co., 1962.

Banaka, William H. *Training in Depth Interviewing.* New York: Harper & Row, Publishers, 1971.

Bardsley, Charles Waring. *A Dictionary of English and Welsh Surnames with Special American Instances.* London, 1901.

Benes, Josef. *O ceskych prijmenich.* Prague: Nakl. Ceskoslovenske Akademie ved, 1962.

Black, Dr. George F. *The Surnames of Scotland, Their Origin, Meaning and History.* New York: New York Public Library, 1968.

Blassingame, John. *Slave Testimony: Two Centuries of Letters, Speeches, Interviews, and Autobiographies.* Baton Rouge: Louisiana State University Press, 1977.

Blockson, Charles L., and Ron Fry. *Black Genealogy.* Englewood Cliffs, N.J.: Prentice-Hall, 1977.

Bragrow, Leo. *History of Cartography,* R.A. Skelton, ed. Cambridge, Mass.: Harvard University Press, 1964.

Camp, Anthony J. *Tracing Your Ancestors in England.* Baltimore, Md.: Genealogical Publishing Co., 1975.

Chapuy, Paul. *Origine des Noms Patronymiques Français.* Paris: 1934.

Child, Heather. *Heraldic Design: A Handbook for Students.* London: G. Bell, 1965.

Chuks-Orji, Ogonna. *Names from Africa, Their Origin, Meaning, and Pronunciation.* New York: Johnson Publishing Co., 1972.

d'Angerville, Count Howard H. *Living Descendants of Blood Royal* (4 vols). London: 1971.

Dauzat, Albert. *Dictionnaire Etymologique des Noms de Famille et Prenoms de France.* Paris: 1951.

Dennys, Rodney. *The Heraldic Imagination.* New York: Crown Publishers, 1976.

Doane, Gilbert H. *Searching for Your Ancestors*, 2d ed. Minneapolis: University of Minnesota Press, 1952.

Everton, George B., ed. *The Handy Book for Genealogists.* Logan, Utah: Everton Publishers, 1971.

Fairchild, Henry Pratt. *Immigration.* New York: Macmillan Publishing Co., 1913.

Fucilla, Joseph Guerin. *Our Italian Surnames.* Evanston: 1949.

Gardner, David E., and Frank Smith. *Genealogical Research in England and Wales.* Salt Lake City, Utah: Bookcraft, 1964.

Gottschald, Max. *Deutsche Namenkunde.* Berlin: Dritte Vermehrte Auslage, 1954.

Greenwood, Val D. *The Researcher's Guide to American Genealogy.* Baltimore, Md.: Genealogical Publishing Co., 1973.

Hill, Roscoe R. *Los Archivos Naciónales de la América Latina.* Havana, 1948.

Hilton, Suzanne. *Who Do You Think You Are? Digging for Your Family Roots.* Philadelphia: Westminster Press, 1977. (Juvenile.)

Jacobus, Donald Lines. *Genealogy as Pastime and Profession.* Baltimore, Md.: Genealogical Publishing Co., 1968.

Kaminkow, Marion, and Kaminkow, Jack. *Original Lists of Emigrants in Bondage from London to the American Colonies, 1719–1744.* Baltimore, Md.: Magna Carta Book Co., 1967.

Karp, Abraham. *Golden Door to America: The Jewish Immigrant Experience.* New York: Viking Press, 1976.

Kazanoff, Benzion C. *A Dictionary of Jewish Names and Their History.* New York: Schocken Books, 1977.

Kirkham, E. Kay. *A Survey of American Church Records.* Logan, Utah: Everton Publishers, 1971.

———. *The Counties of the United States and Their Genealogical Value.* Salt Lake City, Utah: Deseret Book Co., 1975.

———. *The Land Records of America and Their Genealogical Value.* Salt Lake City, Utah: Deseret Book Co., 1964.

———. *Some of the Military Records of America Before 1900: Their Use and Value in Genealogical and Historical*

Research. Salt Lake City, Utah: Deseret Book Co., 1964.

How to Read the Handwriting and Records of Early America, 2d ed. Salt Lake City, Utah: Deseret Book Co., 1964.

Simplified Genealogy for Americans. Salt Lake City, Utah: Deseret Book Co., 1968.

Lister, Raymond. *Antique Maps and Cartographers.* Hamden, Conn.: Shoe String Press, 1970.

MacLysaght, Edward. *A Guide to Irish Surnames.* Dublin: 1964.

Maduell, Charles R. *The Romance of Spanish Surnames.* New Orleans: 1967.

Mann, Thomas Clifford, and Janet Greene. *Over Their Dead Bodies: Yankee Epitaphs & History.* Brattleboro, Vt.: Stephen Green Press, 1962.

Marzio, Peter C., ed. *A Nation of Nations.* New York: Harper & Row, Publishers, 1976

Neubecker, Ottfried. *Heraldry Sources, Symbols and Meaning.* New York: McGraw-Hill Book Co., 1976.

Parker, James. *A Glossary of Terms Used in Heraldry.* Rutland, Vt.: Charles E. Tuttle Co., 1970.

Pine, Leslie Gilbert. *Descendants of Norman Ancestry.* Rutland, Vt.: Charles E. Tuttle Co., 1973.

The Story of Surnames. Aylesbury, Bucks, England: Hazel Watson & Viney, 1965.

International Heraldry. Rutland, Vt.: Charles E. Tuttle Co., 1970.

Puttock, A.G. *A Dictionary of Heraldry and Related Subjects.* Baltimore, Md.: Genealogical Publishing Co., 1970.

Reaney, Dr. P.H. *Dictionary of British Surnames.* England, 1958.

Ribincam, Milton, ed. *Genealogical Research: Methods and Sources.* Washington, D.C.: American Society of Genealogists, 1960.

Rottenberg, Dan. *Finding Our Fathers: A Guidebook to Jewish Genealogy.* New York: Random House, 1977.

Schlesinger, Arthur M. *Paths to the Present.* New York: Macmillan Publishing Co., 1949.

Shumway, Gary L., and William G. Hartley. *An Oral History Primer.* Salt Lake City, Utah: Deseret Book Co., 1974.

Smith, Elsdon Coles. *Dictionary of American Family*

Names. New York: 1956. *Story of Our Names.* New York: Harper & Brothers, 1950.

Smith, Frank, and David Gardner. *Genealogical Research in England and Wales.* (4 vols.) Salt Lake City, Utah: Bookcraft, 1959, 1964, 1976.

Stevenson, Noel C. *Search and Research: The Researcher's Handbook.* Salt Lake City, Utah: Deseret Book Co., 1964.

Stryker-Rodda, Kenn, ed. *Genealogical Research,* vol. 2. Washington, D.C.: American Society of Genealogists, 1971.

Tibon, Gutierre. *Onomastica Hispano Americana.* Mexico, 1961.

Unbegaun, Boris O. *Russian Surnames.* Oxford: Clarendon Press, 1972.

Waitley, Douglas. *Roads of Destiny.* Washington, D.C.: Robert B. Luce, 1970.

Weitzman, David. *Underfoot: An Everyday Guide to Exploring the American Past.* New York: Charles Scribner's Sons, 1976.

Whyte, Donald, ed. *A Dictionary of Scottish Emigrants to the U.S.A.* Baltimore, Md.: Magna Carta Book Co., 1972.

Williams, Ethel W. *Know Your Ancestors.* Rutland, Vt.: Charles E. Tuttle Co., 1960.

Wright, Norman Edgar. *Building an American Pedigree: A Study in Genealogy.* Provo, Utah: Brigham Young University Press, 1974.

APPENDIX 1

STATE-BY-STATE
FAMILY HISTORY HELP LIST

The following is a list of specialty libraries, genealogical societies, and other sources of family history information. For branch libraries for the Church of Jesus Christ of Latter-Day Saints, write to the headquarters at 35 North West Temple St., Salt Lake City, Utah 84150.

LIBRARIES

Alabama

Birmingham Public Library
2026 7th Ave. No.,
Birmingham, 35203

Institute of Genealogical and
   Historical Research,
Samford University Library,
800 Lakeshore Dr.,
Birmingham, 35229

Alaska

Alaska Division of State
   Libraries,
Pouch G, State Capitol,
Juneau, 99801

J. Loussac Library,
427 F St.,
Anchorage, 99501

Arizona

Arizona and the West Library,
318 University of Arizona,
Tucson, 85721

Arizona State Library
1700 W. Washington
Phoenix, 85007

Flagstaff City Library,
11 W. Cherry Ave.
Flagstaff, 86001

Tucson Public Library,
200 S. 6th Ave.,
Tucson, 85701

Arkansas

Little Rock Public Library,
700 Louisiana St.,
Little Rock, 72201

Pine Bluff and Jefferson
County Library,
219 E. 8th Ave.,
Pine Bluff, 71601

California

Bancroft Library,
University of California,
Berkeley, 94720

California State Archives,
Rm. 200, 1020 "0" St.,
Sacramento, 95814

California State Library,
Capitol Mall
Sacramento, 95814

Genealogical Collection of the
San Francisco Public
Library
480 Winston Dr.,
San Francisco, 94132

The Huntington Library,
San Marino, 91108

Long Beach Public Library,
Ocean at Pacific Ave.,
Long Beach, 90802

Los Angeles Public Library,
630 W. Fifth St.,
Los Angeles, 90071

Oakland Public Library,
14th and Oak Sts.,
Oakland, 94612

Pasadena Public Library,
285 E. Walnut,
Pasadena, 91101

Pomona Public Library,
P.O. Box 2271,
Pomona, 91766
(210 Indexes to U.S. Census)

Sutro Library,
480 Winston Dr.,
San Francisco, 94132

Colorado

Boulder Public Library,
1000 Canyon Blvd.,
Boulder, 80302

Colorado Springs Public
Library,
21 Kiowa St.,
Colorado Springs, 80902

Denver Public Library,
1357 Broadway,
Denver, 80203

Historical Society Library,
14th and Sherman,
Denver, 80203

Montrose Public Library,
City Hall,
Montrose, 81401

Norlin Library,
University of Colorado,
Boulder, 80304

Penrose Public Library,
20 N. Cascade,
Colorado Springs, 80902

Tutt Library,
Colorado College,
Colorado Springs, 80903

Connecticut

Beardsley & Memorial
Library,
Munro Pl.,
Winsted, 06098

Connecticut State Library,
231 Capitol Ave.,
Hartford, 06115

Godfrey Memorial Library,
134 Newfield St.,
Middletown, 06457

Hartford Public Library,
500 Main St.,
Hartford, 06103

Otis Library,
261 Main St.,
Norwich, 06360

Phoebe Griffin Noyes Library
Lyme St.,
Lyme, 06371

Delaware

Division of History,
Department of State,
Hall of Records,
Dover, 19901

The Public Archives,
Hall of Records,
Dover, 19901

District of Columbia

Genealogical Department,
Library of Congress Annex,
Washington, 20540

National Archives,
Washington, 20408

Florida

Florida State Library,
Supreme Court Bldg.,
Tallahassee, 32304

Jacksonville Public Library,
122 N. Ocean St.,
Jacksonville, 32202

Miami-Dade Public Library,
1 Biscayne Blvd., North,
Miami, 33132

Orlando Public Library,
10 N. Rosalind Ave.,
Orlando, 38201

P.K. Yonge Library of Florida
History,
University of Florida,
Gainesville, 32601

Palm Beach County
Genealogical Library,
Box 1746,
W. Palm Beach, 33402

State Library,
R.A. Gray Building,
Tallahassee, 32301

Tampa Public Library,
900 N. Ashley St.,
Tampa, 33602

Georgia

Atlanta Public Library,
1 Margaret Mitchell Sq.,
Atlanta, 30303

Bradley Memorial Library,
Bradley Dr.,
Columbus, 31906

Brunswick Regional Library,
208 Gloucester St.,
Brunswick, 31521

Carnegie Library,
607 Broad St.,
Rome, 30161

Decatur-DeKalb Library,
215 Sycamore St.,
Decatur, 30030

Georgia Department of
    Archives and History,
330 Capitol Ave.,
Atlanta, 30334
(Free booklet: "Genealogy and
    History Research in
    Georgia")

Georgia State Library,
301 State Judicial Bldg.,
Capitol Hill Stn.,
Atlanta, 30334

Georgia State University
    Archives,
104 Decatur St., S.E.,
Atlanta, 30303

Lake Lanier Regional Library,
Pike St.,
Lawrenceville, 30245

Piedmont Regional Library,
Winder, 30680

Savannah Public Library,
2002 Bull St.,
Savannah, 31401

Washington Memorial Library,
1180 Washington Ave.,
Macon, 31201

Hawaii

Brigham Young University,
Hawaii Campus,
55-220 Hulanui St.,
Laie, 96762

DAR Memorial Library,
1914 Makiki Hts. Dr.,
Honolulu, 96822

Library of Hawaii,
King and Punchbowl Sts.,
Honolulu, 96813

Idaho

Boise State University Library,
Boise, 83725

Idaho State University Library,
Pocatello, 83209

Illinois

Illinois State Archives,
Archives Bldg.,
Springfield, 62706
(Free booklet: "Counties of
    Illinois, Their Origin and
    Evolution")

Illinois State Historical
    Library,
Old State Capitol,
Springfield, 62706

Newberry Library,
60 W. Walton St.,
Chicago, 60610

Peoria Public Library,
107 N.E. Monroe St.,
Peoria, 61602

Rock Island Public Library,
Rock Island, 61201

Rockford Public Library,
215 N. Wyman St.,
Rockford, 61101

University of Illinois Library,
Urbana, 61801

Vogel Genealogical Rescarch
    Library,
305 1st St.,
Holcomb, 61043

Indiana

Public Library of Ft. Wayne,
Ft. Wayne, 46802

State Library,
140 N. Senate St.,
Indianapolis, 46204
Free check of 1850 census.

Iowa

Iowa Genealogical Library,
Iowa Dept. History and
    Archives,
E. 12th Street and Grand Ave.,
Des Moines, 50319

Kansas

Bethel Historical Library,
Bethel College No.,
Newton, 67114

Garden City Public Library,
210 N. 7th,
Garden City, 67846

Johnson County Library,
8700 W. 63rd St.,
Shawnee Mission, 66202

Public Library,
Independence, 67301

Public Library,
6th & Minnesota Sts.,
Kansas City, 66101

Wichita City Library,
220 S. Main St.,
Wichita, 67202

Kentucky

Breckinridge County Public
    Library,
Hardinsburg, 40143
(Special Collections)

Western Kentucky University
    Library,
Bowling Green, 42101

Louisiana

Hill Memorial Library,
Louisiana State University,
Baton Rouge, 70803

Howard Tilton Library,
Map and Genealogy Rm.,
Tulane University,
New Orleans, 70118

Louisiana State Library,
State Capitol,
Baton Rouge, 70804

New Orleans Public Library,
219 Loyola Ave.,
New Orleans, 70140

Quachita Parish Public Library,
1800 Stubbs Ave.,
Monroe, 71201

Shreve Memorial Library,
424 Texas St.
Shreveport, 71120

Tangipahoa Parish Library,
Amite, 70422

Maine

Maine State Library,
State House,
Augusta, 04330

Public Library,
145 Harlow St.,
Bangor, 04401

Maryland

Enoch Pratt Free Library,
400 Cathedral St.,
Baltimore, 21201

Hall of Records,
College Ave. & St. Johns St.,
Annapolis, 21401

Maryland State Library,
361 Rose Blvd.,
Annapolis, 21401

Massachusetts

Boston Public Library,
Box 286,
Boston, 02117

Massachusetts State Library,
Beacon Hill,
Boston, 02155

Secretary of the
Commonwealth,
Public Documents Division,
State House,
Boston, 02133
(Free booklets on history of
counties and towns)
(Every library in Massachusetts
has a wealth of historical
and genealogical material.)

Michigan

Detroit Public Library,
5201 Woodward Ave.,
Detroit, 48202
(Local history and genealogy)

Flint Public Library,
1026 E. Kearsley,
Flint, 48502

Grand Rapids Public Library,
111 Library St., N.E.,
Grand Rapids, 49502

Herrick Public Library,
300 River Ave.,
Holland, 49423

Michigan Department of
Education,
State Library,
Box 30007,
Lansing, 48909
Publication: *Family Trails*

Minnesota

Folke Bernadette Memorial
Library,
Gustavus Adolphus College,
St. Peter, 56082

Minneapolis Public Library,
300 Nicolet Ave.,
Minneapolis, 55401

Public Library,
90 W. 4th,
St. Paul, 55102

Rolvaag Memorial Library,
St. Olaf College,
Northfield, 55057

University of Minnesota
Library,
Minneapolis, 55455

Mississippi

Attala County Library,
328 Goodman St.,
Kosciusko, 39090

Department of Archives and
History,
Archive and History Bldg.,
Capitol Green,
Jackson, 39205
(Free booklet: "Research in
the Mississippi Department
of Archives")

Evans Memorial Library,
Aberdeen, 39730

Lauren Rogers Memorial
Library,
Box 1108,
Laurel, 39440

Missouri

Heritage Library,
135 E. Pine St.,
Warrensburg, 64093

Kansas City Public Library,
311 E. 12th St.,
Kansas City, 64106

Kent Library,
Southeast Missouri State
College,
Cap Girardeau, 63701

Missouri State Library,
308 E. High St.,
Jefferson City, 65101

Records and Archives,
Office of Secretary of State,
Capitol Bldg.,
Jefferson City, 65101

Riverside Regional Library,
Box 389,
Jackson, 63755

St. Louis Public Library,
1301 Olive St.,
St. Louis, 63103

Springfield Public Library,
Reference Department and
Shepard Room
397 E. Central St.,
Springfield, 65801

Montana

Parmly Billings Memorial
Library,
510 N. Broadway,
Billings, 59101

Public Library,
106 W. Broadway St.,
Butte, 59701

State University Library,
Bozeman, 59717

Mansfield Library,
University of Montana,
Missoula, 59812

Public Library,
Pine and Pattee Sts.,
Missoula, 59801

State University Library,
Missoula, 59801

Nebraska

Alliance Public Library,
202 W. 4th St.,
Alliance, 69301

Nebraska D.A.R. Library,
202 W. 4th St.,
Alliance, 69301

Nebraska State Historical
   Society Library,
1500 R. St.,
Lincoln 68508

Omaha Public Library,
215 S. 15th St.,
Omaha, 68102

Public Library,
136 S. 14th St.,
Lincoln, 68508

University of Nebraska
   Library,
Lincoln, N.E., 68503

Nevada

Las Vegas Public Library,
400 E. Mesquite Ave.,
Las Vegas, 89101

University of Nevada Library,
Reno, 89507

Washoe County Library,
Reno, 89507

New Hampshire

City Library,
Carpenter Memorial Bldg.,
405 Pine St.,
Manchester, 03104

Dartmouth College Archives,
Baker Memorial Library,
Hanover, 03755

Dover Public Library,
73 Locust St.,
Dover, 03820

New Hampshire State Library,
20 Park St.,
Concord, 03303

New Jersey

Atlantic City Free Library,
Illinois and Pacific,
Atlantic City, 08401

Morris Genealogical Library,
228 Elberon Ave.,
Allenhurst, 07711

New Jersey State Library,
Archives and History Bureau,
185 W. State St.,
Trenton, 08625
(Free booklet: "A Guide to
   Source Materials in the New
   Jersey State Library")

New Mexico

New Mexico State Library,
301 Don Gasper,
Santa Fe, 87501

Public Library,
Albuquerque, 87501

University of New Mexico
Library,
Albuquerque, 87106

New York

Adriance Memorial Library,
93 Market St.,
Poughkeepsie, 12601

Buffalo and Erie County Public
Library,
Lafayette Square,
Buffalo, 14203

Columbia University,
Journalism Library,
New York, 10027

Flower Memorial Library,
Genealogical Committee,
Watertown, 13601

James T. Olin Library,
Cornell University,
Ithaca, 14851

New York Public Library,
5th Ave. & 42nd Sts.,
New York, 10016

New York State Library,
Albany, 12224

Queens Borough Public
Library,
89-11 Merrick Blvd.,
Jamaica, 11432

Roswell P. Flower Genealogy
Library,
229 Washington St.,
Watertown, 13601

Syracuse Public Library,
335 Montgomery St.,
Syracuse, 13202

North Carolina

Division of Archives,
Office of Archives and
History,
State Department of Art,
Culture and History,
109 E. Jones St.,
Raleigh, 27611
(Free booklet: "Genealogical
Research in the North
Carolina Archives")

North Carolina State Library,
109 E. Jones St.,
Raleigh, 27611

Public Library of Charlotte and
Mecklenburg Counties,
310 N. Tryon St.,
Charlotte, 28202

Rown Public Library,
201 W. Fisher St.,
Salisbury, 28144

University of North Carolina,
Drawer 870,
Chapel Hill, 27514

North Dakota

Public Library,
Fargo, 58102

Public Library,
Grand Forks, 58201

Public Library,
516 Second Avenue,
Minot, 58701

Ohio

Akron Public Library,
55 S. Main St.,
Akron, 44309

American Jewish Archives,
Hebrew Union College,
Clifton Ave.,
Cincinnati, 45220

Cincinnati Public Library,
800 Vine St.,
Cincinnati, 45202

Cleveland Public Library,
325 Superior Ave.,
Cleveland, 44114

Dayton and Montgomery
　Counties Public Library,
215 E. 3rd St.,
Dayton, 45406

Ohio Historical Society
　Library,
1-17 and 17th Ave.,
Columbus, 43211

Ohio State Library,
65 S. Front St.,
Columbus, 43215

Portsmouth Public Library,
1220 Gallia St.,
Portsmouth, 45662

Public Library of Columbus,
96 S. Grant Ave.,
Columbus, 43215

Public Library of Youngstown,
305 Wick Ave.,
Youngstown, 44503

Toledo Public Library,
Historical and Genealogical
　Department,
325 Michigan St.,
Toledo, 43624

University of Cincinnati
　Library,
Cincinnati, 45221

Warder Public Library,
137 E. High St.,
Springfield, 45502

Oklahoma

Carnegie Public Library,
Fifth and B. Sts.,
Lawton, 73501

Oklahoma Department of
　Libraries,
200 NE 18,
Oklahoma City, 73105

Oklahoma City Library,
109 Capitol,
Oklahoma City, 73105

Public Library,
Muskogee, 74401

Public Library
220 S. Cheyenne,
Tulsa, 74103

State D.A.R. Library,
Historical Bldg.,
Oklahoma City, 73105

Tulsa Central Library,
400 Civic Center,
Tulsa, 74103

University of Oklahoma
    Library,
Norman, 73069

Oregon

Oregon State Archives,
1005 Broadway, N.E.,
Salem, 97301

Oregon State Library,
State Library Building,
Summer and Court Sts.,
Salem, 97310

Portland Library Association,
801 S.W. 10th Ave.,
Portland, 97205

University of Oregon Library,
Eugene, 97403

Pennsylvania

Altoona Public Library,
"The Pennsylvania Room"
1600 5th Ave.,
Altoona, 16602

Carnegie Library,
4400 Forbes Ave.,
Pittsburgh, 15213

Centre County Library,
203 N. Allegheny St.,
Bellefonte, 16823

Citizens Library,
55 S. College St.,
Washington, 15301

Fackenthal Library,
Franklin and Marshall College,
Lancaster, 17602

Franklin Institute Library,
Benjamin Franklin Parkway
    and 20th St.,
Philadelphia, 19103

Free Library of Philadelphia,
Logan Square,
Philadelphia, 19141

Friends Library,
Swarthmore, 19081

Lutheran Theological Seminary
    Library,
Mt. Airy,
Philadelphia, 19119

Pennsylvania Historical and
    Museum Commission,
Div. of Archives,
Box 1026,
Harrisburg, 17108

Pennsylvania State Library,
Walnut and Commonwealth,
Harrisburg, 17126

Rhode Island

Providence Public Library,
229 Washington St.,
Providence, 02903

Rhode Island State Archives,
314 State House,
Providence, 02900

Rhode Island State Library,
82 Smith,
State House,
Providence, 02903

South Carolina

Free Library,
404 King St.,
Charleston, 29407

Greenville County Library,
300 College St.,
Greenville, 29601

Public Library,
Rock Hill, 29730

Public Library,
S. Pine St.,
Spartanburg, 29302

Richland County Public
Library,
1400 Sumter St.,
Columbia, 29201

South Carolina Archives
Department,
1430 Senate St.,
Columbia, 29201

South Carolina Library,
University of South Carolina,
Columbia, 29208

South Carolina State Library,
1500 Senate St.,
Columbia, 29201

South Dakota

Alexander Mitchell Public
Library,
519 S. Kline St.,
Aberdeen, 57401

Carnegie Free Public Library,
10th and Dakota Sts.,
Sioux Falls, 57102

State Historical Library,
Memorial Bldg.,
Pierre, 57501

University of South Dakota
Library,
Vermillion, 57069

Tennessee

Chattanooga Hamilton County
Bicentenial Library,
Genealogy/Local History
Department,
1001 Broad St.,
Chattanooga, 37402

Cossitt-Goodwyn Library,
33 S. Front St.,
Memphis, 38103

McClung Historical
Collection,
East Tennessee History-
Genealogy Center,
600 Market St.,
Knoxville, 37902

Memphis Public Library,
1850 Peabody,
Memphis, 38104

Memphis State University
Library,
Mississippi Valley Collection,
Memphis, 38104

Public Library of Nashville,
222 8th Ave., N.,
Nashville, 37203

Tennessee State Library and
  Archives,
403 7th Ave. N.,
Nashville, 37219

Texas

Catholic Archives to Texas,
1600 Congress Ave.,
Austin, 78801

Clayton Library for
  Genealogical Research,
5300 Caroline,
Houston, 77004

Dallas Public Library,
Texas History and Genealogy
  Department,
1515 Young St.,
Dallas, 75201

El Paso Genealogical Library,
3651 Douglas,
El Paso, 79903

El Paso Public Library,
Document Genealogy Dept.,
501 N. Oregon St.,
El Paso, 79901

Fort Worth Public Library,
300 Taylor St.,
Fort Worth, 76102

Genealogical Research
  Library,
4524 Edmondson Ave.,
Dallas, 75205

Houston Public Library,
500 McKinney Ave.,
Houston, 77002

Texas State Library,
1201 Brazos St.,
Austin, 78711

Tyrrel Public Library,
695 Pearl St.,
Beaumont, 77701

Waco Public Library,
1717 Austin Ave.,
Waco, 76701

Utah

Brigham Carnegie Library,
26 E. Forest,
Brigham City, 84302

Brigham Young University
  Library,
Provo, 84601

Cedar City Public Library,
Cedar City, 84720

Dixie Genealogical Library,
St. George, 84770

Genealogical Library,
Genealogical Society of the
  Church of Jesus Christ of
  Latter-day Saints,
35 North West Temple,
Salt Lake City, 84150

Ogden Public Library,
Ogden, 84402

Public Library,
Manti, 84642

Public Library,
Springville, 84663

University of Utah Library,
Salt Lake City, 84112

Utah State Historical Society
Library,
300 Rio Grande,
Salt Lake City, 84101

Vermont

Genealogical Library,
Bennington Museum,
Bennington, 05201

Public Library,
Court St.,
Rutland, 05701

University of Vermont Library,
Burlington, 05401

Vermont Department of
Libraries, Law and
Documents,
111 State St.,
Montpelier, 05602

Vermont Historical Society
Library,
Pavilion Office Bldg.,
109 State St.,
Montpelier, 05602

Virginia

Albermarle County Historical
Library,
220 Court Square,
Charlottesville, 22901

Alderman Library,
University of Virginia,
Charlottesville, 22903

College of William and Mary
Library,
Williamsburg, 23185

Commonwealth of Virginia,
Virginia State Library,
1101 Capitol,
Richmond, 23219

E. Lee Trinkle Library,
University of Virginia,
Fredericksburg, 22402

Kirn Norfolk Public Library,
301 E. City Hall Ave.,
Norfolk, 23510

Menno Simons Historical
Library,
Eastern Mennonite College,
Harrisonburg, 22801

Virginia Historical Society
Library,
P.O. Box 7311,
Richmond, 23221

Washington

Challam County Museum
Library,
223 East 4th Street.,
Port Angeles, 98362

Regional Public Library,
7th and Franklin Sts.,
Olympia, 98501

Seattle Public Library,
4th and Madison,
Seattle, 98104
(Contains Genealogical
Collection of the State
Library.)

Spokane Public Library,
W. 906 Main Ave.,
Spokane, 99201

University of Washington
Library,
Seattle, 98105

Washington State Historical
Society Library,
State Historical Bldg.,
315 N. Stadium Wy.,
Tacoma, 98403

Washington State Library,
State Library Bldg.,
Olympia, 98501

West Virginia

Cabell County Public Library,
900 5th Ave.,
Huntington, 25701

Department of Archives and
Historical Library,
Cultural Center,
Capitol Complex,
State of West Virginia Library,
Charleston, 25305

Huntington Public Library,
Huntington, 25701

West Virginia Collection,
University of West Virginia,
Morgantown, 26506

Wisconsin

Beloit Public Library,
409 Pleasant St.,
Beloit, 53511

Milwaukee Public Library,
814 W. Wisconsin Ave.,
Milwaukee, 53202

Public Library,
Wausau, 54401

University of Wisconsin,
The Milwaukee Library,
Box 604,
Milwaukee, 53211

Wyoming

Laramie County Public
Library,
Cheyenne, 82001

Western History and Archives
Department,
University of Wyoming,
Laramie, 82070

Wyoming State Archives and
History Department,
State Office Bldg.,
Cheyenne, 82001

Wyoming State Library,
Supreme Court Bldg.,
Cheyenne, 82001

GENEALOGICAL
SOCIETIES

Alabama

Alabama Genealogical Society,
Inc.
AGS depository,
Samford University Library
800 Lakeshore Dr.,
Birmingham, 35229
Publication: *Bulletin*

Birmingham Genealogical
Society,
Box 2432,
Birmingham, 35201
Publication: *Trails*

East Alabama Genealogical
Society,
c/o Mrs. J.H. Strothan,
Drawer 1351
Auburn, 36830
Publication: *Tap Roots*

Mobile Genealogical Society,
Box 6224,
Mobile, 36606
(Large collection of heraldry,
origin of names)

Alaska

Anchorage Genealogy Society,
Box 100412,
Anchorage, 99510

Arizona

Apache Genealogical Society,
Box 1084,
Sierra Vista, 85635

Arizona State Genealogical
Society,
Box 42075,
Tucson, 85733-2075

Arkansas

Ark-La-Tex Genealogical
Assn., Inc.,
P.O. Box 4462,
Shreveport, LA, 71104
Publication: *The Genie*

Arkansas Genealogical
Society,
Box 908,
Hot Springs, 71092
Publication: *Arkansas Family
Historian*

Madison County Genealogical
Society,
P.O. Box 427,
Huntsville, 72740
Publication: *Musings*

Northeast Arkansas
Genealogical Association,
314 Vine St.,
Newport, 73112
Publication: *Arkansas
Genealogical Register*

Northwest Arkansas
Genealogical Society,
P.O. Box K,
Rogers, 72756
Publication: *The Backtracker*

California

California State Genealogical
  Alliance,
c/o Nancy Kepley,
19765 Grand Ave.,
Lake Elsinore, 92330

California Genealogical
  Society,
Box 77105,
San Francisco, 94107-0105

Contra Costa County
  Genealogical Society,
Box 910,
Concord, 94522

Fresno Genealogical Society,
Box 1429,
Fresno, 93716-1429
Publication: *Ashtree Echo*

Genealogical Society of
  Riverside,
Box 2557,
Riverside, 92516
Publication: *Lifeliner*

Genealogical Society of Santa
  Cruz County,
Box 72,
Santa Cruz, 95063

Hi Desert Genealogical
  Society,
15476-9 Sixth St.,
Victorville, 92392

Jewish Genealogical Society of
  Los Angeles,
Box 25245,
Los Angeles, 90025

Los Californianos,
Box 5155,
San Francisco, 94101

Orange County Genealogical
  Society,
Box 1587,
Orange, 92668

Paradise Genealogical Society,
Box 460,
Paradise, 95969-0460

Redwood Genealogical
  Society,
Box 645,
Fortuna, 95540
Publication: *Redwood
  Researcher*

Sacramento German
  Genealogical Society,
Box 660061,
Sacramento, 95866

San Diego Genealogical
  Society,
2925 Kalinna St.,
San Diego, 92104
Publication: *Leaves & Saplings*

Southern California
  Genealogical Society,
Box 4377,
Burbank, 91502
Publication: *The Searcher*

Sutter-Yuba Genealogical
  Society,
Box 1274,
Yuba City, 95991

Colorado

Boulder Genealogical Society,
Box 3246,
Boulder, 80303

Colorado Council of
   Genealogical Societies,
P.O. Box 24379,
Denver, 80224-0379

Larimer County Genealogical
   Society,
600 S. Shields,
Fort Collins, 80521

Connecticut

Connecticut Genealogical
   Society,
P.O. Box 435,
Glastonbury, 06033
Publication: *Connecticut
   Nutmegger*

Stamford Genealogical
   Society,
Box 249,
Stamford, 06904
Publication: *Connecticut
   Ancestry*

Delaware

Delaware Genealogical
   Society,
505 Market Street Mall,
Wilmington, 19801
Publication: *Journal*

District of Columbia

National Genealogical Society,
4527 17th St. North,
Arlington, 22207-2363

Florida

Florida Genealogical Society,
Box 18624,
Tampa, 33609
Publication: *Journal*

Jewish Genealogical Society of
   South Florida,
c/o Herbert Unger,
8045 SW 197th Ave.
#313
Miami, 33173

Palm Beach County
   Genealogical Society,
Box 1746,
W. Palm Beach, 33402
Publication: *Ancestry*

Polk County Genealogical
   Society,
Box 1719,
Bartow, 33830

Southern Genealogist's
   Exchange Society,
Box 2801,
Jacksonville, 32203

Georgia

African-American Family
   Historical Association,
Box 115268,
Atlanta, 30310
(Meetings, newsletters,
projects)

Georgia Genealogical Society,
Box 38066,
Atlanta, 30334

Idaho

Idaho Genealogical Society,
Box 326,
Grangeville, 83530

Illinois

Chicago Genealogical Society,
Box 1160,
Chicago, 60690
Publication: *Chicago
Genealogist*

Cumberland and Coles County
Genealogical Society,
Rt. 1, Box 141,
Toledo, 62468
Publication: *Happy Hunter*

Decatur Genealogical Society,
Box 2205,
Decatur, 62526
Publication: *Central Illinois
Genealogical Quarterly*

Genealogical Society of
Southern Illinois,
c/o Logan College,
Carterville, 62918
Publication: *Newsletter*

Great River Genealogical
Society,
c/o Quincy Public Library,
Quincy, 62302

Illiana Genealogical Society,
Box 207,
Danville, 61832

Iroquois County Genealogical
Society,
Old Courthouse Museum,
103 W. Cherry St.,
Watseka, 60970

Knox County Genealogical
Society,
Box 13,
Galesburg, 61402-0013
Publication: *Quarterly*

Lexington Genealogical
Society,
304 N. Elm St.,
Lexington, 61753

Moultrie County Genealogical
Society,
Box MM,
Sullivan, 61951

Peoria Genealogical Society,
Box 1489,
Peoria, 61655
Publication: *Prairie Roots*

Sangamon County
Genealogical Society,
Box 1829,
Springfield, 62705
Publication: *The Circuit Rider*

Indiana

Illiana Jewish Genealogical
Society
c/o Sharon Graur Blitstein
3033 Bob-O-Link Road,
Flossmoor, 60422

Genealogical Section of the
Indiana Historical Society,
140 N. Senate Ave.,
Indianapolis, 46204
Publication: *Hoosier
Genealogist*

Pulaski County Genealogical
  Society,
RR 4, Box 121,
Winamac, 46996

Iowa

Iowa Genealogical Society,
Box 7735,
Des Moines, 50322
Publication: *Hawkeye Heritage*

Lee County Genealogical
  Society,
Box 303,
Keokuk, 52632

Kansas

Finney County Genealogical
  Society,
P.O. Box 592,
Garden City, 67846

Fort Hayes Kansas
  Genealogical Society,
c/o Fort Hayes Kansas College
  Library,
Hays, 67601

Heritage Genealogical Society,
Box 73,
Neodeska, 66757
Publication: *Quarterly*

Johnson County Genealogical
  Society,
P.O. Box 8057,
Shawnee Mission, 66208

Kansas Genealogical Society,
Box 103,
Dodge City, 67801
Publication: *The Treesearcher*

Montgomery County
  Genealogical Society,
Box 444,
Coffeyville, 67337
Publication: *The Descender*

Riley County Genealogical
  Society,
2005 Claflin Road,
Manhattan, 66502
Publication: *Kansas Kin*

Topeka Genealogical Society,
P.O. Box 4048,
Topeka, 66604-0048

Kentucky

Kentucky Genealogical
  Society,
Box 153,
Frankfort, 40601
Publication: *Bluegrass Roots*

West-Central Kentucky Family
  Research Association,
Box 1932,
Owensboro, 42302
Publication: *Kentucky Family
  Records*

Louisiana

Ark-la-Tex Genealogical
  Association,
Box 4462,
Shreveport, 71104
Publication: *Arka-La-Tex
  Newsletter*

Genealogical Research Society
  of New Orleans,
Box 51791,
New Orleans, 70150
Publication: *New Orleans
  Genesis*

Louisiana Genealogical
   Society,
Box 3454,
Baton Rouge, 70821
Publication: *Register*

Maine

Maine Genealogical Society,
Box 221,
Farmington, 04938

Maryland

Maryland Genealogical
   Society,
201 West Monument St.,
Baltimore, 21201

Mid-Atlantic Germanic
   Society,
c/o Phyliss Lott
12111 Mt. Albert Rd.,
Ellicott City, 21043

Massachusetts

New England Historic and
   Genealogical Society,
101 Newberry St.,
Boston, 02116
Publication: *The Register*

Michigan

Detroit Society for
   Genealogical Research,
Detroit Public Library,
5201 Woodward Ave.,
Detroit, 48202
Publication: *Research
   Magazine*

French-Canadian Heritage
   Society,
c/o Library of Michigan,
Box 30007,
Lansing, 48909

Kalamazoo Valley
   Genealogical Society,
Box 4051,
Kalamazoo, 49041

Mid-Michigan Genealogical
   Society,
3800 Glasgow Dr.,
Lansing, 48910

Muskegon County
   Genealogical Society,
Hackley Library,
316 W. Webster Ave.,
Muskegon, 49440
Publication: *Family Tree Talk*

Saginaw Genealogical Society,
c/o Saginaw Public Library,
505 Janes Ave.,
Saginaw, 48507
Publication: *Timbertown Log*

Western Michigan Genealogical
   Society,
Grand Rapids Public Library,
Grand Rapids, 49503
Publication: *Michigana*

Minnesota

Anoka County Genealogical
   Society,
1900 3rd Ave.,
Anoka, 55303

Minnesota Genealogical
  Society,
P.O. Box 16069,
St. Paul, 55116
Publication: *Minnesota
  Genealogist*

Range Genealogical Society,
Box 388,
Chisholm, 55768
Publication: *Northland
  Newsletter*

Mississippi

Aberdeen Genealogical
  Society,
Aberdeen, 39730

Mississippi Genealogical
  Society,
Box 5301,
Jackson, 39216
Publication: *Newsletter*

Missouri

The Heart of America
  Genealogical Society,
c/o Missouri Valley Rm.,
Kansas City Public Library,
311 E. 21st St.,
Kansas City, 64106
Publication: *Kansas City
  Genealogist*

Ozarks Genealogical Society,
Box 3494,
Springfield, 64804
Publication: *OZAR'KIN*

St. Louis Genealogical
  Society,
1695 S. Brentwood Blvd.,
Suite 203,
St. Louis, 63144

West Central Missouri
  Genealogical Society,
705 Broad St.,
Warrensburg, 64093
Publication: *The Prairie
  Gleaner*

Montana

Yellowstone Genealogy
  Forum,
c/o Parmly Billings Library,
510 N. Broadway,
Billings, 59101

Nebraska

Fort Kearny Genealogical
  Society,
Box 22,
Kearny, 68847

Madison County Genealogical
  Society,
Box 347,
Norfolk, 68701

North Platte Genealogical
  Society,
Box 1452,
North Platte, 69101
Publication: *Newsletter*

Nevada

Nevada State Genealogical
  Society,
Box 1192,
Reno, 89515

New Hampshire

New Hampshire Society of
   Genealogists,
Box 633,
Exeter, 03833
Publication: *Genealogical
   Record*

New Jersey

Genealogical Society of New
   Jersey,
P.O. Box 1291,
New Brunswick, 08093

New Mexico

New Mexico Genealogical
   Society,
Box 8283,
Albuquerque, 87198-8330
Publication: *New Mexico
   Genealogist*

New York

Colonial Dames of America,
421 East 61st St.,
New York, 10021

Jewish Genealogical Society,
   Inc.,
Box 6398,
New York, 10128

New York Genealogical and
   Biographical Society,
122-126 E. 58th St.,
New York, 10022

Ulster County Genealogical
   Society,
P.O. Box 333,
Hurley, 11443

North Carolina

Genealogical Society of the
   Original Wilkes County,
Wilkesboro, 28659

North Carolina Genealogical
   Society,
Box 1492,
Raleigh, 27602
Publication: *The Journal*

NC-VA Piedmont Genealogical
   Society,
Box 2272,
Danville, VA, 24541

North Dakota

Bismarck-Mandan
   Genealogical Society,
Box 485,
Bismarck, 58501

Mouse River Loop Genealogy
   Society,
Box 1391,
Minot, 58702-1391
Publication: *Record*

Ohio

Ashtabula County Genealogical
   Society,
Henderson Library,
54 E. Jefferson St.,
Jefferson, 44047
Publication: *Ancestor Hunt*

Lake County Genealogical
   Society,
Morley Public Library,
184 Phelps St.,
Painsville, 44077

Miami Valley Genealogical
Society,
Box 1364,
Dayton, 45401

Northwestern Ohio
Genealogical Society,
P.O. Box 17066,
Toledo, 43615

Ohio Genealogical Society,
Box 2625,
Mansfield, 44906
Publication: *OGS Newsletter*

Ohio Genealogical Society,
P.O. Box 2625,
Ashland, 44906
Publication: *Ohio Records and
Pioneer Families*

West Augusta Genealogical
Society,
1510 Prairie Dr.,
Belpre, 45714
Publication: *Newsletter*

Oklahoma

Oklahoma Genealogical
Society,
Box 12986,
Oklahoma City, 73157
Publication: *Quarterly*

Tulsa Genealogical Society,
Box 585,
Tulsa, 74101
Publication: *Tulsa Annals*

Oregon

Coos Bay Genealogical
Forum,
Box 1067,
Coos Bay, 97459

Genealogical Forum of
Portland,
1410 S.W. Morrison,
Rm. 812,
Portland, 97205

Mt. Hood Genealogical
Forum,
Box 208,
Oregon City, 97045
Publication: *The Trackers*

Oregon Genealogical Society,
Box 10306,
Eugene, 97440-2306
Publication: *Quarterly*

Rogue Valley Genealogical
Society,
125 S. Central Ave.,
Medford, 97501
Publication: *Rogue Digger*

Williamette Valley
Genealogical Society,
Box 2083,
Salem, 97308
Publication: *Beaver Briefs*

Pennsylvania

Erie Society for Genealogical
Research,
Box 1403,
Erie, 16512
Publication: *Keystone Kuzzins*

Genealogical Society of
Pennsylvania,
1300 Locust St.,
Philadelphia, 19107
Publication: *Genealogy
Magazine of Pennsylvania*

Western Pennsylvania
Genealogical Society,
4338 Bigelow Blvd.,
Pittsburgh, 15213

Rhode Island

Rhode Island Genealogical
Society,
P.O. Box 7618,
Warwick, 02887-7618

South Carolina

South Carolina Genealogical
Association,
P.O. Box 1442,
Lexington, 29072
Publication: *Lexington
Genealogical Exchange*

South Dakota

Rapid City Society for
Genealogical Research,
Box 1495,
Rapid City, 57701
Publication: *Black Hills
Nuggets*

Tennessee

Mid-West Tennessee
Genealogical Society,
Box 3343,
Jackson, 38301
Publication: *Family Findings*

Tennessee Genealogical
Society,
Box 111249
Memphis, 38111-1249
Publication: *Ansearchin News*

Watauga Association of
Genealogists,
Box 117,
Johnson City, 37605-0117
Publication: *Bulletin*

Texas

Amarillo Genealogical Society,
Amarillo Public Library,
300 E. 4th,
Amarillo, 79189

Austin Genealogical Society,
Box 1507,
Austin, 78767-1507

Central Texas Genealogical
Society,
1717 Austin Ave.,
Waco, 76701
Publication: *Hearts of Texas
Records*

Chaparral Genealogical
Society,
Box 606,
Tomball, 77375
Publication: *The Roadrunner*

Fort Worth Genealogical
Society,
Box 9767,
Ft. Worth, 76107
Publication: *Footprints*

Hispanic Genealogical Society,
Box 810561,
Houston, 77281-0561

McLennan County Society,
1717 Austin Ave.,
Waco, 76701
Publication: *The Family Tree*

Mesquite Genealogical
Society,
Box 165,
Mesquite, 75149

Midland Genealogical Society,
Box 1191,
Midland, 79702
Publication: *The Thorny Trial*

San Angelo Genealogical
Society,
Box 3453,
San Angelo, 76901
Publication: *Stalkin' Kin*

San Antonio Genealogical
Society,
Box 17461,
San Antonio, 78217-0461
Publication: *Our Heritage*

Southeast Texas Genealogical
Society,
c/o Tyrrel Historical Library,
P.O. Box 3827,
Beaumont, 77704
Publication: *Yellowed Pages*

Texas State Genealogical
Society,
2507 Tannehill,
Houston, 77008-3052

Tip O'Texas Genealogical
Society,
Harlingen Public Library,
Harlingen, 78550

Utah

Genealogical Society of Utah,
35 North West Temple,
Salt Lake City, 84150

Utah Genealogical
Association,
Box 1144,
Salt Lake City, 84110
Publication: *Genealogical
Journal*

Vermont

Genealogical Society of
Vermont
Westmister West, RFD 3,
Putney, 05346
Publication: *Branches and
Twigs*

Vermont Genealogical Society,
P.O. Box 422,
Pittsford, 05763
Publication: *Missing Links*

Virginia

American Society of
Genealogists,
2255 Cedar Ln.,
Vienna, 22180

Genealogical Society of
Tidewater,
Box 76,
Hampton, 23669
Publication: *Virginia Tidewater
Genealogy*

Washington

Eastern Washington
Genealogical Society,
Box 1826,
Spokane, 99210
Publication: *Bulletin*

Lower Columbia Genealogical
Society,
Box 472,
Longview, 98632

Olympia Genealogical Society,
Olympia Public Library,
8th and Franklin,
Olympia, 98501

Seattle Genealogical Society,
Box 549,
Seattle, 98111
Publication: *Bulletin*

The Tacoma Genealogical
Society,
Box 1952,
Tacoma, 98401
Publication: *Researcher*

Tri-City Genealogical Society,
Box 1410,
Richland, 99352-1410
Publication: *Bulletin*

Whatcom County Washington
Genealogical Society,
P.O. Box 1493,
Bellingham, 98227-1493

Yakima Valley Genealogical
Society,
Box 445,
Yakima, 98907
Publication: *Bulletin*

West Virginia

Marion County Genealogical
Club, Inc.,
Marion County Library,
Monroe St.,
Fairmont, 26554

Wetzel County Genealogical
Society,
Box 464,
New Martinsville, 26155
Publication: *Newsletter*

Wisconsin

Milwaukee County
Genealogical Society,
Box 27326,
Milwaukee, 53227

Wisconsin State Genealogical
Society,
c/o Mrs. John M. Irwin,
2109 20th Ave.,
Monroe, 53566
Publication: *Newsletter*

Wyoming

Cheyenne Genealogical
Society,
Laramie County Library,
Central Ave.,
Cheyenne, 82001

OTHER SOURCES

Alabama

American College of Heraldry
University, 35486

Arizona

Family Historical Society,
Box 5566,
Glendale, 85312

Prescott Historical Society,
W. Gurley St.,
Prescott, 86301

Arkansas

Arkansas Historical
Association,
University of Arkansas,
Fayetteville, 72701

Arkansas History Commission,
One Capitol Mall,
Little Rock, 72201

Carroll County Historical
Society,
Berryville, 72616

Crawford County Historical
Society,
929 E. Main St.,
Van Buren, 72956

Faulkner County Historical
Society,
Conway, 72032

Grand Prairie Historical
Society,
Box 122,
Gillett, 72055

Independence County
Historical Society,
Box 1412,
Batesville, 72501

Pope County Historical
Association,
1120 N. Detroit,
Russellville, 72801

Pulaski County Historical
Society,
P.O. Box 653,
Little Rock, 72203

Washington County Historical
Society,
118 E. Dickson,
Fayetteville, 72701

California

California Historical Society,
2090 Jackson St.,
San Francisco, 94109

Chinese Historical Society,
1050 Sansome,
San Francisco, 94111

Jewish Historical Society of
Orange County,
P.O. Box 2034,
Cypress, 90630

Japanese-American Citizens
League,
1765 Sutter St.,
San Francisco, 94115

Colorado

Historical Society Library,
14th and Sherman,
Denver, 80203

Colorado Historical Society,
Colorado Heritage Center,
1300 Broadway,
Denver, 80203

Connecticut

Connecticut Historical Society,
1 Elizabeth St.,
Hartford 06106

Darien Historical Society,
Old Kings Highway No.,
Darien, 06820

Essex Historical Society,
6 New City St.,
Essex, 06426

Fairfield Historical Society,
636 Old Post Rd.,
Fairfield, 06430

Litchfield Historical Society,
Litchfield, 06759

New Canaan Historical
Society,
13 Oenoke Ridge,
New Canaan, 06480

New Haven Colony Historical
Society,
114 Whitney Ave.,
New Haven, 06510

Trumbull Historical Society,
Trumbull Town Hall,
Trumbull, 06611

Wilton Historical Society,
150 Danbury Rd.,
Wilton, 06897

Delaware

Historical Society of
Delaware,
Old Town Hall,
Wilmington, 19801

District of Columbia

Daughters of the American
Revolution,
1776 "D" St., N.W.,
Washington, 20006

National Society Sons of the
American Revolution,
1000 S. 4th St.,
Louisville, KY., 40203

Florida

Florida Historical Society,
Box 3645,
University Stn.,
Gainesville, 32601

Georgia

Georgia Historical Society,
501 Whittaker St.,
Savannah, 31401

Publications:
Family Puzzlers,
Heritage Papers,
Danielsville, 30633

*Georgia Genealogical
  Magazine*
Box 738,
Easley, S.C. 29640

Georgia Pioneers,
Genealogical Magazine,
Box 1028,
Albany, 31702

Hawaii

Hawaiian Chinese History
  Center,
111 N. King St., Rm. 410,
Honolulu, 96817

Hawaiian Historical Society,
560 Kawaiahao St.,
Honolulu, 96813

Idaho

Idaho Historical Society,
325 State St.,
Boise, 83702

Intermountain Historical
  Society,
Box 788,
McCall, 83638

Nez Perce Historical Society,
P.O. Box 86,
Nez Perce, 83542

Illinois

Chicago Historical Society,
North Ave. and Clark St.,
Chicago, 60614

South Suburban Historical
  Society,
Box 96,
S. Holland, 60473

Swedish Pioneer Historical
  Society,
5125 N. Spaulding Ave.,
Chicago, 60625

Indiana

Family Name Exchange,
P.O. Box 39063,
Indianapolis, 46239

Family Tree and Crests,
6233 Carollton Ave.,
Indianapolis, 46220

Fulton County Historical
  Society,
c/o Shirley Willard,
7th & Pontiac,
Rochester, 46975

Hammond Historical Society,
260 165th St.,
Hammond, 46324

Indiana Historical Society,
315 W. Ohio St.,
Indianapolis, 46202
Publication: *Hoosier
    Genealogist*

Publication:
Indiana Roots,
Box 39063,
Indianapolis, 46239

Iowa

Iowa Department Daughters of
    Union Veterans of Civil
    War,
c/o Sherry Foresman,
Rt. 1, Box 23,
Menlo, 50164

Publication:
Sunday Gazette
"Dear Genie,"
Box 175,
Cedar Rapids, 52406

Kansas

Kansas State Historical
    Society,
Memorial Bldg.,
Topeka, 66603

Publication:
*Midwest Genealogical
    Register,*
Box 1121,
Wichita, 67201

Kentucky

Harrodsburg Historical
    Society,
Box 316,
Harrodsburg, 40330

Kentucky Historical Society,
202 Broadway,
Frankfort, 40601
Publication: *Kentucky
    Ancestors*

Publications:
East Kentuckian,
Box 24202,
Lexington, 40524

Kentucky Genealogist,
3621 Brownsboro Rd., 201B
Louisville, 40207

Louisiana

Publication:
Southern Roots
J&W Publications,
2838 Jody Lane,
Shreveport, 71118

Maine

Camden Historical Society,
80 Mechanic St.,
Camden, 04843

Maine Historical Society,
485 Congress St.,
Portland, 04111

Publication:
Downeast Ancestry,
P.O. Box 398,
Machias, 04654

Maryland

Department of Economic
    Development,
State Office Bldg.,
Annapolis, 21401
(Free historical and
    genealogical literature)

Garret County Historical
    Society,
Courthouse,
Oakland, 21550

Jewish Historical Society of
    Maryland, Inc.,
15 Lloyd St.,
Baltimore, 21202

Maryland Historical Society,
210 West Monument St.,
Baltimore, 21201

Publication:
*Maryland and Delaware
    Genealogist,*
Box 352,
St. Michaels, 21663

Publication:
Rootbound,
Family Historians,
Box 25 CWF,
Ft. George G. Meade,
20755

Massachusetts

American Antiquarian Society,
185 Salisbury St.,
Worcester, 01609

Danvers Historical Society,
Danvers, 01923

Massachesetts Historical
    Society,
1154 Boylston St.,
Boston, 02215

Massachusetts Mayflower
    Descendants,
101 Newberry St.,
Boston, 02116

Nantucket Historical
    Association,
Box 1016,
Nantucket, 02554

Old Colony Historical Society,
66 Church Green,
Taunton, 02780

Michigan

Detroit Historical
    Commission,
5401 Woodward Ave.,
Detroit, 48202

Flat River Historical Society,
302 S. Lafayette St.,
Greenville, 48838

Michigan Historical
    Commission,
505 State Office Bldg.,
Lansing, 48913

Midland County Historical
    Society,
1710 W. St. Andrews Dr.,
Midland, 48640

Publications:
*Kalamazoo Valley Family
    Newsletter,*
Box 405,
Comstock, 49041

Newsletter,
French Canadian Heritage
   Society of Michigan,
Box 30007,
Lansing, 48909

Minnesota

American Swedish Institute,
2600 Park Ave.,
Minneapolis, 55407

Brown County Historical
   Society,
New Ulm, 56073

Minnesota Historical Society,
690 Cedar St.,
St. Paul, 55101

Norwegian-American
   Historical Society,
Northfield, 55057

Olmsted County Historical
   Society,
Box 6411,
Rochester, 55901

Mississippi

Periodical:
*Mississippi Genealogical
   Exchange,*
P.O. Box 16609,
Jackson, 39206

Missouri

Concordia Historical Institute,
301 DeMun Ave.,
St. Louis, 63105

Johnson County Historical
   Society,
Warrensburg, 64093
Publication: *The Bulletin*

Missouri Baptist Historical
   Society,
Jewell College Library,
Liberty, 64068

Missouri Territorial Pioneers,
3929 Milton Dr.,
Independence, 64055

Moniteau County Historical
   Society,
California, 65018

State Historical Society,
Hitt & Lowry Sts.,
Columbia, 65201

Publications:
Missouri Pioneers,
1824 S. Harvard,
Independence, 64052

The Researcher,
Box 206,
Chillicothe, 64601

Montana

Montana Historical Society,
225 N. Roberts St.,
Helena, 59601

Nebraska

Nebraska State Historical
   Society,
1500 R. St.,
Lincoln, 68508

Nevada

Nevada State Historical
  Society,
Box 1192,
Reno, 89501

New Hampshire

New Hampshire Historical
  Society,
30 Park St.,
Concord, 03301

New Jersey

Gloucester County Historical
  Society,
17 Hunter St.,
Woodbury, 08096

Monmouth County Historical
  Society,
70 Court St.,
Freehold, 07728 ·

New Jersey Historical Society,
230 Broadway,
Newark, 07104

Publication:
AVOTAYNU
International Review of Jewish
  Genealogy,
Box 1134,
Teaneck, 97666

New York

American Italian Congress,
111 Columbia Hts.,
Brooklyn, 11201

Colonial Dames of America,
421 E. 61st St.,
New York, 10021

DeWitt Historical Society,
116 N. Cayuga St.,
Ithaca, 14850

Dutchess County Historical
  Society,
Box 88,
Poughkeepsie, 12602

General Society of Colonial
  Wars,
122 E. 58th St.,
New York, 10022

Historical Society of
  Middletown,
25 East Ave.,
Middletown, 10940

Holland Society,
122 E. 58th St.,
New York, 14304

Huguenot Historical Society,
14 Forest Glen Rd.,
New Paltz, 12561

Jefferson County Historical
  Society,
228 Washington St.,
Watertown, 13601

Leo Baeck Institute German-
  Jewish Families,
129 E. 73rd St.,
New York, 10021

Long Island Historical Society,
Pierpont and Clinton Sts.,
Brooklyn, 11201

New York Historical
Association,
170 Central Park West,
New York, 10024

New York State Historical
Association,
Fenimore House, Lake Rd.,
Cooperstown, 13326

Onondaga Historical
Association,
311 Montgomery St.,
Syracuse, 13202

Polish-American Information
Bureau,
55 W. 42nd St.,
New York, 10036

Russian Historic and
Genealogic Society,
971 1st Ave.,
New York, 10022

Southhold Historical Society
Southhold,
Long Island, 11971

Staten Island Historical
Society,
Richmondtown,
Staten Island, 10301

Suffolk County Historical
Society,
Riverhead,
Long Island, 11901

Supervisor of Historical Sites,
State Education Bldg.,
Albany, 12224
(Free booklet: "Historic Sites
of New York State")

Wayne County Historical
Society,
21 Butternut St.,
Lyons, 14489

Publication:
Yesteryears,
3 Seymour St.,
Auburn, 13021

North Carolina

Historic Foundation of the
Presbyterian and Reformed
Churches,
Montreat, 28757

Publication:
Carolina Genealogist,
Heritage Papers
Danielsville, GA, 30633

North Dakota

State Historical Society of
North Dakota,
Liberty Memorial Bldg.,
Bismarck, 58501

Ohio

Cincinnati Historical Society,
Eden Park,
Cincinnati, 45202

Ohio Historical Society,
I-17 and 17th Avenue,
Columbus, 43211

Twinsburg Historical Society,
Twinsburg, 44087

Washington County Historical
  Society,
402 Aurora St.,
Marietta, 45750
Publication: *Tallow Light*

Western Reserve Historical
  Society,
10825 East Blvd.,
Cleveland, 44106

Publication:
Gateway to the West, Ohio,
c/o Anita Short,
RR 1,
Arcanum, 45304

Oklahoma

Coal County Historical
  Society,
Box 322,
Coalgate, 74538

Five Civilized Tribes Museum,
Agency Hill,
Honor Heights Dr.,
Muskogee, 74401

Oklahoma Historical Society,
2100 N. Lincoln,
Oklahoma City, 73105
Publication: *Chronicles*

Oregon

Oregon Historical Society,
1230 Park Ave. S.W.,
Portland, 97201

Pennsylvania

American Swedish Historical
  Foundation,
1900 Pattison Ave.,
Philadelphia, 19145

Blair County Historical
  Society,
Box 1083,
Altoona, 16603

Bucks County Historical
  Society,
Pine and Ashland Sts.,
Doylestown, 18901

Chester County Historical
  Society,
225 High St.,
West Chester, 19380

Clarion County Historical
  Society,
Courthouse,
Clarion, 16214

Clearfield County Historical
  Society,
104 E. Pine St.,
Clearfield, 16830

Clinton County Historical
  Society,
East Water St.,
Lock Haven, 15370

Cumberland County Historical
  Society,
Box 626,
Carlisle, 17013

Delaware County Historical
   Society,
Box 1036,
Widener College,
Chester, 19013

Elk County Historical Society,
County Courthouse,
Ridgway, 15853

Friends General Conference,
1515 Cherry St.,
Philadelphia, 19102

Historic Schaefferstown,
Box 1776,
Schaefferstown, 17088

Historical Society of
   Pennsylvania,
1300 Locust St.,
Philadelphia, 19107

Historical Society of Western
   Pennsylvania,
4388 Bigelow Bldg.,
Pittsburg, 15213

Historical Society of York
   County,
250 E. Market St.,
York, 17403

Huntingdon County Historical
   Society,
Box 305,
Huntingdon, 16652

Juniata County Historical
   Society,
c/o Shellenberger,
Star Route,
Mifflintown, 17059

Lackawanna County Historical
   Society,
232 Monroe Ave.,
Scranton, 18510

Lehigh County Historical
   Society,
414 Walnut St.,
Allentown, 18102

Lutheran Historical Society,
Gettysburg, 17325

Methodist Historical Center,
326 New St.,
Philadelphia, 19106

Mifflin County Historical
   Society,
17 N. Main St.,
Lewistown, 17044

Monroe County Historical
   Society,
9th and Main Sts.,
Stroudsburg, 18360

Muncy Historical Society,
131 S. Main St.,
Muncy, 17756

Northampton County Historical
   Society,
101 S. 4th St.,
Easton, 18042

Northumberland County
   Historical Society,
1150 Front St., North,
Sunbury, 17801

Pennsylvania German Society,
Box 97,
Breinigsville, 18031

Schuylkill County Historical
Society,
14 N. 3rd St.,
Pottsville, 17901

Scottish Historical and
Research Society of the
Delaware Valley,
102 St. Paul's Road,
Ardmore, 19003

Scotch-Irish Society of the
U.S.A.,
3 Parkway, 20th fl.,
Philadelphia, 19102

Somerset Historical Society,
Box 533,
Somerset, 15501

Rhode Island

Newport Historical Society,
82 Touro St.,
Newport, 02840

Rhode Island State Historical
Society,
52 Power St.,
Providence, 02906

South Carolina

Huguenot Society of South
Carolina,
94 Church St.,
Charleston, 29401

Publication:
*South Carolina Magazine of
Ancestral Research,*
Box 21766,
Columbia, 29221

South Carolina Historical
Society,
1500 Old Town Rd.,
Charleston, 29407
Publication: *South Carolina
Historical Magazine*

South Dakota

South Dakota State Historical
Society,
Memorial Bldg.,
Pierre, 57501

Tennessee

East Tennessee Historical
Society,
500 W. Church Ave.,
Knoxville, 37902-2505
Publication: *Echoes*

West Tennessee Historical
Society,
157 S. Fenwick Rd.,
Memphis, 38111

Publication:
River Counties,
610 Terrace Dr.,
Columbia, 38401

Texas

Texas Catholic Historical
Society,
3812 Lafayette,
Fort Worth, 76107

Texas State Historical
Association,
Box 8011,
University Stn.,
Austin, 78712

West Texas Historical Society,
Alpine, 79830

Publication:
Nase Dejiny,
The Magazine of Czech
Genealogy,
P.O. Box 45,
Hallettsville, 77964

Utah

Brigham Young University
Family History Services,
Fulrath House,
Provo, 84607

Utah State Historical Society,
603 E. South Temple,
Salt Lake City, 84102

Vermont

Vermont Historical Society,
Pavilion Office Bldg.,
109 State St.,
Montpelier, 05602

Virginia

Augusta County Historical
Society,
Box 686,
Staunton, 24401

Clark County Historical
Association,
Berryville, 22611

Fairfax Historical Society,
Box 415,
Fairfax, 22030

King and Queen Historical
Society,
Newtown, 23126

Norfolk Historical Society,
c/o Chesapeake Public Library
300 Cedar Road,
Chesapeake, 23320

Publication:
The Virginia Genealogist,
Box 4883,
Washington, D.C. 20008

Washington

Ft. Vancouver Historical
Society,
Box 1834,
Vancouver, 98663

State Capital Historical
Association
211 W. 21st Ave.,
Olympia, 98501

West Virginia

Jackson County Historical
Society,
P.O. Box 22,
Ripley, 25271

West Virginia Historical
Society,
Cultural Center
Capitol Complex,
Charleston, 25305

Wisconsin

State Historical Society of
Wisconsin,
University of Wisconsin,
816 State St.,
Madison, 53706

Wyoming

Publication:
Bits and Pieces,
Box 746,
Newcastle, 82701
(Covers N.D., S.D.,
Wyoming and Montana)

APPENDIX 2

GENEALOGICAL PUBLISHERS AND BOOKSTORES

The growth of interest in genealogy has stimulated publishing on the subject as well as the opening of bookstores with specialties in this area. The following list contains the names of some of the more established bookstores and genealogical publishers by geographical area. Most of the stores specialize in genealogical works that have a strong regional appeal, although their collections frequently contain more extensive material. As with other aspects of genealogy, letters of inquiry and detective work will uncover surprising treasures in many of these places. Most of the publishers and bookstores listed supply catalogs on request. Many are free; some have a small charge.

Northeast

Car-Del-Scribe
Box 746
Burlington, VT 05401

Connecticut Society of
   Genealogists, Inc.
Box 305
West Hartford, CT 06107

Genealogist's Bookshelf
Box 468, 330 E. 85th St.
New York, NY 10028

Hoenstine Book Mart
Box 208
Holidaysburg, PA 16648

George S. MacManus
   Company
2022 Walnut St.
Philadelphia, PA 19103

New England Historic and
   Genealogical Society
101 Newbury St.
Boston, MA 02116

New York Public Library
Grand Central Station, Box
2747
New York, NY 10017

Charles E. Tuttle Company,
Inc.
Rutland, VT 05701

South

American Association for State
and Local History
132 9th Ave. North
Nashville, TN 37208

Boarderland Books
Anchorage, KY

Genealogical Book Company
521-23 St. Paul's Pl.
Baltimore, MD 21202

Genealogical Publishing
Company
521-523 St. Paul's Pl.
Baltimore, MD 21202

Holmes-Corey Antiquities
Box 115 M
Marco Island, FL 33937

Kentucky Publishing Company
153 Cherokee Park
Lexington, KY 40503

Magna Carta Book Company
5324 Beaufort Ave.
Baltimore, MD 21215

Polyanthos, Inc.
822 Orleans St.
New Orleans, LA 70116

Reprint Company
154 W. Cleveland Park Dr.
Spartanburg, SC 29303

Southern Historical Press
Box 229
Easley, SC 29640

Walton-Folk Americana
330 Cherokee St.
Kennesaw, GA 30144

Midwest

Bland Books
401 N.W. 10th St.
Fairfield, IL 62837

The Bookmark
Box 74
Knightstown, IN 46148

Gale Research Company
Book Tower
Detroit, MI 48226

Heritage Resource Center
Box 26305
Minneapolis, MN 55426

Hoosier Heritage Press
520 N. Campbell St.
Indianapolis, IN 46219

Southwest

Ancient Book Shop
Box 986
Santa Fe, NM

West

The Augustan Society
Hartwell Company
1617 W. 261st St.
Harbor City, CA 90710

Brigham Young University
 Press
205 University Press Bldg.
Provo, UT 84602

Dawson Book Shop
550 S. Figueroa St.
Los Angeles, CA 90017

Deseret Book Company
44 E. South Temple
Salt Lake City, UT 84110

Everton Publishers, Inc.
Box 368
Logan, UT 84321
(Also, computerized "Roots
 Cellar" and Family File
 containing a half-million
 names)

Hawkes Publishing, Inc.
156 W. 2170 South
Salt Lake City, UT 84115

Heritage Research Institute
964 Laird Ave.
Salt Lake City, UT 84105
(Origins of names)

Saddleback Book Shop
Box 10393
Santa Ana, CA 92771

San Francisco Historical
 Records
1204 Nimitz Dr.
Colma, CA 94015

APPENDIX 3

MAP SOURCES FOR GENEALOGISTS

Northeast

Colonial Maps
490 Beverly Rd.
Teaneck, NJ 07666

Courtland New York
   County Maps
Courtland Historical Society
Courthouse, 3rd fl.
Courtland, NY

Onandega Historical Asso-
   ciation
311 Montgomery St.
Syracuse, NY 13202
(1793 Map of Central New
   York)

State of Pennsylvania
Department of Internal
   Affairs
Harrisburg, PA
(Free genealogical map of
   Pennsylvania counties)

Swann Galleries
117 E. 24th St.
New York, NY

District of Columbia

United States Government
   Printing Office
Superintendent of Docu-
   ments
Washington, D.C. 20025
(Catalog of maps)

Midwest

Maps of 19th Century
   United States
G. A. Noble
Drawer E
Hiawatha, IA 52233

Kenneth Nebenzahl
   Company
333 N. Michigan Ave.
Chicago, IL 62521

Maps of Sweden
Anderson's Butik
Box 151
Lindsborg, KS 67456

Southwest

Oklahoma Planning
   Commission
Oklahoma Department of
   Highways
Oklahoma City, OK
(Free map of Civil War
   activities in Indian Terri-
   tory)

Texas State Historical Maps
Drawer 3885
San Angelo, TX 76901

West

Germany Central Tourist
   Association
323 Geary St.
San Francisco, CA 94102
(Free map of West
   Germany)

John Howell
434 Post St.
San Francisco, CA 94102

Karta Americana
7212 4th N.W.
Seattle, WA 98117

Karta Europa
7212 4th N.W.
Seattle, WA 98117

Pacific Coast Map Service
11470 Long Beach Bl.
Lynwood, CA 90262

Roadmaps-Thru-History
Box 90622
Los Angeles, CA 90009

Miscellaneous

Department of Highways
State capitol
Each state
(State maps with cem-
   eteries)

APPENDIX 4

SPECIAL IMMIGRANT
PASSENGER LISTS

Because passenger lists are so valuable for genealogical purposes, many have been published privately by genealogical
and historical societies or by publishers who specialize in
such research books, and they can be found in most genealogical library collections. Among the most important are
the following:

John Hotten, *The Original List of Persons of Quality Who
Went from Great Britain to the American Plantations,
1600-1700*

Ralph Strassburger, *Pennsylvania German Pioneers: Port of
Philadelphia from 1727 to 1808*

John Evjen, *Scandinavian Immigrants in New York, 1630-
1674*

John Farmer, *A Genealogical Register of the First Settlers
of New England*

Jack Kaminkow, *A List of Emigrants from England to
America, 1719-1759*

Charles Browning, *Welsh Settlement of Pennsylvania*

Samuel Joseph, *Jewish Immigration to the United States
from 1881 to 1910*

Israel Rupp, *A Collection of Thirty Thousand Names of
German, Swiss, Dutch, French, and Other Immigrants
in Pennsylvania from 1727 to 1776*

Donald Yoder, *Emigrants from Wyer Hemberg; the Adolf
Gerber Lists*

APPENDIX 5

MAJOR PORTS OF ENTRY FOR IMMIGRANTS

Passenger lists for these ports are available in the National Archives in Washington, D.C., and its branches.

NAME OF SEAPORT OR DISTRICT	PASSENGER LISTS
Alexandria, Virgina	1820–1852
Annapolis, Maryland	1849
Baltimore, Maryland	1820–1909
Bangor, Maine	1848
Barnstable, Massachusetts	1820–1826
Bath, Maine	1825–1832, 1867
Boston, Massachusetts	1820–1943
Bristol and Warren, Rhode Island	1820–1824, 1828, 1843–1871
Charleston, South Carolina	1820–1829, 1906–1945
Galveston, Texas	1846–1871
Jacksonville, Florida	1804–1845
Kennebunk, Maine	1820–1827, 1842
Key West, Florida	1837–1868, 1898–1945
Marblehead, Massachusetts	1820–1852
Miami, Florida	1899–1945
Mobile, Alabama	1820–1862, 1904–1945
Nantucket, Massachusetts	1820–1862
New Bedford, Massachusetts	1823–1899, 1902–1942
New Orleans, Louisiana	1820–1945
New York, New York	1820–1942

Newport, Rhode Island	1820–1875
Plymouth, Massachusetts	1821–1843
Providence, Rhode Island	1820–1867, 1911–1943
Richmond, Virginia	1820–1844
St. Augustine, Florida	1820–1827, 1870
Savannah, Georgia	1820–1868, 1906–1945

APPENDIX 6

LIST OF <u>MAYFLOWER</u> PASSENGERS

An asterisk denotes the passengers whose family line has been traced by modern genealogists. If you think you have a *Mayflower* ancestor, you should check with the New England Historic and Genealogical Society.

John Carver and his wife Katherine
Desire Minter
John Howland* and Roger Wilder, two man-servants
William Latham, a boy
Jasper More, a child
William Brewster* and his wife Mary* with two sons Love* and Wrasling, and a boy called Richard More*
Edward Winslow* and his wife Elizabeth with two man-servants George Sowle* and Elias Story; also a little girl called Ellen More
William Bradford* and his wife Dorothy
Isaak Allerton* and his wife Mary with three children, Bartholomew, Remember* and Mary*, and a servant boy, John Hooke
Samuel Fuller* and a servant, called William Butten
John Crakston and his son John Crakston
Captain Myles Standish* and his wife Rose
Christopher Martin and his wife, and two servants, Salamon Prower and John Langemore
William Mullines and his wife, and two children, Joseph and Priscilla*, and a servant, Robart Carter
William White and Susana* his wife and a son called Resolved*, one other son born on the ship called Peregriene* and two servants named William Holbeck and Edward Thomson

Steven Hopkins* and his wife Elizabeth* and two children,
Giles* and Constanta* by a former wife; and Damaris
and Oceanus by this wife; and two servants, called Edward Doty* and Edward Litster

Richard Warren*

John Billinton* and his wife Elen* and two sons, John and
Francis*

Edward Tillie and his wife Ann and two children that were
their cousins, Henery Samson* and Humillity Coper

John Tillie and his wife and their daughter Eelizabeth*

Francis Cooke* and his son John*

Thomas Rogers and his son Joseph*

Thomas Tinker and his wife and a son

John Rigdale and his wife Alice

James Chilton and his wife and their daughter Mary*

Edward Fuller and his wife and Samuell*, their son

John Turner and two sons

Francis Eaton* and his wife Sarah, and Samuell* their son

Moyses Fletcher

John Goodman

Thomas Williams

Digerie Preist

Edmond Margeson

Peter Browne*

Richard Britterige

Richard Clarke

Richard Gardenar

Gilbart Winslow

John Alden*, a cooper hired at Southhampton

John Allerton and Thomas English, both seamen

INDEX

FACT

is stranger than

FICTION